The Persona and Journey Map Playbook

Designing Human-Centered Artifacts to Inspire and Drive Change

Andrew Schall

Apress®

The Persona and Journey Map Playbook: Designing Human-Centered Artifacts to Inspire and Drive Change

Andrew Schall
Boca Raton, FL, USA

ISBN-13 (pbk): 979-8-8688-0892-0					ISBN-13 (electronic): 979-8-8688-0893-7
https://doi.org/10.1007/979-8-8688-0893-7

Copyright © 2024 by Andrew Schall

This work is subject to copyright. All rights are reserved by the Publisher, whether the whole or part of the material is concerned, specifically the rights of translation, reprinting, reuse of illustrations, recitation, broadcasting, reproduction on microfilms or in any other physical way, and transmission or information storage and retrieval, electronic adaptation, computer software, or by similar or dissimilar methodology now known or hereafter developed.

Trademarked names, logos, and images may appear in this book. Rather than use a trademark symbol with every occurrence of a trademarked name, logo, or image we use the names, logos, and images only in an editorial fashion and to the benefit of the trademark owner, with no intention of infringement of the trademark.

The use in this publication of trade names, trademarks, service marks, and similar terms, even if they are not identified as such, is not to be taken as an expression of opinion as to whether or not they are subject to proprietary rights.

While the advice and information in this book are believed to be true and accurate at the date of publication, neither the authors nor the editors nor the publisher can accept any legal responsibility for any errors or omissions that may be made. The publisher makes no warranty, express or implied, with respect to the material contained herein.

>	Managing Director, Apress Media LLC: Welmoed Spahr
>	Acquisitions Editor: Shiva Ramachandran
>	Development Editor: James Markham
>	Project Manager: Jessica Vakili

Cover designed by eStudioCalamar

Distributed to the book trade worldwide by Apress Media, LLC, 1 New York Plaza, New York, NY 10004, U.S.A. Phone 1-800-SPRINGER, fax (201) 348-4505, e-mail orders-ny@springer-sbm.com, or visit www.springeronline.com. Apress Media, LLC is a California LLC and the sole member (owner) is Springer Science + Business Media Finance Inc (SSBM Finance Inc). SSBM Finance Inc is a **Delaware** corporation.

For information on translations, please e-mail booktranslations@springernature.com; for reprint, paperback, or audio rights, please e-mail bookpermissions@springernature.com.

Apress titles may be purchased in bulk for academic, corporate, or promotional use. eBook versions and licenses are also available for most titles. For more information, reference our Print and eBook Bulk Sales web page at http://www.apress.com/bulk-sales.

Any source code or other supplementary material referenced by the author in this book is available to readers on GitHub (https://github.com/Apress). For more detailed information, please visit https://www.apress.com/gp/services/source-code.

If disposing of this product, please recycle the paper

Table of Contents

About the Author xv

Preface xvii

Acknowledgments xxiii

Chapter 1: Representing Our Users 1
    Human-Centered Design: Putting People at the Center of the Experience 2
        Personas in Human-Centered Design: Understanding Users for Better Solutions 5
        Understanding the Path Forward with Journey Maps 11
        Key Takeaways 18

Chapter 2: Why Most Personas Fail 21
    An Obituary for Sally 22
    A Persona Postmortem 23
        Lack of Trust and Relevancy 23
        Neglect 24
        Isolation 24
    What Are the Symptoms of a Sick Persona? 25
    Aspects of Personas That Are Adverse to Your Persona's Health 26
        Irrelevant Information 27
        Vague Information 27
        Overgeneralized and Stereotypical Information 28
        Hyperspecific Information 29
        Unsupported Information 30

TABLE OF CONTENTS

Too Much of a Good Thing Can Harm Your Persona 31
    Redundancies and Confusion 31
    Difficulties in Maintaining Focus and Prioritizing 32
    Challenges with Maintaining Numerous Personas 32

Bad Personas Can Make the Organization Sick 33
    Distractions—Paying Attention to the Wrong Details 33
    Misinformation—Misleading or Wrong Information 34
    Distrust—Lack of Trust in Persona Information 34
    Disengagement—Losing Interest in the Persona (and the End User) 34

A Cure for the Common Persona 35
    Quality over Quantity 35
    Relevant to the Organization 35
    Balancing Specificity with Generalization 36
    Establishing Trust 36

Key Takeaways 36

Chapter 3: Flying to New Heights: The Concept of Altitudes 39

A Fog Preventing Organizational Alignment 39

The Concept of Altitudes 41

Using Altitude-Based Artifacts in Human-Centered Design 42

The Relationship Between Altitudes, Personas, and Journey Maps 46
    High Altitude Examples 47
    Low Altitude Examples 48

The Persona Spectrum 50

Key Takeaways 52

TABLE OF CONTENTS

Chapter 4: Developing Persona Characteristics That Matter 55
Setting Up a Persona Attribute Framework 56
    Calibrate Your Organization's Altimeter 56
    Represent Attributes at Each Altitude Level 58
    Set Altitude Levels 58
Starting Broad: Identifying Major User Groups 60
Narrowing Focus: Utilizing the Altitude Framework to Generate Personas 62
    Lower Altitude Personas 64
    Conduct a User Attribute Alignment Workshop 66
    Considerations for an Organization with Existing Personas 68
Key Takeaways 68

Chapter 5: Building a Persona Family Tree 71
The Risks of Not Defining an Organization-Wide Persona Strategy 72
A Persona Strategy Provides Transparency and Alignment 72
    Collaborating on a Persona Strategy 73
Visualize Your Organization's Personas 73
    Creating the Foundation 74
    Creating the Primary Branches 75
    Creating Secondary Branches 75
    Growing the Tree Over Time 75
    Other Ways to Visualize Your Organization's Personas 76
    Persona Relationship Mapping Resources 78
Key Takeaways 79

Chapter 6: Researching Your Personas 81
Planning Your User Research Strategy 82
Define Your Research Objectives 82
    Use Proto Personas to Identify Hypotheses About Your Users 83
    Decide on Whether to Focus on Current or Aspirational Users 83

TABLE OF CONTENTS

Choose Research Methods 84
- Utilize Existing Knowledge 84
- Learn from Subject Matter Experts 85
- Take an Iterative Approach to Research 86

Use Mixed Methods and Triangulate Your Data 87

Identifying Your Users 88
- How Do You Know Who Your Users Are? 88
- Types of User Data 88
- Classifying User Types by Behavior 89

Surveys 92
- Large-Scale Surveys Can Cast a Wide Net and Provide Statistical Validity 92
- Capture Low Altitude Persona Details with Branching Logic ... 93
- Limitations of Surveys 94

Understanding Your Users 94

Interviews 95
- The "3 P's" Questioning Method 96
- Using a Funnel Approach for Your Interview Questions 97
- Be Careful of Leading Questions 99
- Knowing When You've Reached Saturation 100

Recruiting Representative Participants 101
- Creating a Screener 101
- Screening for Specific Users 101

The Power of Using Attitudinal Data with Behavioral Data 103

Analyzing Your Data 104
- Keeping Track of Your Findings 104
- Identify Trends 105
- Key Takeaways 107

TABLE OF CONTENTS

Chapter 7: Synthesizing Data to Inform Your Personas 109
Creating Themes 110
Determining Which Themes to Inform Your Personas 111
Using Themes to Identify Similarities and Differences between Personas 111
Understanding Themes on a Spectrum 117
Key Takeaways 123

Chapter 8: Constructing Your Personas 125
Benefits of an Effective Persona 126
Persona Construction Strategy 126
Empathetic 127
Actionable 127
Contextual 127
Scannable 128
Building Out Your Persona 128
Provide an Introduction to Your Persona with a Cover Page 128
Getting into the Details of Goals and Tasks 134
Going Deeper to Understand Contextual Factors 138
Implications and Considerations 142
Key Takeaways 147

Chapter 9: Designing Your Personas 149
Creating a Template for Your Personas 150
Different Levels of Design Fidelity 150
Using Atomic Design Patterns 152
Creating a Visual Hierarchy 157
Using Photos to Represent the Persona 163
Key Takeaways 169

vii

TABLE OF CONTENTS

Chapter 10: Conducting Research to Understand Your User's Journey 171

Planning User Research 172

Define Your Research Objectives 172

Selecting Research Methods 173

Behavioral Data 174

    Identifying Behavior Patterns with Analytics 174

Observing Users with Session Replays 176

Observing Users in Real Time 178

    Conducting a Contextual Inquiry 179

    Tips for Conducting a Contextual Inquiry Session 181

    Identifying People, Places, and Things 182

Attitudinal Data 185

Key Takeaways 186

Chapter 11: Synthesizing Data to Inform Your Journey Map 189

Using Data to Understand the User's Behaviors in Context 190

    Data Organization 191

    Sketching Out Each Participant's Journey 193

    Identifying Common Journey Experiences 198

    Identifying Common Themes 200

    Integrating Other Data Sources into Your Journey Map Research 201

    Keeping Track of Unanswered Questions 203

    Taking a Collaborative Approach to Research Synthesis 205

    Validate and Iterate Your Preliminary Journey Concept 210

    Key Takeaways 211

TABLE OF CONTENTS

Chapter 12: Creating a Flight Path for Your Journey Map 213
Charting the Course for the Journey Ahead 214
    Finding the Right Altitude 215
    Identifying a Place to Take Off 220
    Identifying a Place to Land 221
    Using Milestones to Break Down Phases 223
    Using Actions as Progress Markers in the Flight Path 223
    Key Takeaways 225

Chapter 13: Adding Contextual Layers to Your Journey Map 227
Representing the Quality of the Experience 228
    Quantifying the Experience with an Experience Quality Score 229
Representing Root Causes of an Experience 237
    Using the "5 Whys" Analysis Technique 237
    Alignment with Mental Models 238
    Usability 244
    Other Factors That Can Impact an Experience 245
    Emotion Classification 249
    Minimizing Turbulence in Your Journey Map 251
    Key Takeaways 252

Chapter 14: Designing Your Journey Map 253
Journey Map Construction Strategy 254
    Contextual Framing 254
    Scannable 254
    Actionable 254
    Empathetic 255

TABLE OF CONTENTS

Creating a Structure for Your Journey Map 255
    Designing Components and Templates 255
    Setting the Stage 256
    Visualizing the Journey 260
    Visualizing Experience Quality Scores 262
    Insights Track: Highlighting Root Causes and Effects 263
    Bringing It All Together: The Complete Journey Map 270
    Key Takeaways 272

Chapter 15: Keeping Your Personas and Journey Maps in the Air 275

Measuring the Impact 276
    Key Performance Indicators 277
    Defining Your Key Players and Their Goals 277
    Measuring Performance 278
    Indicators 281

Articulating Goals with Solutions 282
    Develop a Hypothesis Statement 283

Representing KPIs in Personas and Journey Maps 286
    Create an Action Plan for Infusing KPIs into Personas and Journey Maps 287

Growing Organizational Knowledge 288
    Knowledge Systems 289
    Evolving Personas and Their Journeys over Time 297
    Key Takeaways 303

Chapter 16: Using Personas and Journey Maps with Other Artifacts 305

Using Personas with Other Personas 306
    Utilizing Research Insights Across the Persona Family Tree 306
    Identifying Commonalities and Differences 307

- Designing Holistic and Inclusive Experiences 308
- Feedback and Iteration 309
- Using Journey Maps with Other Journey Maps 310
  - End-to-End Continuum 310
  - Consistent Persona and Overarching Goal 310
  - Connecting Journey Maps 311
- Product-Centric Artifacts 312
  - User Stories 312
  - User Story Mapping 314
  - Jobs-to-Be-Done (JTBD) 315
  - Ecosystem Maps 316
  - Service Blueprints 318
- Establishing the Who, What, and How 319
- Key Takeaways 320

Chapter 17: Charting Future Courses for Your Journey Maps 323

- Why You Should Envision the Ideal User Experience 324
  - Strategic Focus 325
  - Innovation and Competitive Advantage 325
  - User-Centric Culture 325
  - Stakeholder Alignment 326
- Defining the Future Based on Insights and Practical Solutions 326
  - Rooted in Current Reality 327
  - Directly Address Pain Points 328
  - Clear Articulation of Solutions 328
  - Feasibility and Practicality 329
  - Measurable Improvements 329

TABLE OF CONTENTS

The Journey of a Nightmare Flight Experience 330
    Current State Journey Map 331
The Improved Future Experience 334
    Future State Journey Map 335
Creating a Future State Journey Map Based on a Current State Journey Map 337
    Align to a Specific Altitude 337
    Extract Insights from the Current State Journey Map 337
    Conduct a Workshop to Align on Pain Points and Solutions 338
    Develop the Future State Journey Map 342
    Final Review and Alignment 342
Creating a Bridge from the Current to the Optimal Future State 342
    Current State: Establishing the Foundation 343
    Near-Term Solution: Constructing Initial Pillars 343
    Mid-Term Solution: Refining and Strengthening 344
    Far-Term Solution: Ensuring Long-Term Stability 344
    Optimal Future State: Continuous Monitoring and Improvement 344
Key Takeaways 345

Chapter 18: Launching a User Artifact Program 347
Align Phase: Planning and Stakeholder Engagement 348
    Program Management 349
    Stakeholder and Leadership Interviews 350
    SME "Deep Dive" Interviews 351
Assess Phase: Inventory and Gap Analysis 351
    Inventory Existing Artifacts and Knowledge 351
    Review Current Data 352

TABLE OF CONTENTS

Enable Phase: Documenting Processes and Resources 352
    Provide Templates 353
    Develop Documentation 353
Education Phase: Workshops and Ongoing Support 354
    Orientations and Workshops 354
    Ongoing Support and Guidance 356
Design Phase: Creating User Artifacts 356
    Iterative Development 357
Refine Phase: Continuous Feedback and Expansion 357
    Feedback and Refinement 357
    Updating and Expanding Artifacts 358
    Measuring Effectiveness 358
Engagement Strategies: Tying the Program to Organizational Goals 359
    Align with Organizational Goals 359
    Focus on Team Outcomes 359
    User-Driven Experience 359
Key Takeaways 360

Index **363**

About the Author

Andrew Schall has over 20 years of experience as a UX leader, researcher, and strategist. He has collaborated with renowned organizations such as Citibank, Harley Davidson, The New York Times, National Institutes of Health, Office Depot, and Southwest Airlines. He currently leads a rockstar team of UX researchers at ServiceNow focusing on creating the next generation of employee-centered experiences.

Andrew previously served as the Senior Director of Experience Design Research at Mayo Clinic, where he led a team dedicated to revolutionizing healthcare experiences. At Mayo Clinic, he pioneered a new strategy for creating personas and journey maps to deeply understand user needs and guide product and service experience roadmaps. He has shared his innovative approach at numerous seminars and events, including UXDX and UXPA.

Andrew loves to share his knowledge and insights with the UX community. He co-authored the book *Eye Tracking in User Experience Design* and contributed to the book *Measuring the User Experience*. As the Director of Publications for UXPA, he oversees the *Journal of User Experience* and *UX Magazine*. Andrew is an experienced instructor teaching courses in user experience and Human-Computer Interaction (HCI). He is an adjunct faculty member at the Maryland Institute College of Art (MICA) and has previously taught at Brandeis University, University of Washington, and Cornell University.

Preface

Why I Wrote This Book

In the ever-evolving field of user experience design, one recurring frustration has been the frequent abandonment of meticulously researched, designed, and presented personas and journey maps. Time and again, I observed these valuable artifacts—intended to guide and inspire—being sidelined or rendered ineffective. This recurring pattern, coupled with the proliferation of generic personas adorned with clichéd stock photo portraits, superficial backgrounds, and irrelevant details, sparked a deep sense of dissatisfaction in me.

It became clear that a meaningful connection between the needs of users and the strategic goals of businesses was missing. There had to be a better way to create personas and journey maps—one that goes beyond superficial attributes and truly reflects the complexities of human experience. This realization led me to rethink and redefine how we approach these critical tools.

The Persona and Journey Map Playbook is my response to this challenge. This book is born from my desire to see organizations develop personas and journey maps that are not just theoretical exercises but practical assets that drive real, human-centered decision-making. It is designed to address the gaps I have observed and to offer a fresh, actionable perspective on creating artifacts that genuinely support both user needs and business objectives.

PREFACE

Inside this playbook, you will find

- **Practical Guidance**: Step-by-step instructions on creating detailed, effective personas and journey maps that resonate with both users and stakeholders.

- **Innovative Techniques**: New methods and approaches to ensure that your personas and journey maps are grounded in reality and offer tangible benefits.

- **Real-World Examples**: Examples designed to bridge the divide between theory and practice, making the process engaging and accessible.

My hope is that this resource will help you navigate the complexities of persona and journey map creation with greater clarity and purpose. By fostering a mindset deeply attuned to the human experience, we can create tools that not only guide but also inspire, driving meaningful change in our organizations.

Thank you for embarking on this journey with me. Together, let's strive to transform the way we approach human-centered design and make a meaningful impact in our organizations.

What This Book Will Cover

This book is designed as a step-by-step guide for understanding and applying personas and journey maps in Human-Centered Design (HCD). For those embarking on this journey, I recommend reading the book in a linear order, as each chapter builds on the previous ones, providing a cohesive framework for mastering these essential tools. As you start creating your own personas and journey maps, you'll find it valuable to revisit specific chapters for guidance and deeper insights.

Here's an overview of what each chapter covers.

Understanding the Foundations

Chapter 1: Representing Our Users
Start with the foundational principles of HCD, exploring the roles of personas and journey maps. Understand their history, evolution, and importance in creating user-centered solutions.

Chapter 2: Why Most Personas Fail
Learn about common pitfalls in persona creation and how to avoid them. We dissect typical issues and provide insights into diagnosing and fixing flawed personas.

Chapter 3: Flying to New Heights: The Concept of Altitudes
Discover how to balance detail and context in personas and journey maps. The concept of altitudes helps you find the right level of granularity for effective representation.

Crafting Personas

Chapter 4: Developing Persona Charactcristics That Matter
Delve into the attributes that make up a persona, akin to the building blocks of human DNA. Learn to define and organize these characteristics to create meaningful personas.

Chapter 5: Building a Persona Family Tree
Visualize relationships among personas with a persona tree, helping you address the right user types and grow your understanding of diverse user needs.

Chapter 6: Researching Your Personas
Understand the importance of user research in persona creation. Discover methods for uncovering genuine user behaviors, motivations, and pain points.

Chapter 7: Synthesizing Data to Inform Your Personas
Explore data synthesis techniques, such as Venn diagrams and visualization methods, to identify shared traits and distinctions among personas.

Chapter 8: Constructing Your Personas
Get practical guidance on assembling personas and combining research findings into comprehensive profiles that support user understanding.

Chapter 9: Designing Your Personas
Use a modular approach to persona design, breaking down personas into reusable components based on atomic design patterns and visual principles.

Mapping the User Journey

Chapter 10: Conducting Research to Understand Your User's Journey
Investigate research methods for journey mapping, focusing on understanding user goals and the paths they take to achieve them.

Chapter 11: Synthesizing Data to Inform Your Journey Map
Organize and analyze data to create journey maps that highlight key themes and trends, identifying opportunities for improvement.

Chapter 12: Creating a Flight Path for Your Journey Map
Structure your journey maps with clear waypoints and milestones, ensuring a consistent and effective representation of user journeys.

Chapter 13: Adding Contextual Layers to Your Journey Map
Enhance your journey maps with contextual layers, exploring user experiences, mental models, and interactions to provide a comprehensive view.

Chapter 14: Designing Your Journey Map
Develop journey maps using a structured, modular approach, incorporating atomic design patterns and visual principles for clarity and impact.

Strategies for a Successful Persona and Journey Maps Program

Chapter 15: Keeping Your Personas and Journey Maps in the Air
Learn strategies for maintaining the relevance and dynamism of your personas and journey maps, adapting to evolving user behaviors and organizational needs.

Chapter 16: Using Personas and Journey Maps with Other Artifacts
Discover how to integrate personas and journey maps with other design tools like user stories, ecosystem maps, and service blueprints.

Chapter 17: Charting Future Courses for Your Journey Maps
Create future state journey maps to envision ideal user experiences. Ground your designs in practical realities, prioritizing solutions to improve user journeys.

Chapter 18: Launching a User Artifact Program
Finally, learn how to implement a successful user artifact program in your organization. From planning and alignment to engagement and refinement, this chapter provides a roadmap for continuous improvement and user-driven success.

By following this playbook, you'll be equipped with the knowledge and skills to create and utilize personas and journey maps effectively, driving meaningful and human-centered design in your organization.

Acknowledgments

I am deeply grateful to Lisa Semidey, Caroline Little, and Noah Ward for helping me to think through the complexities of reinventing a new approach to personas and journey maps. Your insights and reality checks ensured my ideas stayed grounded and practical.

I extend my heartfelt thanks to Adam Perlin and Diana Glozman for refining my words and providing invaluable guidance throughout the writing of this book. Your support has been instrumental in shaping the final product.

To the team at Apress, your enthusiasm for this project and your dedication to providing a platform for my thoughts have made this journey possible. Thank you for believing in this work and giving it a place to reach the world.

I am eternally grateful to my family for their love and support. Special thanks to my husband, Reid, for his continual patience, and to my mom, for always believing in me and making me feel loved every day.

Finally, this book is dedicated to the memory of our pug, Lucy, who lived to the grand old age of 17. She was the sweetest dog ever, and I miss her greatly.

CHAPTER 1

Representing Our Users

In this chapter, you'll explore the key concepts of Human-Centered Design (HCD) and understand the roles of personas and journey maps within this approach. We'll cover the foundational principles of HCD, including the importance of empathy, user understanding, and collaborative design. Additionally, you'll learn about the history and evolution of personas and journey maps and how these tools have become essential for creating human-centered solutions. This overview will provide a solid grounding in how personas and journey maps contribute to designing effective and meaningful experiences.

CHAPTER 1   REPRESENTING OUR USERS

Human-Centered Design: Putting People at the Center of the Experience

Human-centered design (HCD) is an approach to problem-solving and innovation that prioritizes the needs, behaviors, and preferences of end-users throughout the design and development process. It places people at the center of design thinking, emphasizing empathy, collaboration, and iterative problem-solving to create solutions that meet user needs.

The 10 key principles and elements of HCD are

1. Empathy

    At the core of HCD is the practice of empathizing with the people for whom you are designing. This involves understanding their experiences, motivations, frustrations, and goals through research.

2. Humans in the Center

   HCD embodies the belief that solutions should be designed for and by the people who will use them. It challenges assumptions and encourages designers to involve users in the design process, ensuring that the end product or service aligns with their real-world needs.

3. Deep Understanding

   HCD involves a significant amount of research to fully understand the user. It includes gaining an understanding of their lives and experiences, as well as their goals and challenges.

4. Collaborative

   HCD promotes cross-functional collaboration. Teams often include members with diverse backgrounds, such as designers, researchers, engineers, and marketers. This interdisciplinary approach encourages a variety of perspectives and expertise to contribute to the design process.

5. Creative Problem-Solving

   HCD encourages creative thinking to solve complex problems. Designers use brainstorming, ideation, and other creative techniques to generate innovative solutions that address user needs and challenges.

6. Continuous Feedback

   Feedback from users is a continuous source of guidance in HCD. Designers actively seek input from users and stakeholders at every stage of the

CHAPTER 1   REPRESENTING OUR USERS

design process. Feedback informs design decisions and helps ensure that the final solution aligns with user expectations.

7. Holistic

    HCD takes a holistic view of the user experience, considering not only the product or service itself but also the broader context in which it will be used. This includes the physical environment, social factors, and the emotional impact on users.

8. Ethical and Inclusive

    HCD emphasizes the importance of ethical considerations and inclusivity. Designers aim to create solutions that are accessible and considerate of diverse user groups, avoiding bias and discrimination.

9. Ongoing Assessment

    After a solution is implemented, HCD practitioners assess its impact on users and the broader community. This ongoing evaluation helps ensure that the solution continues to meet user needs and provides value over time.

10. Iterative Design

    HCD embraces an iterative process, continually refining and improving design solutions based on user feedback. Iterative improvement ensures that designs evolve to better meet user needs and adapt to changing contexts or requirements.

By prioritizing empathy, collaboration, and iterative processes, HCD aims to create solutions (such as products, services, and experiences) that are not only functional but also meaningful and enjoyable for users.

Personas in Human-Centered Design: Understanding Users for Better Solutions

Personas used in HCD embody the collective individuals that you are designing for. The concept of personas representing a population has a long history that predates modern experience design practices.

The Origins of Personas in Human-Centered Design

Alan Cooper is often credited with being the father of modern-day user personas. He wrote about his early work in personas during the 1980s and 1990s before it was common for product teams to visualize the people they designed for. In the early 1990s, Cooper introduced the concept of goal-directed design and advocated for a user-centered approach focused on understanding and addressing user goals rather than just technical requirements. In his influential book *The Inmates Are Running the Asylum*, Cooper explained his concept of personas to represent users. He emphasized the importance of understanding users' goals, motivations, and behaviors to design software that truly met their needs. Cooper introduced the term "persona" to describe these user archetypes, emphasizing the creation of fictional characters to represent different user groups.

The Story of Chuck, Cynthia, and Rob

In an early project using personas, Alan used the names Chuck, Cynthia, and Rob to represent three different user types.

CHAPTER 1   REPRESENTING OUR USERS

Alan described these fictitious characters to help his team understand the unique roles and activities that these individuals perform.

> Chuck was an analyst who used ready-built templates and reports. Cynthia was an analyst, too, and she used similar ready-built templates. But Cynthia also wrote her own templates, which she gave to Chuck to use. Rob was the IT manager who supported both Rob and Cynthia. He could optimize Cynthia's templates, but he would never originate or use them.

Personas turned out to be a great success. Alan reported that members of his team would often refer to their personas by name, such as asking, "What would Cynthia do?" or " Is this something Chuck would understand?" during meetings.

As the concept of personas gained traction in the user experience community, designers recognized its value in guiding design decisions, promoting empathy, and ensuring that user needs were at the forefront of the design process. Creating personas based on research and data became a standard approach in HCD design.

Over the years, the use of personas has evolved and diversified. Personas have become more sophisticated, incorporating not only demographic data but also psychographic information, user goals, pain points, and context of use. They are now commonly used in various design disciplines, including product and service design, to create user-centered solutions. Today, personas are a standard tool in HCD design, helping teams create products and services that better align with user needs and goals.

The Composition of a Persona

Personas are created using attributes that represent a particular type of user. Personas can come in many different configurations and levels of detail. Examples of components that are often used in personas to represent the user include

- **Background**: Historical and current events that help to establish context for the user's experiences. This can include past and current jobs, living situations, and life milestones.

- **Demographics**: Generalizable population characteristics that can be used to classify the user into defined segments. This can include age, gender, education, socioeconomic status, and geographic location.

- **Goals and Needs**: What a user wants to achieve and what is needed to be able to successfully reach their goal. An example goal could be paying taxes online and the need to have access to tax software and copies of the most recent income records.

- **Knowledge and Experience**: The information and mental models that a user has related to accomplishing their goals. This can include technology proficiency, depth of subject matter knowledge, and prior experiences.

- **Motivations**: Primary drivers that can influence the user to take action. This can include attributes like cost savings, convenience, and social recognition.

- **Challenges and Pain Points**: Impediments that make it difficult for a user to achieve their goals. This can include constraints on time, limited resources, and lack of knowledge.

We will dive deeper into the components of a persona and how to use them in Chapter 6.

Creating detailed personas based on these components helps UX designers make informed decisions, prioritize features, and create human-centered design solutions. It also ensures that the design process remains focused on the needs and preferences of the target audience.

An Example of a Typical Persona

Let's examine a persona named Helen, who represents an individual with limited access to the latest technology and low technology literacy.

CHAPTER 1   REPRESENTING OUR USERS

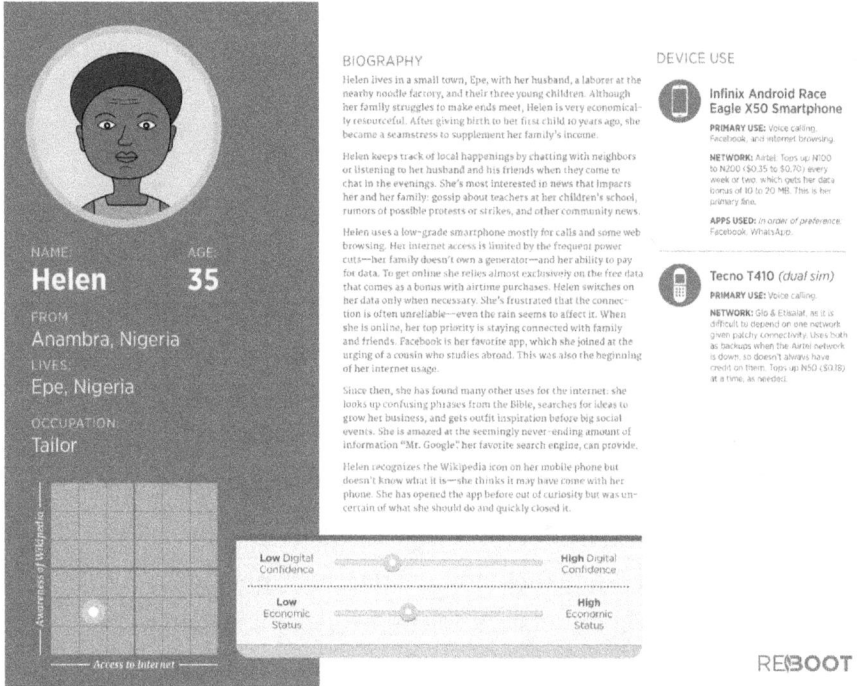

Example of a persona from the Wikimedia Foundation's New Readers project. Created by Reboot, 2016

Helen's backstory helps us understand her living situation and some of the challenges she faces daily. Many of the details in her biography paint a picture of an individual who strongly needs to stay connected with others and be aware of the latest news. Her lack of a reliable and affordable Internet connection makes it difficult to accomplish these goals. She is interested in using the Internet but has limited experience and knowledge of how to do so.

This persona helps us empathize with individuals like Helen and understand some barriers that must be considered when creating future experiences supporting Helen's goals. It's important to keep in mind that Helen is a fictional character who is used to embody the characteristics of this type of person. The content reflected in this persona is the result of extensive ethnographical research and interviews with many people in similar situations, which are used to create a composite sketch representing the most common attributes of this audience.

How Personas Are Used in HCD

In the human-centered design process, personas are typically used in the following ways:

- **Discovery**: Personas are created based on extensive research, including user interviews, surveys, observations, and behavioral data. This foundational discovery research helps identify common traits, behaviors, and needs among different user groups.

- **Empathy and Understanding**: Throughout the design process, team members reference personas to gain a deeper understanding of the user perspective. This empathy-driven approach ensures that design decisions reflect the actual needs of the user.

- **Concept Ideation**: Personas guide discussions during brainstorming and ideation sessions. It prompts designers to ask questions like, "How would this persona interact with this feature?" to generate ideas that align with user needs.

- **Iterative Design**: As the design evolves, personas help evaluate the success of design solutions by measuring how well they meet the needs and goals of the target users. Personas are instrumental in evaluating prototypes and in usability testing. They help focus testing scenarios and recruit users who match the personas, ensuring realistic and representative feedback.

Personas help teams maintain focus on the user throughout the entire HCD process. They provide a means to better connect with the user we are designing for and consider the impact of the experience we create. A journey map is a natural companion to personas in HCD. Journey maps articulate how users will achieve their goals and how the persona's attributes shape the experience created within the journey.

Understanding the Path Forward with Journey Maps

Journey maps are visual representations that document and illustrate the user's experience while engaging with a product, service, or system. These visualizations provide a detailed narrative of a user's step-by-step interaction, highlighting key touchpoints, emotions, and pain points throughout the journey. Journey maps play a crucial role in understanding, empathizing with, and improving the user experience in HCD.

CHAPTER 1   REPRESENTING OUR USERS

The Origins of Journey Maps in Human-Centered Design

The origins of journey mapping can be traced back to the broader fields of design thinking, customer experience, and service design. In the late 20th century, organizations began recognizing that understanding the customer journey was vital for success. Over 30 years ago, Chip Bell and Ron Zemke created one of the first known customer journey maps after exploring customer experience issues at a large telecommunications company. They conducted user research with customers and presented the findings by displaying them in sequence on the conference room walls.[1] These early uses for journey maps helped organizations understand how to analyze and optimize the end-to-end customer experience.

The Composition of a Journey

The core building blocks of a journey map provide the infrastructure to understand what happens as a user attempts to achieve a specified goal. All represented activities in a journey happen in a sequential and usually linear progression based on how a user would experience them. Here is an example of a journey map representing a persona's usage of Wikipedia:

---

[1] The Father of Customer Journey Mapping, Chip Bell, Talks Driving Innovation Through Customer Partnership, The Intercom Blog. https://www.intercom.com/blog/videos/customer-service-expert-chip-bell/#:~:text=Chip%20Bell%20is%20an%20author,how%20to%20engage%20with%20them

CHAPTER 1   REPRESENTING OUR USERS

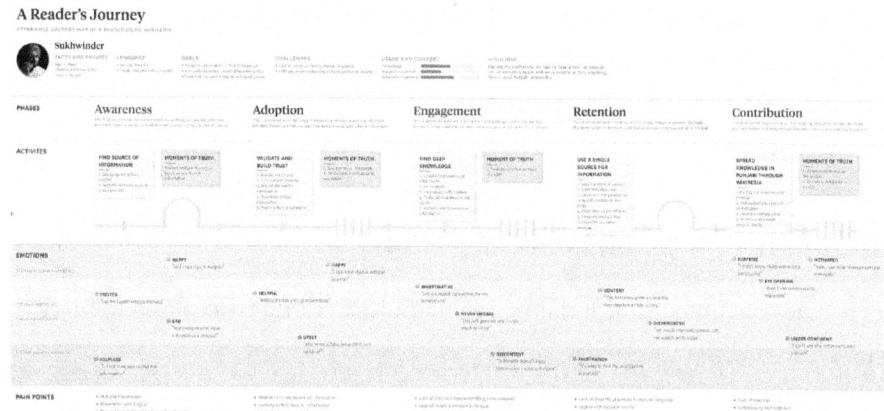

Example of a journey map by the Wikimedia Foundation and Obvious India in 2019

Journey maps can come in many different configurations and levels of detail. The most common components needed to represent the user's experience include

- **Goals**: Each journey represents an overall goal that the user wants to accomplish. The steps in the journey highlight the actions the user takes toward achieving this goal. Goals can also be broken out by specific phases in the journey. The end of the journey typically represents a successful outcome where a user can achieve their overall goal.

- **Phases**: Journey maps typically divide the user experience into broad phases representing major milestones. These phases comprise steps, which are the moments where users engage with the system.

- **Steps**: At each phase, journey maps detail the user's actions. These can include physical actions, digital interactions, or decision-making processes.

13

CHAPTER 1   REPRESENTING OUR USERS

- **Pain Points**: Journey maps highlight any pain points and challenges users encounter along their journey. They identify opportunities for improvement or enhancement in the user experience.

An Outline of a Simple Journey Map

Let's examine the simplified journey of an individual who plans to book a cruise vacation.

Phase: Inspiration and Research

Steps:

- Starts researching cruise destinations and cruise lines online
- Reads reviews and watches videos of cruises
- Decides on a specific destination and cruise line

Phase: Booking Process

Steps:

- Visits the cruise line's website and selects the desired cruise
  - **Pain Point**: Filters related to selecting a specific departure date aren't available, requiring the user to spend extra time reviewing cruises that aren't applicable.
- Selects the cabin type and then selects a room
  - **Pain Point**: The map interface does not let the user zoom in or out to see where their room is located on the ship.
- Adds passenger details

Phase: Confirmation and Payment

Steps:

- Reviews the confirmation details and checks the itinerary
  - **Pain Point**: The user is surprised to find out that there is a non-refundable deposit required before they can complete their reservation.
- Completes the payment process
- Reviews the booking confirmation email

Journey maps often represent the most common workflows and pain points that users typically experience. This information is uncovered through qualitative and quantitative insights collected before creating the journey map. This journey has a clearly defined endpoint determined by the user's indicated goal (i.e., successfully booking a cruise). It is essential to realize that all journeys are part of a continuum and can be used to represent both short and longer-term goals. For example, the journey could have extended into trip preparation and departure phases or the onboard cruise ship experience.

How Journey Maps Are Used in HCD

Teams use journey maps to better understand how users accomplish their goals by examining the touchpoints that make up their experience. They can help product experience teams to

- **Understand and Align**: By providing details and context, a journey map will help teams gain a shared understanding of how users achieve their goals within a given experience.

- **Identify Gaps**: By visualizing the entire journey, teams will spot gaps in the user experience or areas where user needs are not adequately addressed.

- **Prioritize Initiatives**: Journey maps help prioritize design efforts by highlighting critical moments in the user journey that significantly impact user satisfaction and overall success.

- **Collaborate Cross-Functionally**: Journey maps facilitate collaboration among cross-functional teams within an organization, ensuring everyone shares a common understanding of the user experience and aligns their efforts accordingly.

- **Test Solutions**: Journey maps can shape the goals for usability testing, helping teams create scenarios and tasks that reflect real-world user interactions. They also serve as benchmarks for evaluating design changes and their impact on the user experience.

It's important to note that the creation and utilization of journey maps are iterative processes. Teams often revisit and update journey maps as they gather more user data and insights over time. This continuous refinement ensures that the product meets evolving user needs and expectations. Journey maps also play a pivotal role in human-centered design, as they encourage a deeper exploration of user emotions, pain points, and motivations throughout their journey. They are effective communication tools, allowing teams to convey complex user experiences to stakeholders and decision-makers, promoting buy-in and support for human-centered design efforts.

CHAPTER 1   REPRESENTING OUR USERS

Pitfalls in Persona and Journey Map Development

Some have criticized personas and journey maps for not adding sufficient value or not being particularly relevant to an organization. This can be directly attributed to the incorrect strategies that teams have previously taken to create these artifacts.

Fictitious Personas Representing Real Users

Traditionally, it has been best practice to create an imaginary individual to represent the user to generate empathy and make the persona feel like a real person. This persona was given a name, a family, hobbies, and often a personality.

Generating fake characters to represent personas in human-centered design creates several challenges. These fabricated individuals are prone to overgeneralization and fantasy. They often simplify the rich diversity of real user populations into one-dimensional, unrealistic characters, which can result in design decisions that cater to imagined stereotypes rather than real needs. Moreover, these fake individuals aren't genuine people despite being assigned names and fabricated backgrounds. They lack the depth, context, and complexity that real users possess.

Designing products based on such artificial constructs can lead to disconnects between the product and users' actual experiences, ultimately compromising human-centered design principles. Using fake personas can result in inauthentic, misguided design choices that fail to address real user needs while perpetuating harmful stereotypes and generalizations.

Assumption-Driven Journey Maps

Journey maps can be misrepresented if the workflows they represent are created from the perspective of the business rather than how a user experiences it. Business-centric journey maps can perpetuate biases and assumptions not grounded in real user data. They often fail to capture the nuances of user interactions and the emotional aspects of the journey. Journey maps based on business perspectives rather than actual user research can undermine the core principles of empathy, leading to a less effective and inaccurate understanding of the user's experiences.

Solutioning over Understanding Problems

By their nature, product teams are solution-driven entities responsible for addressing both business and user needs. Rushing to create solutions without first understanding the user is a common pitfall in product development that can have detrimental consequences. Focusing on solutions prematurely can result in teams investing time and resources in developing features or designs based on assumptions or guesswork rather than actual user needs. This approach can result in products misaligned with user expectations, leading to suboptimal user experiences, low adoption rates, and wasted resources.

There is a missed opportunity when user understanding is bypassed in order to expedite the creation of a new product or feature. Skipping this foundational step can hinder collaboration and alignment within cross-functional teams, as the absence of a shared user perspective can lead to conflicting priorities and divergent design decisions.

Key Takeaways

- Human-centered design (HCD) is an approach that prioritizes the needs, behaviors, and preferences of end-users. It emphasizes empathy, collaboration, and iterative problem-solving to create solutions that truly meet user needs.

CHAPTER 1   REPRESENTING OUR USERS

- Principles of HCD include empathy, humans at the center, deep understanding of users, cross-functional collaboration, creative problem-solving, continuous feedback, a holistic view, ethical and inclusive design, and ongoing assessment of solutions.

- Personas in HCD represent user archetypes created to better understand and communicate the needs of different audience groups. They help promote empathy with users, ensure user-centric design decisions, and guide the design process.

- Journey maps are visual representations of the user experience, highlighting key touchpoints, emotions, and pain points throughout the user's interaction with a product, service, or system. They aid in identifying gaps, prioritizing design efforts, fostering cross-functional collaboration, and guiding usability testing and evaluation.

- Current failures in persona and journey map development include fictitious personas, assumption-driven journeys, and the tendency to rush into solutions without first understanding user needs, leading to inauthentic, misguided design choices and suboptimal user experiences.

In the next chapter, you will learn why most personas fail and ways to ensure you provide your organization with the most accurate, insightful, and valuable information about our users.

19

CHAPTER 2

Why Most Personas Fail

Why do so many personas fail to have a lasting impact on the organization? The root causes of this failure lie in the current practices used to create personas. This chapter describes common failures associated with industry personas and how to diagnose "sick" personas that could hurt an organization's overall health. To illustrate these issues, we will take a closer look at a persona called Sally.

CHAPTER 2   WHY MOST PERSONAS FAIL

An Obituary for Sally

We are greatly saddened to report the recent death of the persona Sally, the On-the-Go Regional Sales Associate. Here is the story of her birth, life, and untimely death.

The day started with the latest quarterly update, during which the VP of Sales learned about the abysmal sales numbers after a recent redesign of the product landing page. In an effort to identify and fix the issue, the user experience team was tasked with developing a persona that reflects the target audience's needs. The team completed months of qualitative and quantitative research to craft a work of art representing their archetype user. They decided to proclaim her "Sally."

The design team proudly showed Sally off to everyone in the organization and even hung a portrait of her in the company cafeteria amongst Sally's fellow personas. Everyone was overjoyed to learn all about Sally, and the organization's leadership commended the team members for their hard work. The leadership felt certain that Sally would help the organization to finally embrace a human-centered design culture and help them to solve their sales issues.

Several months later, Sally is nowhere to be seen. The product team had been focusing on putting out fires based on a new vision set out by the executive leadership. The design and research teams were overwhelmed by requests to create and test designs based on requirements that the business analysts acquired after speaking with several high-profile customers. The poster of Sally had been taken down in the cafeteria and replaced by a promotion for a company-sponsored Zumba class. The IT department accidentally deleted the contents of a cloud server hosting Sally and her companion personas, but no one seemed to notice.

CHAPTER 2   WHY MOST PERSONAS FAIL

A Persona Postmortem

So what ultimately killed the persona called Sally? At first glance, Sally seems like a very healthy persona that the organization wants to get to know and keep around. However, by performing a postmortem on this persona, we will observe a few causes of an early death. Sally "passed away" due to a series of ailments and missteps that real-life individuals face within organizations.

Lack of Trust and Relevancy

Even though the design team based this persona on user research, no one strongly believed in who Sally was, what she wanted, or how the organization should meet her goals. Stakeholders in the organization harbored perceptions and opinions about Sally that were often based

23

on their own assumptions. The information about Sally did not contain details relevant to the organization's goals or convincingly explain aspects that would have helped the team understand the user. Just because Sally existed did not mean she had a clear purpose in the organization. It was unclear to the stakeholders why they should prioritize Sally's needs over other audiences.

Neglect

Sally suffered from prolonged organizational neglect. No one took the time to "take care" of Sally or regularly see if her needs were being met. Unfortunately, most personas and journey maps are quickly forgotten amongst other organizational priorities and are rarely maintained. A common reason why these artifacts are abandoned is that they eventually no longer represent the current user and do not reflect the latest business objectives. Most personas and journey maps are static, passive documents that, while often visually attractive, do not play an active role in the product or service design life cycle.

Isolation

Sally's demise occurred partly because she was isolated from the user advocacy channels within the organization, which left her feeling unsupported. No one "visited" Sally anymore, and she was separated from the organization's team members who could promote her needs. Personas are often artifacts created to "check a box" as a required milestone in the human-centered design process and aren't frequently used outside the user experience team. Without a reason to regularly reference the persona, the organization focuses on other information to guide its decision-making. Also, without Key Performance Indicators (KPIs) closely tied to the persona, the organization lacks any way of knowing how well it supports its target audience's needs.

CHAPTER 2   WHY MOST PERSONAS FAIL

What Are the Symptoms of a Sick Persona?

Sally's untimely death serves as a reminder of the critical importance of aligning a persona with the organization's needs. Her persona illustrates the negative consequences of failing to align with user needs, neglecting user feedback, and leaving users feeling isolated and unsupported.

If your organization has already created personas, the following are signs that they might not be effective and could be at risk of expiring:

- The persona is nowhere to be seen in project planning sessions
- The persona is not talked about in internal communications
- The persona is not considered in any decisions that would impact the user
- The persona is not regularly measured or reported on

CHAPTER 2   WHY MOST PERSONAS FAIL

Any of these symptoms could indicate that your personas should be revisited to see if the information that they contain supports the current needs of the organization and the user.

Aspects of Personas That Are Adverse to Your Persona's Health

Junk food can be satisfying, but just like in a real person, these empty calories provide little value and often erode our health. To make personas relatable and feel like actual people, designers often introduce fictional elements to make the personas feel like a whole living person.

This extraneous information, like junk food, may initially be appealing or appear to satisfy specific needs, but it is highly problematic for teams using personas to make decisions about the organization's users. The following are some of the most common fictional elements included with personas and why they are problematic.

Irrelevant Information

Including irrelevant information in a persona can lead to confusion and misalignment in decision-making. Irrelevant details distract from the core characteristics and needs of the user, making it difficult for an organization to focus on what truly matters. Decisions based on irrelevant information are unlikely to address the actual concerns and preferences of the target user group, leading to wasted resources and misguided efforts. Your persona might be harboring junk information if it includes anecdotes like these:

- Hobbies and extracurricular activities
- Names of spouses, parents, friends, pet cat, etc.
- Things they liked to do for fun
- Inspirational quotes

Vague Information

Vague information in a persona leaves room for misinterpretation and ambiguity. Decision-makers may struggle to understand users' needs, goals, and pain points accurately. This can result in a lack of clarity in product or service development, marketing campaigns, and user support efforts. Vague information also makes it challenging to measure the success of initiatives since success criteria are not well-defined. A persona contains vague information when it includes one or more of the following:

- Goals that aren't clearly defined or lack a conclusive outcome (e.g., "peace on earth," "live a healthy life," "be a better human being")
- Ambiguous pain points such as "finds technology challenging" without detailing specific issues they face
- Information visualizations without a defined scale (e.g., a chart showing a partially filled-in scale indicating their level of tech savviness)

Overgeneralized and Stereotypical Information

Overgeneralization occurs when attributes are grouped to represent users under broad categories. Often, this information generalizes facts intended to pertain to a group of individuals represented by the persona, but that might not be an attribute for everyone. For example, Sally's persona contains a personality trait that says she is passionate. Still, we can't assume that everyone supposed to be represented by Sally has this same quality or would feel this way in all situations. This can lead to stereotyping and oversimplification of user needs and behaviors. Decision-makers may assume that all users within a category share the same preferences, resulting in products, services, or communications that do not reflect user diversity. This oversimplification can alienate user segments and cause them to disengage. Examples of aspects that tend to be overgeneralized include

- Personality traits (e.g., witty, punctual, energetic, etc.)
- Personal preferences (e.g., favorite shampoo brands)

CHAPTER 2 WHY MOST PERSONAS FAIL

- Personal habits (e.g., morning person)
- Frustrations that anyone would have (e.g., long waits, overly complex things, time-consuming things)

While personas should be based on facts about the user population, demographics can be overgeneralized. Attributes should be carefully considered that best reflect all representative users being of a certain age, gender, race, or socioeconomic status, and designers should be aware of their own biases so that they can put them aside.

Hyperspecific Information

Hyperspecification occurs when attributes are too specific to represent a generalized population adequately. This information only pertains to specific individuals represented by the persona that would not be a universal attribute for everyone in a particular group. This can lead to an overly narrow perspective of a user's demographics, backgrounds, and behaviors. Decision-makers may assume that all users within a category share these specific attributes, resulting in products, services, or communications that do not resonate with the larger user population. Examples of details that are typically too specific for a persona include the following:

- Home location (e.g., Boca Raton, Florida)
- Age (e.g., 25 years old)
- Marital status
- Employer (e.g., Acme Corporation)
- Years of work experience (e.g., 18 years as an Acme employee)
- Unique scenarios (e.g., Sally's boss expects her to be online by 7:15 a.m. PST)

There are situations where certain types of specific information are relevant. For example, if your team were designing a new dating app, relationship status and age would be useful to know. However, these details would be inappropriate for personas used to design engineering software.

Unsupported Information

When a persona lacks supporting evidence and is not backed by research, it becomes unreliable and potentially misleading. Decision-makers may make choices based on assumptions or unfounded opinions about users, leading to incorrect conclusions. Unsupported information can erode trust in the persona's accuracy and credibility, making gaining buy-in for user-centric strategies challenging.

The purpose of creating personas is to provide a deep understanding of different user groups so that organizations can tailor their strategies and offerings accordingly. Irrelevant, unsupported, vague, or overgeneralized information undermines this purpose, hindering the organization's ability to make informed decisions and effectively meet user needs. To maximize the value of personas, it is essential to ensure that the information included is relevant, well-supported by data and research, precise, and representative of the true diversity of the user base.

CHAPTER 2   WHY MOST PERSONAS FAIL

Too Much of a Good Thing Can Harm Your Persona

A collection of personas representing the organization's target audiences can be a strength in understanding the broad range of user needs that an organization must meet. However, many teams that have adopted the concept of personas continually generate personas to support new initiatives and usually lack a clear persona governance strategy. Having too many personas can be detrimental to the "health" of individual personas needed to represent the unique needs of each audience.

Redundancies and Confusion

Too many personas can create confusion within the organization. It is common in large organizations for different teams and departments (e.g., marketing, CX, UX, sales, operations, etc.) to create their own personas in a vacuum, representing the same or similar audiences. This creates redundancies and potentially introduces conflicting information about the same user group. Different teams or departments may interpret and respond to the needs of various personas differently, leading to inconsistencies in product development, marketing, and support efforts. It also makes it difficult to understand a particular user's journey as that person interacts across the organization's entire product and service ecosystem.

Difficulties in Maintaining Focus and Prioritizing

Too many personas make it challenging for the organization to prioritize and allocate resources effectively. A single persona may become muddled or overshadowed by many other personas, making it difficult for the organization to maintain a coherent and unified approach to address the needs of any of its personas successfully. Decision-makers may find it difficult to decide which user persona to prioritize, leading to a lack of clear focus on addressing specific user needs.

Challenges with Maintaining Numerous Personas

Creating and maintaining numerous personas requires significant time, effort, and resources. Regularly updating and validating these personas to reflect changing user behaviors and preferences can become burdensome. The sheer volume of personas may result in outdated or inaccurate information, which can further hinder the organization's ability to make informed decisions about Sally and other users.

An excessive number of organizational personas leads to a lack of focus, confusion, and practical challenges in maintaining and updating them. This will ultimately harm a personas "health," as their specific needs will not receive the attention and resources needed for their optimal user experience. To address this, organizations should strike a balance by focusing on a manageable number of personas that represent key user segments accurately and align with their strategic goals and resources.

CHAPTER 2   WHY MOST PERSONAS FAIL

Bad Personas Can Make the Organization Sick

These ill-formed personas can make an organization "sick," leading to various negative consequences. Here's how these considerations contribute to organizational health issues:

Distractions—Paying Attention to the Wrong Details

Bad personas can be distracting because they often include irrelevant information. Decision-makers may focus on superficial details about the persona, diverting attention from critical user needs. When organizations pay attention to the wrong details in a persona, they may invest resources in addressing issues that are not truly important to the target audience, leading to inefficiencies and misaligned strategies.

CHAPTER 2   WHY MOST PERSONAS FAIL

Misinformation—Misleading or Wrong Information

Bad personas can contain misinformation, providing incorrect or misleading information about the user. This misinformation can lead to misguided decision-making and ineffective strategies. When misinformation is discovered, trust in the persona's accuracy is eroded, causing decision-makers to question the reliability of user personas and potentially undermining the entire persona-based approach.

Distrust—Lack of Trust in Persona Information

When bad personas are created and used, decision-makers may lose trust in the information presented in them. They may begin to doubt the validity of user research and persona development processes. Teams that distrust a persona's information can make decisions without considering user needs, resulting in products, services, or marketing campaigns that miss the mark and fail to engage the target audience effectively.

Disengagement—Losing Interest in the Persona (and the End User)

Decision-makers and teams may become disinterested in personas that do not provide valuable insights or accurate representations of users. When teams lose interest in personas, they are less likely to advocate for user-centric approaches, which can result in a decline in overall user satisfaction and loyalty.

Badly created personas negatively impact an organization, causing distractions, spreading disinformation, fostering distrust in user data, and ultimately leading to disengagement from user-centered strategies.

Creating and using personas based on accurate and reliable user research is essential to maintain organizational health, ensuring that decision-makers can trust and act upon the information provided.

A Cure for the Common Persona

It is possible to avoid contagions that commonly infect your personas and ensure that newly created personas have a long shelf life. Personas should be formed as part of a strategy that considers both the organization's and the user's goals.

Quality over Quantity

Organizations should prioritize and focus on the personas that align with most users. Once designers create these core personas, they should develop a deliberate strategy to identify and create personas that map to other types of users (see Chapter 5 on creating persona trees). Too many personas lead to confusion, dilution of resources, and challenges in maintaining accuracy. Focusing on fewer, well-researched personas that represent key user segments is more effective than trying to account for every possible type of user.

Relevant to the Organization

Personas should focus on information that directly impacts organizational alignment and decision-making. Aligning personas to business goals and those accountable for achieving such goals will ensure that personas receive the attention of executives, managers, and others responsible for prioritizing resources. Irrelevant or distracting details lead to organizational disengagement, as teams may lose interest in using personas that don't provide valuable insights. To prevent disengagement, personas must be thoughtfully constructed to offer actionable information that guides human-centric strategies and decision-making.

Balancing Specificity with Generalization

It is important to strike a balance between specificity and generalization when representing the details of a persona. Overly specific information can make seeing common themes within a represented user group challenging, while overly generalized information may not provide sufficiently actionable insights. A well-crafted persona strikes this balance, capturing the right level of detail to be useful while avoiding a specificity that renders it too granular or niche.

Establishing Trust

Trust is paramount when using personas to inform decisions. Unsupported or erroneous insights within personas can erode trust in the persona-based approach and lead to misguided strategies. Ensuring that a persona's information is accurate and based on sound research is essential for maintaining the trust of stakeholders.

Key Takeaways

Reasons Why Most Personas Fail:

- **Lack of Trust and Relevance**: Personas often fail when stakeholders do not believe the information in them or do not understand how they relate to organizational priorities.

- **Neglect and Isolation**: Personas are abandoned or forgotten when they aren't regularly updated and are isolated from decision-making processes.

- **Inclusion of Irrelevant Information**: Personas can fail when they contain irrelevant, unsupported, vague, overgeneralized, or hyperspecific details that detract from core user needs.

Recommendations to Prevent Persona Failure:

- **Prioritize Relevance and Trust**: Create personas aligned with organizational goals and support them with robust research to build trust in their accuracy.

- **Balanced Specificity**: Strike a balance in persona details to create personas that are actionable and useful for decision-making.

- **Quality Over Quantity**: Focus on a manageable number of well-researched personas rather than creating too many, which can lead to confusion and resource dilution.

In the next chapter, you will learn about altitudes to conceptualize the various detail and context levels needed to accurately represent a persona and its journey.

CHAPTER 3

Flying to New Heights: The Concept of Altitudes

Many organizations struggle to understand their users and align on a unified strategy to meet user needs. Determining the right level of detail is an essential part of a persona and journey map strategy. In this chapter, you will learn about altitudes to conceptualize the various detail and context levels needed to accurately represent a persona and its journey.

A Fog Preventing Organizational Alignment

Heavy fog covers most organizations, making it difficult for the various parts to see, understand, and align. Occasionally, these parts temporarily collide in the mist, and this is where initiatives are typically formed. This alignment is often short-lived, and once these projects are underway, the fog thickens, producing a lack of clarity caused by miscommunication, misinterpretation, and misinformation.

CHAPTER 3   FLYING TO NEW HEIGHTS: THE CONCEPT OF ALTITUDES

A human-centered approach to design requires that all parts of an organization understand and align on who the user is and what that user's needs are. This can be challenging given the following:

- The user is not consistently defined in the same way by the various teams involved.

- The knowledge about the user is fragmented and not represented by the same details.

- The organization is separated into functional silos that do not look at the user's entire experience.

- Different roles in the organization focus their attention on big-picture solutions while others are in the weeds solving narrowly focused problems.

To address these problems, a new framework is necessary to build an infrastructure for personas and journey maps. These can help the organization understand the user with the right level of detail and context to support decision-making. Once everyone in the organization understands the user in the same way, the organizational fog will begin to lift.

CHAPTER 3   FLYING TO NEW HEIGHTS: THE CONCEPT OF ALTITUDES

The Concept of Altitudes

Flying gives us a new perspective on a landscape because we are seeing the world from a different vantage point. Think about the last time that you were on a flight. The plane reaches its cruising altitude, the pilot turns off the fasten seatbelt sign, and you take your first look out the window. What do you see?

You can see far and wide across the landscape below at this height. Your view gives you the broadest range of observations, such as mountain ranges, lakes, cities, farmland, rivers, and deserts. These are the same kinds of observable features that astronauts view from space. While observing Earth from these high altitudes, we often contemplate how small we are and truly appreciate the grand scale of our world and ecosystem.

CHAPTER 3   FLYING TO NEW HEIGHTS: THE CONCEPT OF ALTITUDES

As your flight moves across the landscape, you see different environments, structures, and identifiable characteristics that help you form a mental model of the geography from the beginning to the end of your journey. These characteristics can establish milestones and prominent points of reference to understand where you are and which direction you are going.

When the plane begins its initial descent, you start to see details that weren't possible earlier in your flight. If you are landing in a populated area, you may begin to see commercial and residential properties, highways, parks, and boats on the water. These characteristics help you see how humans have organized their spaces and better understand how things are interconnected.

On the final approach, people and buildings emerge in starker view, appearing before you in greater detail but with a much narrower focus of view. The vehicles on the road no longer look like tiny ants, and you can likely determine the make and model of certain cars. You can read billboards and large road signs. When the plane's landing gear finally touches the ground, your viewpoint returns to the granular level of detail you see every day.

Increasing and decreasing altitudes provide a telescoping lens for viewing various levels of detail and context. When applied to personas and journey maps, organizations can use altitudes to understand the user from varying perspectives and adjust to the best level for alignment on solutions.

Using Altitude-Based Artifacts in Human-Centered Design

Personas and journey maps are used as artifacts to align on who the user is and what they need to accomplish to achieve their goals. They also provide the context and path to reaching a successful outcome.

High altitude artifacts help the entire organization align on the most common attributes representing their users. They can ensure that different parts of an organization are making decisions based on the same information and help organizations look more holistically at how we support users who are tied to the success and future of the organization.

Mid altitude artifacts help teams within a departmental group focus on the details that inform product and service roadmaps.

Low altitude artifacts help inform product requirements and features. They help the team focus on use cases that pertain to certain populations in specific use cases.

Let's examine how these artifacts might help an e-commerce company within the travel industry. In this example, we will focus on a core type of user central to this organization's business model. The highest level persona for this organization is the traveler.

CHAPTER 3   FLYING TO NEW HEIGHTS: THE CONCEPT OF ALTITUDES

The traveler's goals are to

- Find transportation for an upcoming trip.
- Evaluate available options.
- Purchase the trip.

High altitude artifacts help everyone in the organization gain a shared perspective on the core needs of anyone booking travel and the phases of that experience. This alignment can ensure a common frame of reference as members of the organization begin to support the various needs of the different types of travelers from the beginning to the end of their journey. Let's look at a lower altitude persona with more specific needs: a persona representing a business traveler who needs to book a flight for a work trip.

CHAPTER 3   FLYING TO NEW HEIGHTS: THE CONCEPT OF ALTITUDES

The business traveler's goals are to

- Find transportation for an upcoming work trip.
- Evaluate available options based on flight schedule, company-preferred airline, and pricing based on company policy.
- Purchase the trip using a corporate credit card.
- Receive an emailed receipt to submit with an expense report.

The mid altitude persona provides additional context for these users such as potential reasons for their trip, considerations for evaluating their travel options, and purchasing needs. Other personas of the same altitude (such as a leisure traveler) would share the same basic needs but possess key differentiators that the team would need to consider. Finally, let's look at the lowest altitude persona for this organization: a small business traveler looking to change a booked flight at the last minute while using his smartphone at the airport on his day of travel.

The small business traveler's goals in this particular situation are as follows:

- Find last-minute transportation options for a booked trip due to a change in a client's schedule.
- Evaluate options based on the airline's flight schedule, seat availability, and the most cost-effective option.
- Utilize the browser on their smartphone to locate their reservation, change their existing flight, and pay any cost difference with their new itinerary.

This persona still has all of the needs of the high- and mid-level personas, but possesses additional unique needs related to this type of business and travel situation. Considerations for this type of persona include the level of urgency, budget constraints, and environment. Low altitude artifacts help teams think through more complex use cases that could have experience design, operational, and technical implications.

The Relationship Between Altitudes, Personas, and Journey Maps

In our postmortem of the Sally persona, we identified information about Sally that negatively affected our ability to understand and design for a particular type of individual. The Sally persona contained aspects that were both incredibly narrow and hyperspecific, as well as generalities and cliches. This persona was not sufficiently grounded in relevant details that would help define requirements nor broad enough to consider the wider implications for users of this type. When we apply the concept of altitudes, we can see how the information represented in a persona and journey map changes to support different levels of understanding about the user.

CHAPTER 3   FLYING TO NEW HEIGHTS: THE CONCEPT OF ALTITUDES

High Altitude Examples

A high altitude persona includes details that represent the audience's most common attributes. It highlights consistencies that help understand the goals, needs, and pain points shared by all users represented by this persona. The persona below captures the core attributes of a salesperson and details what a typical individual in a sales role needs to succeed. For example, building a client pipeline, closing deals, and maintaining client relationships are all goals for any salesperson persona.

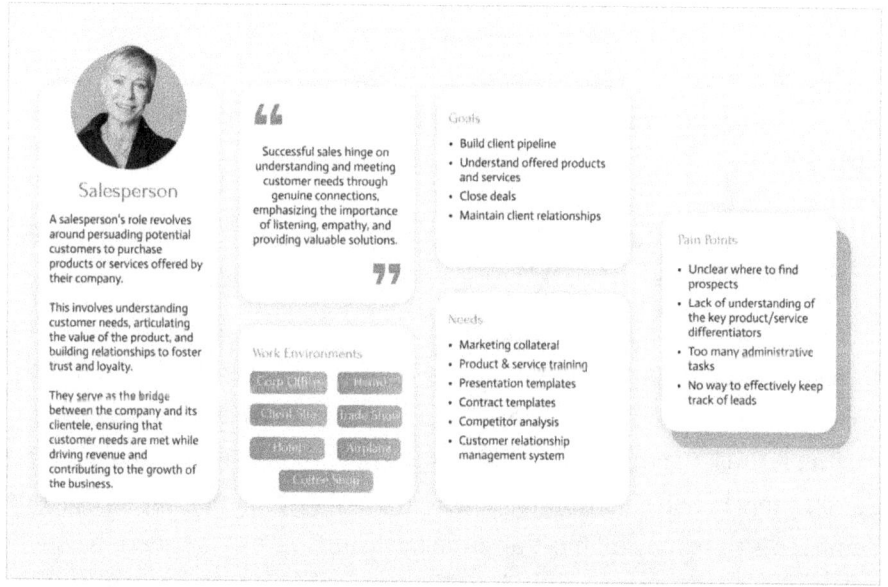

A journey map written at the same high altitude helps to understand the common milestones and steps that all personas of this type would take to achieve their goal. This journey map highlights all of the milestones necessary for a salesperson to complete a sale with a new client.

47

CHAPTER 3   FLYING TO NEW HEIGHTS: THE CONCEPT OF ALTITUDES

Persona	Salesperson				
Goal	**Complete the Sales Process for a New Client**				
Milestones	Prospecting & Research	Initial Contact & Qualification	Presentation & Demonstration	Negotiation & Closing	Onboarding & Follow-Up
Tasks	• Identify potential leads through different channels • Research and gather information about leads to tailor the approach	• Reach out to leads via various means (calls, emails, social media) • Qualify leads by understanding their needs and evaluating fit	• Arrange meetings or demos to showcase the product/service • Address any concerns or objections raised by the prospect	• Discuss pricing, terms, and customization • Secure the deal and finalize the transaction	• Ensure smooth onboarding for the client • Maintain communication for long-term relationships and potential upselling opportunities
Painpoints	• Difficulty in finding accurate and updated contact information for leads • Lack of information about the lead's specific needs or challenges, leading to a generic approach	• Facing rejection or lack of response from leads despite multiple attempts to connect • Difficulty in qualifying leads due to vague or unclear responses about their needs	• Technical issues or glitches during demos affecting the quality of the pitch • Inability to address all concerns raised by the prospect, leading to doubts	• Challenges with aligning pricing or terms with the prospect's expectations • Prolonged decision-making processes or unexpected objections at the final stages	• Challenges with maintaining communication post-sale due to multiple client engagements • Handling client dissatisfaction or issues without a clear resolution strategy

Like our in-flight experience analogy, this high altitude perspective provides the broadest viewpoint for organizations to achieve a unified alignment on who this user is and how to support them along their journey.

Low Altitude Examples

In contrast, a low altitude persona focuses on the unique needs of a targeted audience. It provides a more specific context and helps identify aspects that may require additional considerations. In this example, the persona represents the attributes of a salesperson new to the organization, in a remotely based role, and responsible for obtaining new small business clients. This persona still has the same basic attributes and needs as any salesperson on the team but has unique needs that must be considered when designing for this audience.

CHAPTER 3   FLYING TO NEW HEIGHTS: THE CONCEPT OF ALTITUDES

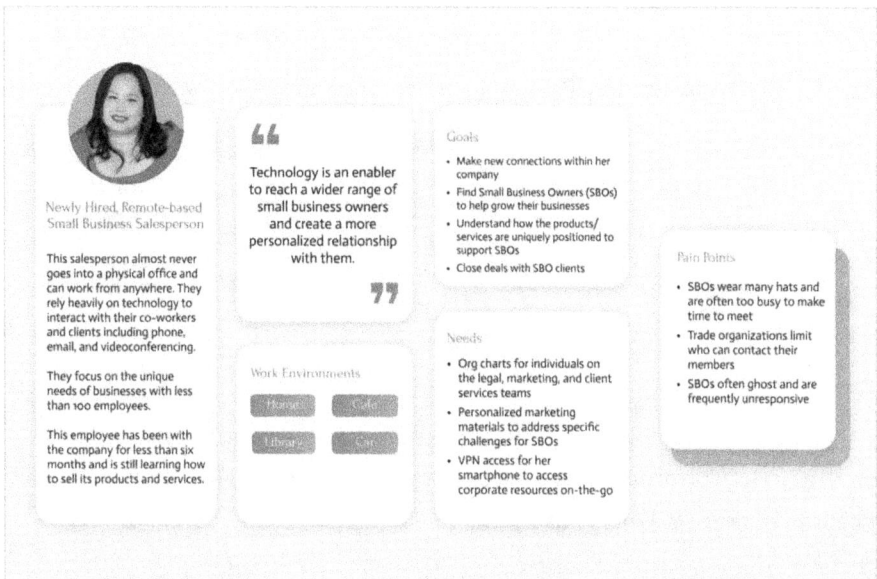

To support this persona's primary goal of obtaining new clients, they have needs related to being a new employee and methods to find suitable clients who are small business owners.

An accompanying low altitude journey map includes the same milestones and represents the same goal of obtaining a new client as the higher altitude version. The activities within each milestone are more contextual to the circumstances of a persona who is working remotely, learning a role and ways of working at a new company, and encountering the challenges of selling to small business owners.

49

CHAPTER 3   FLYING TO NEW HEIGHTS: THE CONCEPT OF ALTITUDES

Using the concept of altitudes to design your personas and journeys allows you to examine the right level of detail to help drive alignment and decision-making within your team.

The Persona Spectrum

Representing users at many altitudes may have you reaching for an air sick bag. Instead of generating many personas and journey maps to represent every aspect of your users, altitudes can make it much easier to establish a common view and a consistent framework.

A small set of high altitude personas can help represent the overarching types of audiences that an organization needs to support. From there, you can break down the audiences into subsets of the higher altitude persona. This can be represented by a set of mid altitude personas that provide a deeper level of context and unique needs while still inheriting the traits of the higher altitude persona. Lower altitude personas are reserved for use cases that require the team to understand highly specific subsets of these user groups.

CHAPTER 3   FLYING TO NEW HEIGHTS: THE CONCEPT OF ALTITUDES

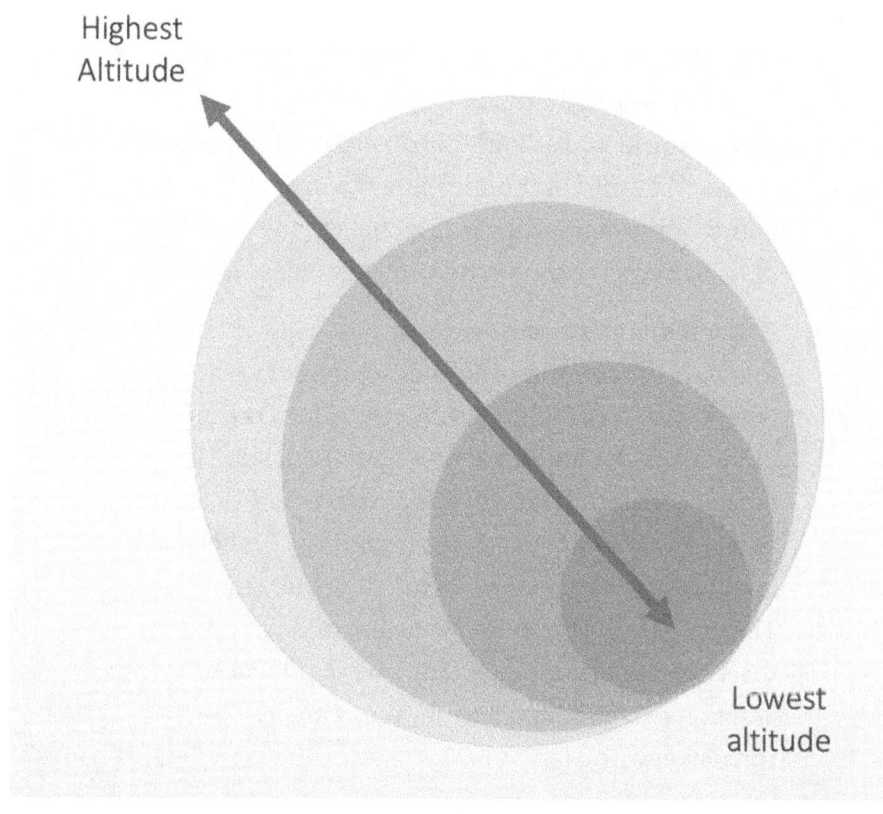

Visualizing the relationship between personas at each altitude helps an organization understand the broader and more specific needs it needs to address. This also economizes the creation of personas by only creating personas at lower altitudes as a specific need arises and enables organizations to utilize information gained from higher altitudes.

No matter how many personas the organization will ultimately need to create, it is necessary to construct a framework for building a hierarchy to show the connections between each persona. The easiest way to visualize this hierarchy is to create a tree structure. Creating a persona tree is essential to building your organization's persona strategy. You will learn how to make a persona tree for your organization in Chapter 5.

CHAPTER 3 FLYING TO NEW HEIGHTS: THE CONCEPT OF ALTITUDES

Key Takeaways

- **Organizational Alignment and the Fog**: You may have experienced a common issue in many organizations that is considered a "fog" that obstructs alignment. Fog is caused by miscommunication, misinterpretation, and misinformation, making it challenging for different parts of the organization to work together effectively.

- **Altitudes as a Framework**: Consider a new framework that uses the concept of altitudes—similar to the perspective on a flight—to understand users from different angles and at varying levels of detail. The concept of altitudes enables teams to establish a common view and consistent framework for personas and journey maps across a team or organization. This helps ensure that everyone is working from the same understanding of the user experience and that personas and journey maps are used in a consistent way.

- **Higher Altitudes vs. Lower Altitudes**: High altitude personas and journey maps provide a broad perspective and focus on common attributes, while low altitude personas and journey maps delve into unique, user-specific needs and situations.

- **Alignment and Decision-Making:** High altitude artifacts can serve as tools to foster alignment across your organization, enabling different teams to base their decisions on the same information. Mid altitude artifacts inform product and service roadmaps, while low altitude artifacts guide specific product requirements and features.

In the next chapter, you will review the different types of attributes that comprise a persona and understand how these attributes change in context and detail based on the altitude.

CHAPTER 4

Developing Persona Characteristics That Matter

A persona, like the intricate structure of human DNA, is a complex tapestry woven together from a combination of characteristics, experiences, and traits. Like DNA, the organized collection of these attributes creates a uniquely defined type of individual akin to our genetic code. In this chapter, we will begin to define what attributes comprise the building blocks of personas.

CHAPTER 4 DEVELOPING PERSONA CHARACTERISTICS THAT MATTER

Setting Up a Persona Attribute Framework

An organization, and in some cases, individual teams, may have different ways of defining the makeup of their users. The first step before creating personas is to create an agreed upon framework to use to define your personas. The attributes framework will be composed of characteristics that help coordinate the creation of personas at each altitude.

Calibrate Your Organization's Altimeter

At any given moment, air traffic control coordinates thousands of flights. Airspace is divided into different altitudes and airspace classes. Assigning specific altitudes to aircraft helps organize and manage air traffic within

CHAPTER 4   DEVELOPING PERSONA CHARACTERISTICS THAT MATTER

defined airspace sectors. Precise altitude coordination is fundamental to maintaining order, safety, and efficiency in the complex and dynamic air traffic environment. It ensures that aircraft operate within designated airspace in a manner that minimizes risks and maximizes the capacity of the airspace system.

Whether managing flights or personas, an organization needs to think at various altitudes in the same way to ensure a coordinated and successful outcome. A persona's characteristics will vary, but they should all possess distinct differences that help define and clearly distinguish a persona from all the others. Defining levels allows personas with the same detail and context to "live" in established altitudes.

Represent Attributes at Each Altitude Level

In the most basic sense, an attribute is a characteristic that helps to define a persona. A persona may have one or many defining attributes associated with it, depending on why it was created and as determined by stakeholders, subject matter experts, and user research. The types of attributes and their specificity and context will be based on the altitude they are associated with.

Set Altitude Levels

Higher altitude levels should contain broader characteristics representing a wide range of personas. The persona characteristics are more focused, specific, and contextual at lower altitude levels. The height of each defined altitude level may vary and will be different for every organization. Most organizations can represent all their personas within three to four altitude levels. This amount strikes a balance between allowing an organization to consider necessary specificity and context while avoiding personas that become too granular or narrow.

CHAPTER 4   DEVELOPING PERSONA CHARACTERISTICS THAT MATTER

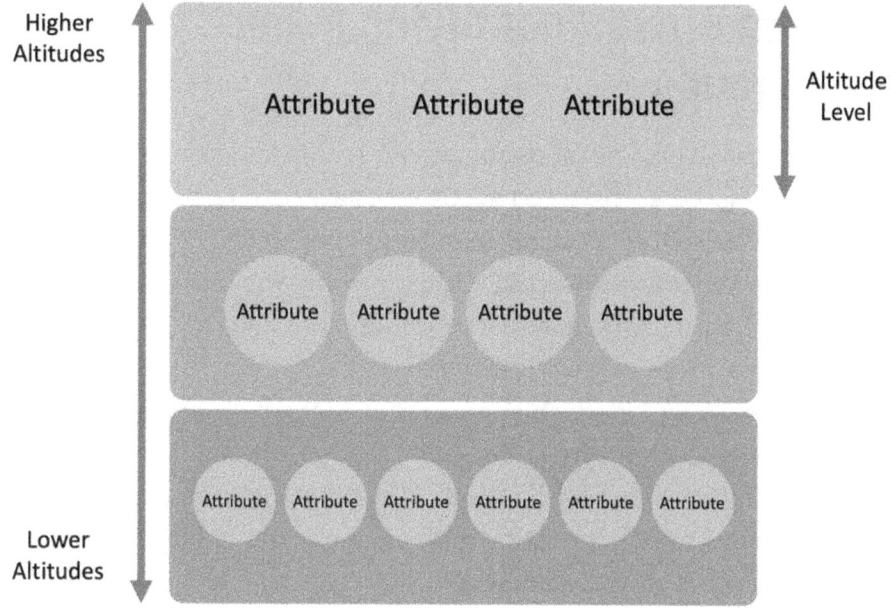

Establishing clearly defined altitudes ensures that personas will be compatible with each other and will share a similar way of thinking about the characteristics that comprise them. For example, a collection of attributes for a team building a mobile game app could include commonalities, including the type of gamer (casual or frequent), account status (current or new), and account level (free or paid). A lower altitude collection might contain more granular details such as device type, operating system version, configuration settings, and communication preferences.

The altitudes help establish a common framework that can scale over time as your organization continues to define additional attributes that help define your users. Once you have aligned the attributes and determined how they relate to each other, you can begin using this framework to define your personas.

CHAPTER 4   DEVELOPING PERSONA CHARACTERISTICS THAT MATTER

Starting Broad: Identifying Major User Groups

Many established organizations already have some understanding of the types of users they serve and might even have existing personas documented. Even if your organization hasn't invested in user research to understand your users, you can still brainstorm who those users might be. While these user types may just be assumptions and could overlook certain groups, they're a good place to start.

You should start with the highest altitude user groups to create a relationship structure for your personas. These groups should represent the largest number of users with the most attributes in common. Let's take the example of a small flower shop business seeking to understand and create experiences for its customers.

CHAPTER 4   DEVELOPING PERSONA CHARACTERISTICS THAT MATTER

Samantha owns the local florist shop in her small rural community. She has been gradually expanding the reach of her business beyond her brick-and-mortar store to fulfill online orders. She has also started to market to other local small businesses that utilize flowers. Last year, she purchased a farm so that she could now supply her business with the flowers it needed herself. Samantha hopes to enter the wholesale flower business as the next growth phase for her business.

In this scenario, Samantha knows that she wants to focus on selling to three unique types of customers: retail consumers, other small businesses, and wholesale businesses. While all of these need to purchase flowers, they have fundamentally different backgrounds, needs, and ways of interacting with Samantha's business.

These customer groups represent three user types, all of whom need to communicate with the shop owner, make purchases, and receive orders. Samantha must understand the similarities and differences between these user groups to make more informed decisions about everything from marketing to how customers can purchase her flowers online.

CHAPTER 4   DEVELOPING PERSONA CHARACTERISTICS THAT MATTER

Narrowing Focus: Utilizing the Altitude Framework to Generate Personas

After you have established altitude levels and the attributes that will be represented, you can begin to generate personas for your organization. High altitude personas should be created first for a strategic and bigger-picture view of the user. Lower altitude personas should be formed using the lower altitude bands that represent specific characteristics of these types of users.

To begin developing her personas, Samantha considered factors impacting how she interacts with her retail and business-to-business (B2B) customers to stick with our current example. She identified occasions that spark the highest number of purchases, such as weddings, funerals, and birthdays. Over half of her customers purchase flowers directly from her local shop, but online purchases have steadily increased. About a third of Samantha's customers have been buying from her for years, but she is looking for opportunities to attract new customers. Her research with wholesale customers indicates that having different payment options is necessary to establish a relationship with her business. Based on these defined altitudes, let's look at the persona attributes representing Samantha's audiences.

CHAPTER 4   DEVELOPING PERSONA CHARACTERISTICS THAT MATTER

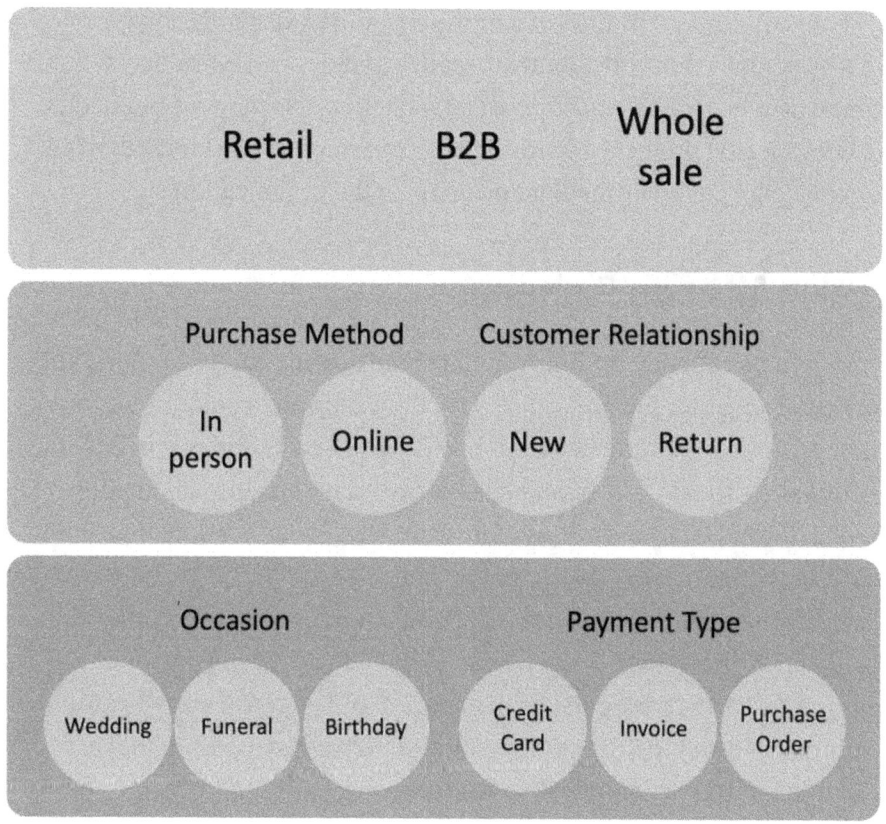

In this example, the highest altitude level represents the three distinct types of customers. The next altitude level represents more specific details and context (e.g., purchase method and customer relationship) that must be considered for each customer. The lowest defined altitude, and therefore the most granular, represents even more specific details and context (e.g., occasion and payment type) that may not be necessary for all personas or situations.

In some cases, a fourth altitude level may be necessary for even more specific situations, such as when an organization must create personas representing certain buyer types for unique sizes, venues, and budgets.

Your established framework should support a structured way to create personas that consider the breadth and depth of your users. Your framework should scale to support new personas as they are needed to address specific projects and initiatives. You might only start with a few personas that are an immediate priority for the organization.

Lower Altitude Personas

Samantha has already established her three target audience groups and now must consider personas based on their unique needs. She knows many customers visiting her store buy flowers as a birthday gift. She highly values these customers because birthdays are annual, making it more likely that she can successfully form long-term relationships with them. Anticipating this, she developed numerous creative bouquets and customizations for these customers. Based on this scenario, Samantha should create a persona for her retail in-person returning customers who purchase birthday gifts. Each aspect of this persona would contain attributes that shape the experiences that Samantha wants to make available for these customers.

CHAPTER 4   DEVELOPING PERSONA CHARACTERISTICS THAT MATTER

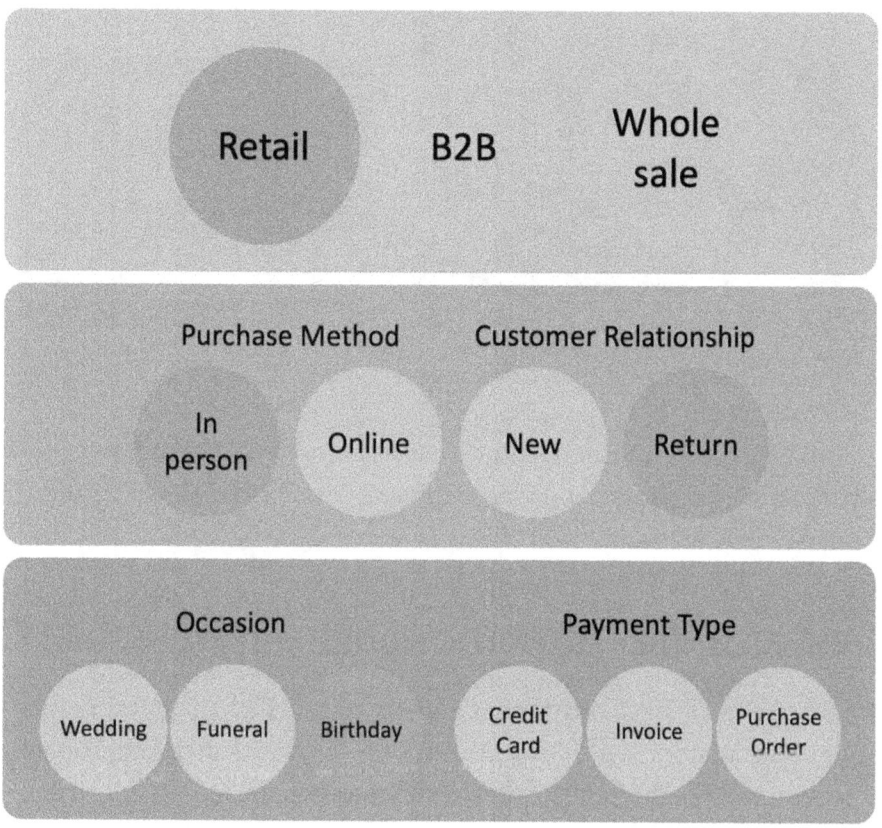

This example persona highlights the attributes representing her target retail customers. This persona will help Samantha focus on catering to the needs of her in-person and returning customers. The additional details of the buying occasion provide further context and the unique needs of a customer purchasing in that specific situation.

CHAPTER 4   DEVELOPING PERSONA CHARACTERISTICS THAT MATTER

Utilizing the established altitude bands helps to ensure that the personas created contain only the attributes needed to make decisions about this type of user.

Conduct a User Attribute Alignment Workshop

Workshops are an engaging format that brings together all departmental groups that support user needs. The process starts with divergent thinking to brainstorm the different attributes that make up the many users the organization supports. This is also a great opportunity to share any existing user research or data about the organization's users. Individuals in the workshop should use either physical or digital sticky notes to document these attributes. The group will then post their notes on a wall or digital board and review them together. At this phase of the activity, participants should not be concerned about exact phrasing or if they are defining attributes that are too broad or narrow.

CHAPTER 4   DEVELOPING PERSONA CHARACTERISTICS THAT MATTER

Converging the group's ideas is the next step to creating a common set of attributes. A facilitator can help to review all the ideas the team generates and create an affinity map to group similar attributes together. The group should use the dot voting technique, where each person uses a set of colored dot stickers to prioritize the most relevant attributes and agree upon the final labels to describe each attribute.

The final step is to take the attributes and create a hierarchy based on the defined altitude bands. Further alignment may be necessary beyond a single workshop activity, but this process brings the organization closer to thinking about users in the same way to define organization-wide personas.

CHAPTER 4 DEVELOPING PERSONA CHARACTERISTICS THAT MATTER

Considerations for an Organization with Existing Personas

Some organizations may already have established personas or criteria for their users. Depending on how narrowly these existing personas are defined, a team may need to deconstruct them to determine their attributes so that they can be used in broader contexts. For example, if job titles define personas, a facilitator should encourage participants to consider what attributes are included in this role. For example, these attributes may include whether an individual works remotely or onsite, the tools they use, and whether they are a part-time or full-time employee. The result is a better understanding of the attributes comprising personas, thereby enabling organizations to broaden their application beyond the existing personas and possibly serve in the creation of new personas that share these attributes.

Key Takeaways

- **Establish a Persona Attribute Framework**: Define an agreed-upon attribute framework that will guide the creation of your personas. Calibrate the organization's "altimeter" to think at various altitudes for a coordinated outcome.

- **Represent Attributes at Each Level**: Define attributes for personas at different altitudes; attributes should vary in specificity and context based on altitude. Set altitude levels with broad characteristics at higher altitudes and more focused, specific characteristics at lower altitudes.

CHAPTER 4   DEVELOPING PERSONA CHARACTERISTICS THAT MATTER

- **Start Broad**: Identify attributes starting with the highest altitude representing the largest user segments with common characteristics.

- **Narrow Focus**: Identify lower altitude attributes with specific characteristics representing a subset of users.

- **Conduct a User Attribute Alignment Workshop**: Hold workshops to unite departmental groups supporting user needs. Use divergent thinking to brainstorm attributes, then converge to create a common set using affinity mapping and dot voting.

In the next chapter, we will explore how to visualize the relationships and hierarchy between various personas at the same and different altitudes.

CHAPTER 5

Building a Persona Family Tree

Establishing a relationship structure for your personas is essential to ensuring that your organization addresses the correct types of users. A persona tree helps you visualize these connections, provides a growth strategy as your organization accounts for a broader user base, and develops a deeper understanding of unique user needs.

CHAPTER 5   BUILDING A PERSONA FAMILY TREE

The Risks of Not Defining an Organization-Wide Persona Strategy

Personas and journey maps are often created in reaction to an organizational need. Often, these artifacts are initiated for a narrowly defined project and are siloed within a team. Before long, the organization generates many unrelated project-specific personas and journey maps. A lack of awareness may lead to different teams creating nearly identical artifacts for their needs, wasting time and resources. Without coordination, teams may create artifacts utilizing varying levels of detail or context, making them less useful across initiatives and less applicable to other teams within the organization.

A Persona Strategy Provides Transparency and Alignment

Having a shared plan for personas benefits the entire organization by providing transparency and alignment in several ways:

- Defines the specific types of users that the organization currently supports.
- Identifies user types with established personas and where there are opportunities to expand the organization's knowledge of a particular group.
- Highlights different perspectives allowing for both a bird's-eye and a ground-level view of the organization's users.
- Identifies opportunities to include additional users for future support and growth.

By visualizing the various types of users the organization supports, a persona tree provides greater clarity and opportunities for cross-functional collaboration to address the same users holistically rather than in siloed departments. This becomes particularly important when an organization seeks to utilize entire journeys and create additional interconnections between them to create an end-to-end service blueprint.

Collaborating on a Persona Strategy

A plan for establishing personas should be done at the organizational level. It should include representatives from user experience, product, IT, marketing, sales, support, and any other team with customer touchpoints. An agreed upon framework should consist of all of the primary user groups the organization supports and should be scalable to include new types of users and additional attributes of current users that may need to be considered.

Visualize Your Organization's Personas

A tree visualization helps you to see how your personas relate to each other and how they are represented hierarchically. A tree visualization contains several components: foundation, primary, and secondary branches. Your tree's foundation must be solid and should focus on the core, high altitude personas. Primary branches account for key variances in these personas, while secondary branches account for unique attributes that support specific use cases. We examine these components in detail below.

CHAPTER 5   BUILDING A PERSONA FAMILY TREE

Creating the Foundation

The base of your tree will include one or more of your highest-altitude personas. All of the other personas in the tree will be connected to the foundational persona(s) and inherit all its attributes. For example, in Samantha the flower shop owner's persona tree, the foundation includes her business's three primary customer types: retail, B2B, and wholesale. The personas at the base of your tree should very rarely, if ever, change. They represent the users your organization primarily focuses on, and its long-term strategies are centered around these personas. The tree's base would only change if the organization made a fundamental shift to serve an entirely different audience.

Creating the Primary Branches

Primary branches comprise one or more attributes that represent personas at a specific altitude. For example, the primary branches in Samantha's persona tree would include those representing purchase methods (i.e., in-person or online) and customer relationships (i.e., new or returning). The major branches of your tree will rarely change as they represent attributes of your users that almost always need to be considered.

Creating Secondary Branches

Secondary branches represent unique attributes and scenarios that may be important in certain situations. They may include one or more of the attributes represented at a lower level altitude and may not relate to all personas. These additional branches on Samantha's tree include purchase occasion and payment type. Unlike primary branches, they are expected to change and should expand and evolve as the organization learns about its users and new situations emerge. For example, Samantha may expand her business to specialize in other purchasing occasions or find that customers expect more mobile payment options like Apple Pay.

Growing the Tree Over Time

The persona tree helps your organization keep track of the personas it created and indicates placeholders for identified personas that should be developed in the future. Teams should consult the tree before creating a new persona to determine where it fits into the hierarchy and ensure that it doesn't duplicate an existing one. Once an organization establishes its initial tree, it can implement a governance structure to propose new personas.

Questions to consider as your organization begins to build out branches at each altitude:

- Have you accounted for all of the *primary* audiences that the organization serves?
- Have personas been included that are based on the *essential* attributes that define the unique aspects of this audience?
- Can any personas be *combined* to represent a persona at a higher altitude?
- Are there any unique needs requiring a higher altitude persona to be *split up* to represent more specific personas?

Other Ways to Visualize Your Organization's Personas

While the metaphor of a growing tree can help your organization understand your personas' relationships, you don't need a literal tree to map out this structure. Any visualization with a hierarchical or relationship structure can represent the connection between each persona. Below are two other visualization techniques that organizations may utilize to describe the relationships between personas.

Venn Diagrams

A Venn diagram uses overlapping circles to show connection points between similar and different personas. This type of diagram works best for depicting a limited number of personas.

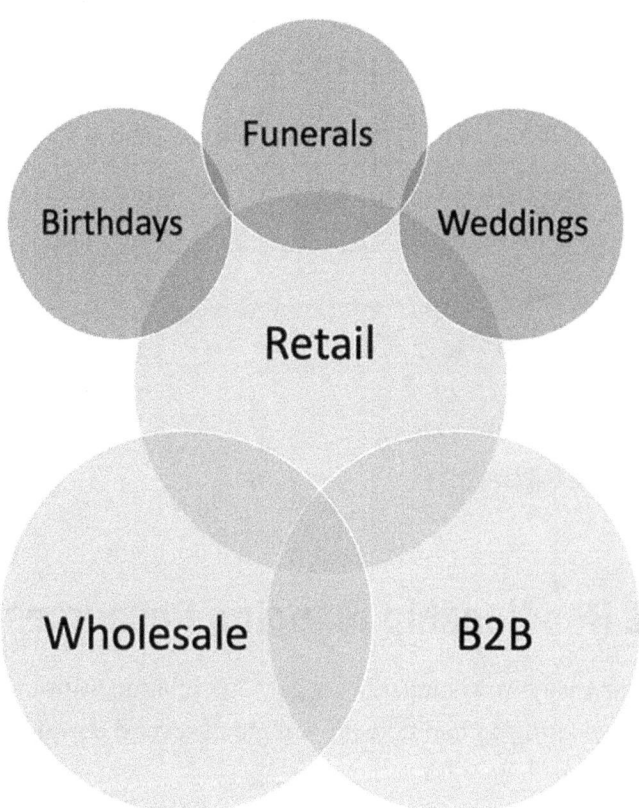

Hierarchy Diagrams

A hierarchy diagram uses interconnected lines between personas and a top-down framework to show each level. This type of diagram works best for organizations with a large number of personas.

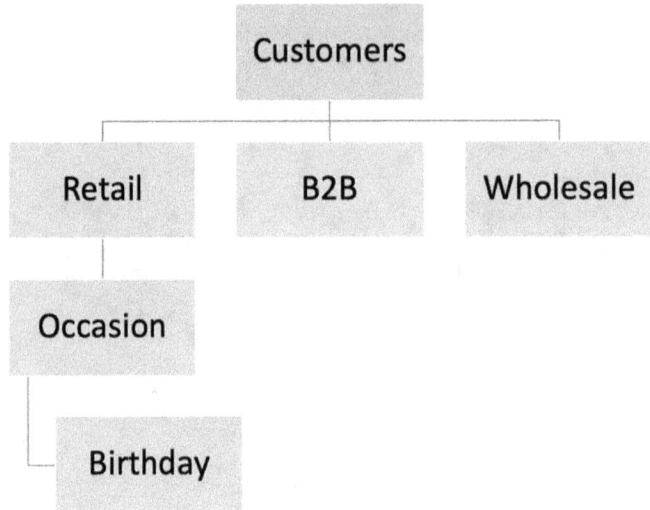

Persona Relationship Mapping Resources

There are many ways to visualize your persona relationships using popular design software, and you can take advantage of several templates that are available for free.

Tree Relationship Templates

Miro template: https://miro.com/templates/prune-the-product-tree/
Figma template: https://www.figma.com/community/file/1277011523626912658

Venn Diagram Relationship Templates

Miro template: https://miro.com/templates/venn-diagram/
Figma template: https://www.figma.com/templates/venn-diagram/
Whatever tool you use must be easy to maintain and update the document as the tree evolves.

Key Takeaways

- **Avoid Siloed Persona Creation:** If your organization creates personas and journey maps in isolation for specific projects, you risk wasting resources and duplicating efforts. Different teams might end up creating nearly identical artifacts without a cohesive strategy. A shared persona strategy brings transparency and alignment across your organization. It helps define user types, identify gaps in your understanding of different groups, and highlight opportunities for future growth.

- **Collaborative Persona Development:** Develop your personas with input from various departments like user experience, product, IT, marketing, sales, and support. A comprehensive framework should include all primary user groups and be flexible enough to accommodate new user types and attributes as needed.

- **Visualizing Personas with a Tree Structure:** Use a tree visualization to map out how your personas relate to each other. This structure includes foundational personas (core users), primary branches (key attributes like purchase methods), and secondary branches (unique scenarios or attributes). This method helps you see the big picture and the specifics of user groups.

- **Maintaining and Evolving Your Persona Tree:** Your persona tree isn't static; it should grow and evolve as you learn more about your users. Review the tree regularly to avoid duplicating personas and ensure it accurately represents your audience. Implement a governance structure to manage new personas and updates.

- **Alternative Visualization Methods:** While the tree metaphor is useful, consider other visualization methods like Venn diagrams for smaller groups of personas or hierarchy diagrams for a large number of personas. These methods can help you understand and communicate the relationships between different user types.

In the next chapter, we will identify user research methods that are used to inform a persona's attributes.

CHAPTER 6

Researching Your Personas

User research acts as a compass to guide you through creating your personas. Using a mixed-methods approach, the genuine behaviors and needs of the target audience are revealed. Research helps transform personas from generic archetypes to informed and empathetic representations by understanding users' motivations and pain points. This data-driven approach ensures that the final personas accurately reflect the real people your organization is designing for.

CHAPTER 6   RESEARCHING YOUR PERSONAS

Planning Your User Research Strategy

The research strategy used to inform the design of your personas should include the following steps:

1. Define your research objectives.
2. Choose research methods.
3. Determine who your target audience is.
4. Gather data about your users.
5. Analyze the collected data to identify patterns, trends, and insights.

The first step in the process is to define clear learning goals for your research activities.

Define Your Research Objectives

Your research aims to provide facts and objective data to inform the creation of your personas. Defining clear research objectives ensures that all your activities focus on identifying the right kind of insights that can be directly plugged into your personas. Your research goals should be

- **Specific**: Narrowly focused as opposed to more exploratory and open-ended goals. The specificity should be based on the altitude level of the persona you plan to create.

- **Relevant**: Practical insights that the team needs to know to create experiences for the persona, instead of things that would be nice to know or to provide interesting anecdotes.

- **Measurable**: There should be a way to triangulate your data and validate insights to ensure that they accurately reflect the intended persona.

Use Proto Personas to Identify Hypotheses About Your Users

A proto persona is a preliminary representation of a potential user based on initial assumptions or hypotheses about their characteristics, needs, and behaviors. When creating proto personas, you're essentially making educated guesses about who your users might be and what they might need. These assumptions serve as hypotheses that can be tested through user research.

These proto personas may be created as part of a team brainstorming activity to capture ideas from your team that will be validated during user research. Make sure to indicate that any artifacts created from these activities are merely preliminary so that individuals do not confuse them with the final research-based personas.

Decide on Whether to Focus on Current or Aspirational Users

When creating a proto persona, an organization must decide whether to utilize current or aspirational personas. Most proto personas reflect the assumed needs of your existing users. In our previous example of Samantha and her flower shop business, we focused on personas related to her current customers who represent retail and B2B.

Proto personas can also be generated for users that your organization does not currently serve. Aspirational personas represent users that a product or service aims to attract or engage in the future as part of an organization's growth strategy. Used to drive innovation and future development, aspirational personas inspire new features and functionalities by understanding the needs of potential users. Research for aspirational personas can include users of analogous experiences, competitor products, and external market data. In our previous example of Samantha, she aspires to grow her business to support a new type of persona representing a wholesale customer. Understanding this new audience will require her to learn about individuals outside her existing customer base.

Choose Research Methods

All of the information used to create your personas should be based on a combination of primary and secondary research methods.

Utilize Existing Knowledge

Secondary research utilizes existing knowledge and can jumpstart your discovery process and reduce the time and resources needed to construct your personas. Your organization may already have lots of information about its users. This information might be based on prior user research, market research, analytics data, or industry reports. Before using existing knowledge for your personas, make sure to assess its quality and applicability:

- What type of research helped to inform these insights?
- What is the level of rigor associated with the research?
- How closely does it match the target audience of the persona?
- How recently was this information collected?

When using existing insights, make sure to cite the source of your research so that you can refer back to the original source as needed.

Learn from Subject Matter Experts

Interviewing subject matter experts (SMEs) as part of your research is a valuable starting point for understanding users. SMEs possess specialized knowledge and deep insights about a domain or industry. They often have direct experience with users, enabling them to provide nuanced perspectives and valuable context that can be used to identify typical user behaviors or challenges that users may encounter.

SMEs can include individuals with diverse backgrounds and roles such as

- Industry experts
- Executives
- Internal employees who are also end users
- Content owners and instructional designers
- Customer support staff
- Sales team members
- Trainers

SMEs can serve as effective surrogates in your research if they have direct experience interacting with the target audience, but you should limit how much you rely on their insights. Be aware that SMEs can be biased and may reflect their personal opinions and preferences. Don't assume that this person is a typical end user. Here are some example interview questions for different types of SMEs that work at a healthcare startup company:

Sales Team

- How many nurses and admin staff do most of your clients have at their office?
- What specific pain points come up during your discussions with clients?

Internal Medical Team

- Tell me about your experiences using our organization's products in your clinical practice.
- How well does the product's current workflow match how you work at your practice?

Customer Support Team

- What are the primary reasons that clients contact support?
- What are the common questions that clients ask?

After an initial set of interviews, an SME can continue to serve as a valuable partner in the persona creation process, helping to explain further and validate insights gained about the user.

Take an Iterative Approach to Research

Understanding the users who represent your personas is not a one-and-done activity. Initial discovery research sets the foundation for further research that can help widen and deepen your organization's knowledge. You should first focus on understanding the larger commonalities of your high altitude personas and then gradually expand and deepen that knowledge with more focused research aimed at your lower altitude personas. Your organization should invest in a knowledge management platform for storing and retrieving insights, such as Dovetail, EnjoyHQ, and Condens.

CHAPTER 6 RESEARCHING YOUR PERSONAS

Use Mixed Methods and Triangulate Your Data

A mixed-methods approach in user research involves using multiple data sources or research methods to augment findings and ensure the credibility of insights. It enables a comprehensive understanding of users by incorporating various perspectives and dimensions, such as qualitative insights from interviews and quantitative data from surveys or analytics. This holistic view helps uncover deeper insights into user behaviors, preferences, and needs.

Data triangulation is the identification of patterns and themes across different datasets. Researchers can find consistent trends and commonalities by analyzing data from multiple sources, providing valuable insights that inform persona creation.

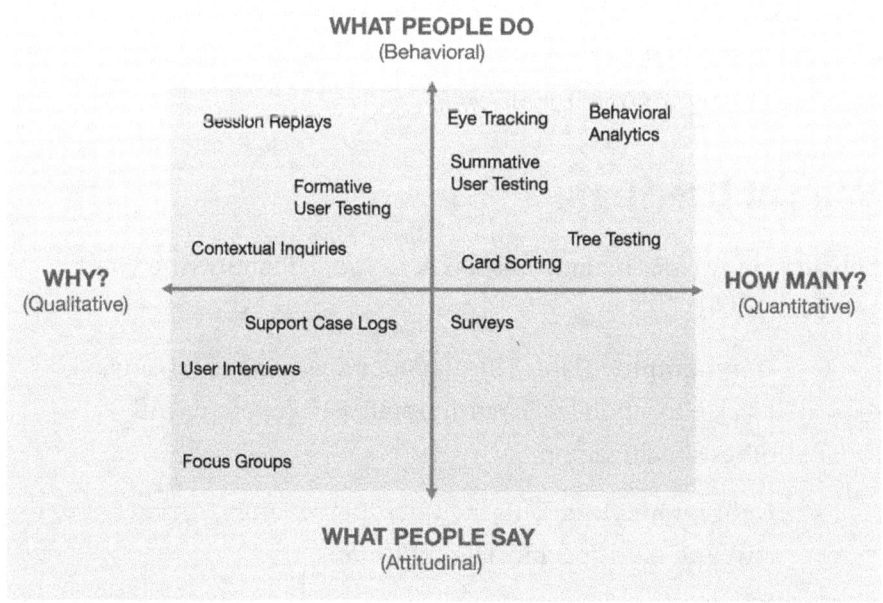

Based on the diagram, Landscape of User Research Methods by Christian Rohrer

Every research method has its limitations and biases. Using a mixed-methods approach and data triangulation increases confidence in the findings by cross-referencing and validating insights from different sources, reducing the risk of drawing inaccurate conclusions. This ensures that insights are more robust and representative of the user population, enhancing the credibility and reliability of the personas developed. When stakeholders see that insights are supported by diverse evidence, they are more likely to trust and act upon the personas during decision-making processes.

Identifying Your Users
How Do You Know Who Your Users Are?

Your organization is likely storing a large amount of information about its current users. There is also a wealth of external sources about different populations and industries. You should focus your research on objective data sources to help classify your users.

Types of User Data

There are many types of data that can help you to identify who your users are:

- **Demographic Data:** This includes age, gender, income level, education level, marital status, occupation, and other similar factors.
- **Geographic Data:** This includes their country, region, city, and even specific neighborhoods.

- **Behavioral Data:** This includes information on how customers interact with your brand, such as their purchase history, frequency of purchases, average order value, products or services they prefer, and their preferred communication channels.

- **Technographic Data:** This type of data focuses on your customers' technology use, such as the devices they own, the social media platforms they frequent, and their online behavior.

- **Transaction Data:** This includes information on past purchases, including what was purchased, when it was purchased, and how much was spent.

- **Customer Service Interactions:** Reviewing customer service interactions can provide insights into common issues or concerns among your customer base.

Using a combination of these data sources, you can group users based on characteristics that represent who they are.

Classifying User Types by Behavior

Behavioral data refers to information about users and their actions. This could be their background, tendencies, habits, or interactions with particular products or services. It can include how long they spend on a particular page, what features they interact with, how they navigate the product, and whether they can achieve their goals.

CHAPTER 6   RESEARCHING YOUR PERSONAS

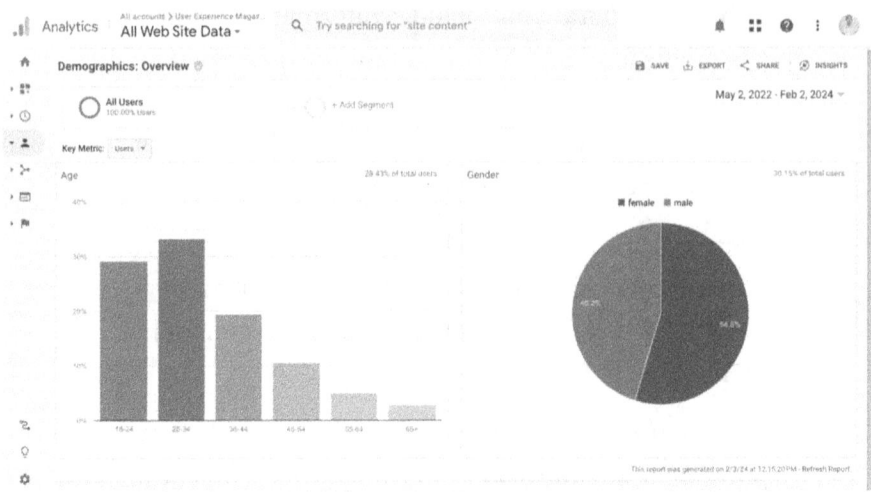

Behavioral data is an objective measurement that is not open to interpretation (e.g., they either submitted a support ticket or they didn't). The power of these metrics lies in volume. Behavioral data collected from analytics platforms aggregate thousands, if not millions, of user actions to paint a clear picture of what users are doing with sample sizes that are usually statistically significant. Understanding whether users have had experience with your products and how often they use them can be an important factor in defining a persona and understanding their mental models.

New vs. Returning Users

- **New Users:** These individuals have recently started engaging with a product or service. They might be unfamiliar with the interface, features, or functionalities. They might require onboarding assistance, introductory tutorials, or tooltips to navigate the platform effectively.

CHAPTER 6   RESEARCHING YOUR PERSONAS

- **Returning Users:** These users have previously engaged with the product or service. They are likely more familiar with the interface, features, and functionalities. They might need less guidance and are more inclined toward advanced features or personalized experiences tailored to their past interactions.

Frequent vs. Infrequent Users

- **Frequent Users:** These users engage with the product or service regularly and spend significant time using it. They are likely to have a deep understanding of its features and functionalities. They might appreciate shortcuts, advanced settings, or power-user tools to optimize their experience further.

- **Infrequent Users:** These users engage with the product or service sporadically or less frequently. They may need reminders, prompts, or simplified workflows to reorient themselves each time they return. Their priorities might lean toward ease of use and quick access to essential features rather than mastering advanced functionalities.

Novice vs. Advanced Users

- **Novice Users:** These users have limited expertise with the product or service. Understanding and utilizing its features effectively may require step-by-step guidance, extensive documentation, or beginner-friendly interfaces. Their interactions might be basic, focusing on core functionalities.

- **Advanced Users:** These users possess in-depth knowledge and are experts with the product. They might seek more advanced features, customization options, or integrations to streamline their workflows and optimize their productivity. They may also appreciate access to APIs, keyboard shortcuts, or expert-level support for complex tasks.

We will revisit users' actions to accomplish their goals in more detail in Chapter 10.

Surveys

Surveys are a flexible method in user research that can be used to collect both behavioral and attitudinal data. By collecting data from a diverse pool of respondents, surveys provide a broader perspective, enabling researchers to identify patterns and trends that inform the creation of high and low altitude personas. Surveys can capture background and demographic information such as age, gender, education, location, and occupation. It can also include behavioral data that details users' habits, priorities, needs, and pain points. This data and behavioral patterns enable researchers to segment users into distinct personas based on shared characteristics and behaviors.

Large-Scale Surveys Can Cast a Wide Net and Provide Statistical Validity

A large sample size improves the reliability and validity of your findings, lessening the risk of biases and ensuring a more representative portrayal of the target audience. Statistical analysis of survey data allows researchers to quantify responses, uncover correlations, identify statistical significance, and draw meaningful conclusions about user characteristics and behaviors. I'd recommend the book *Quantifying the User Experience* by Jeff Sauro and James Lewis for a deeper dive into quantitative metrics.

Capture Low Altitude Persona Details with Branching Logic

Dynamically adjusting the survey flow based on respondents' answers ensures that individuals are directed toward questions to more deeply understand their unique traits. Branching logic enables further exploration of relevant topics, yielding nuanced insights into the behaviors and motivations of these individuals. For example, if a respondent selects that they visit a coffee chain five or more times a week, they would be associated with a high altitude persona of frequent customers. The survey then branches to focus on questions about their experiences at the cafe, coffee preferences, and other aspects associated with that behavior. Honing in on distinct characteristics will help to inform the creation of attributes for your lower altitude personas.

Crafting effective survey questions is beyond the scope of this book. To learn more about that topic, I recommend picking up a copy of Caroline Jarrett's book, *Surveys That Work: A Practical Guide for Designing and Running Better Surveys*.

Limitations of Surveys

Surveys are an unmoderated research method, meaning that data is collected without a researcher directly interacting with a user in real-time. Keep in mind that unmoderated methods have limitations such as:

- Participants can misinterpret questions.
- Participant's answers can't easily be verified.
- There is a limited ability to follow up on answer choices.

Due to these limitations, use interviews to complement your surveys for a more interactive dialog with participants. Surveys are nonetheless a powerful research method that can leverage a large sample size with statistical significance and have the potential to capture insights from a wide demographic.

Understanding Your Users

Once you learn who your users are, you need to understand why they feel the way they do and what drives their behaviors and decisions. Researching the "why" means understanding the underlying reasons users act and behave in the ways that they do. While behavioral data (such as usage or search activity data) provides valuable insights into *what* users do within a product, attitudinal data helps us understand *why* they do it.

This can be obtained through qualitative research methods such as interviews in which users are asked questions that help to understand their thought processes on a particular topic. Speaking with representative participants ensures that the research will provide relevant and accurate insights that can be used to populate your persona.

CHAPTER 6   RESEARCHING YOUR PERSONAS

Interviews

Interviews are a versatile qualitative research method used to gather insights directly from users. Researchers engage in one-on-one conversations with participants to understand their experiences, behaviors, needs, and perspectives related to a product, service, or topic of interest. These interviews are typically semi-structured, meaning there's a predefined list of topics or questions, but the conversation can also evolve organically based on the participant's responses. Through user interviews, researchers delve deeper into participants' thoughts, feelings, and motivations, uncovering valuable insights that inform the design process. Interviews can be conducted in person, over the phone, or through video conferencing, offering flexibility in reaching participants across different locations.

CHAPTER 6   RESEARCHING YOUR PERSONAS

The "3 P's" Questioning Method

The "3 P's" questioning technique is an interviewing strategy designed to reduce biases, ensure that questions and answers are understood, and gain a deeper understanding of the "why." This method comprises three key components: position, parrot, and probe. These techniques foster clearer communication, uncover underlying insights, and facilitate more productive discussions.

- **Positioning** involves asking questions in a deliberate order to guide the flow of conversation and elicit relevant information. This structured approach ensures that a line of questioning isn't accidentally leading or biasing. Funneling is an example of a technique to position questions from a semi-structured to a structured sequence.

- **Parrotting** encourages active listening and comprehension by paraphrasing or restating the respondent's answers in your own words. This confirms that what you thought you heard and understood matches with what the participant was intending to convey.

- **Probing** entails delving deeper into the topic by seeking clarification or additional details along the same line of questioning. By probing further, individuals can unearth nuances, address ambiguities, and gain a more comprehensive understanding of the subject matter.

These three techniques are a powerful method to obtain insights from your user interview participants.

Using a Funnel Approach for Your Interview Questions

The concept of a funnel in user interview questions involves starting with broader, open-ended inquiries and gradually narrowing down to more specific and focused queries. This approach mirrors the shape of a funnel, where the opening is wide and allows for exploration of various topics, while the bottom is narrow and directs attention to specific details. Starting with open-ended questions allows participants to share their thoughts and experiences freely, encouraging the exploration of diverse topics. Gradually narrowing down the focus of the conversation allows researchers to uncover deeper insights into user behaviors, needs, and preferences.

CHAPTER 6   RESEARCHING YOUR PERSONAS

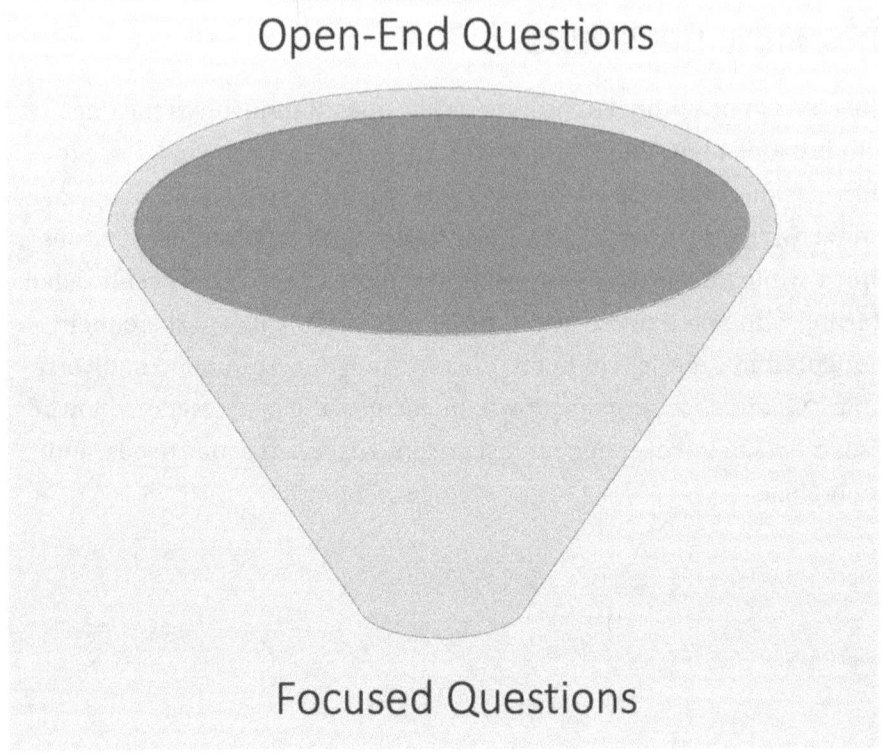

At the top of the funnel, researchers begin with open-ended questions that encourage participants to share their thoughts, experiences, and opinions freely. These questions are exploratory and allow respondents to express themselves without feeling constrained. Examples of open-ended questions include

- "Can you tell me about your typical day at work?"
- "How do you usually approach [task/activity]?"

As the interview progresses, researchers gradually guide the conversation toward more specific topics or areas of interest. This involves asking follow-up questions that delve deeper into particular aspects mentioned by the participant. These follow-up questions help researchers uncover underlying motivations, preferences, and pain points. Examples of follow-up questions include

- "You mentioned that [specific challenge]. Can you elaborate on that?"
- "How does [specific feature] impact your workflow?"

Toward the bottom of the funnel, researchers ask structured questions aimed at eliciting precise information or feedback on particular design elements, functionalities, or concepts. These questions are focused and often require a more direct response from participants.

The funnel approach to user interview questions is a good strategy for guiding conversations in a structured yet flexible manner, enabling researchers to gather comprehensive insights from participants.

Be Careful of Leading Questions

Leading questions and language in user interviews can introduce various risks that may compromise the validity and reliability of the data collected. Leading questions often contain implicit cues or suggestions that steer participants toward a particular response. This can bias participants' answers, leading to skewed or inaccurate data. For example, asking, "Don't you find it challenging to do your taxes?" implies that the individual found his or her taxes challenging and creates an expectation of agreement, potentially influencing the participant's response.

To mitigate these risks, interviewers should strive to use neutral and open-ended language that allows participants to express their thoughts and experiences freely. It's important to avoid implying desired responses or assumptions in the questions and to maintain a non-judgmental and objective demeanor throughout the interview process.

Further examples of leading and neutral language:

- **Leading Language:** Tell me about the problems that you are having with your team members. (This assumes the individual is experiencing problems with his or her team).

- **Neutral Language:** Tell me about your experiences working with your team members. (This allows the individual to answer the question without building in potentially false premises/biases.)

Pilot testing questions and obtaining feedback from colleagues help identify and address potential biases or leading language before conducting the actual interviews. Overall, conducting user interviews with careful attention to language and question formulation is essential for obtaining accurate and meaningful insights from participants.

Knowing When You've Reached Saturation

Saturation in user research refers to the point at which new data ceases to provide additional or substantially different insights or information. It means that you have reached a sufficient understanding of a topic and that further interviews are unlikely to yield significant new findings.

User researchers assess saturation through various means, including the repetition of themes or patterns across interviews, the absence of new information in successive interviews, or the researcher's judgment based on the depth and richness of the data collected. Achieving saturation is important for ensuring the validity and reliability of research findings, as it indicates that the study has comprehensively explored the topic and captured the diversity of participant perspectives.

Recruiting Representative Participants

You should conduct your research with individuals who will provide the most accurate representation of your personas. Use defined attributes as a starting point to identify the types of users to recruit. Use a screener to ensure that participants match the target persona.

Creating a Screener

A participant screener in user research identifies individuals who meet specific criteria for research studies, ensuring quality, representativeness, efficiency, and alignment with objectives. It streamlines recruitment, maintains data relevance, and minimizes bias, ultimately enabling the collection of meaningful insights from participants with relevant characteristics and experiences.

Screening for Specific Users

Let's take the example of a cruise company that is planning to conduct research to better understand its primary persona: the cruise ship traveler. This high altitude persona would include a wide representation of individuals who may book cruise travel.

CHAPTER 6   RESEARCHING YOUR PERSONAS

This screener would include questions that identify both attitudinal attributes, such as their thoughts on booking a cruise online, and behavioral questions, such as how often they have taken a cruise in the last six months. Here are some questions that could be used to identify and recruit participants for this study:

- Have you ever booked a cruise vacation before?
- Are you currently considering booking a cruise vacation within the next six months?
- When planning a cruise vacation, what factors are most important to you? (e.g., destination, price, activities onboard, amenities, cruise line reputation)
- What methods have you used to book your cruise (e.g., website, phone, travel agent)

- What online platforms or websites do you typically use when researching or booking cruise vacations?
- How comfortable are you with using online booking tools or websites to plan and book vacations?
- How much time do you usually spend researching and planning your vacation before making a booking decision?

When conducting research for lower altitude personas, we need to target types of users with specific recruitment questions. For example, if we were looking to create a persona for solo cruise travelers who are loyal to a particular brand, we would need to add additional questions such as:

- Do you usually travel on cruises alone, with a partner, with family, or with friends?
- Which cruise lines do you typically travel on?

Recruiting participants with very specific criteria can be challenging, but it is essential that your research insights accurately portray the users that will comprise your persona.

The Power of Using Attitudinal Data with Behavioral Data

The goal of understanding the "what" and "why" is to help identify behavior patterns and the root causes for the actions that the user takes. Combining these strategies allows teams to make informed decisions based on triangulated data.

Each method has strengths and weaknesses, and there is no one right approach to utilizing them. To get started with an overview of the most common research methods used in UX, I recommend reading *Measuring the User Experience* by Bill Albert and Tom Tullis.

CHAPTER 6   RESEARCHING YOUR PERSONAS

Analyzing Your Data

It's tempting to start constructing personas and looking for solutions to address their problems as soon as you begin to discover insights about them. To avoid jumping to conclusions, your research process should ensure that you finish collecting all data and then take the time to objectively review your findings. Taking structured notes, tagging data, and grouping findings are the precursors to synthesizing your insights.

Keeping Track of Your Findings

Use Tags to Identify and Keep Track of Your Findings

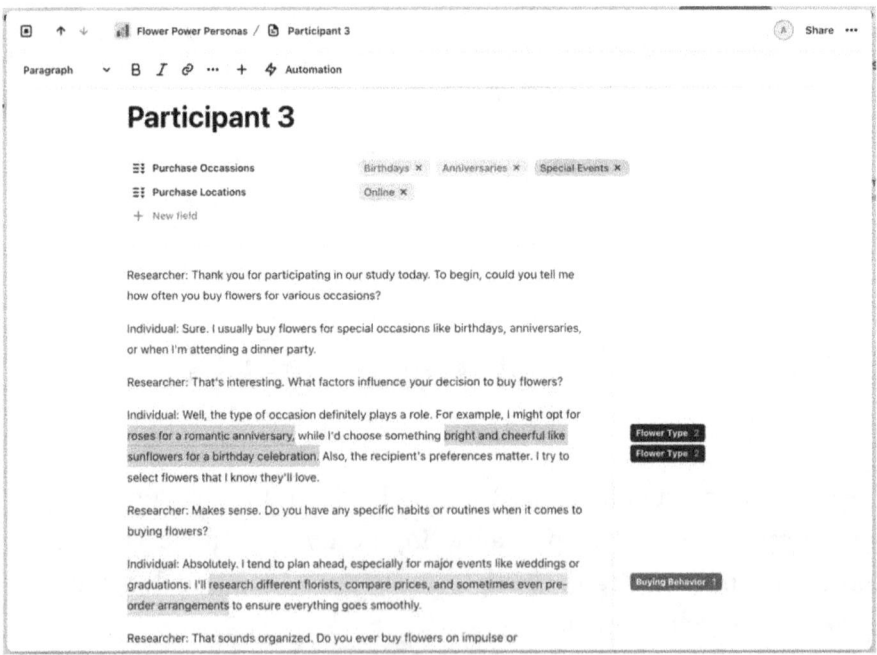

CHAPTER 6   RESEARCHING YOUR PERSONAS

Using Predetermined and Ad Hoc Tags

Your tagging strategy can include predefining a set of categories or identifiers before data collection begins. This approach offers the advantage of providing structure and consistency to the analysis process. If multiple researchers are involved in data collection, preset tags can facilitate collaboration by providing a standardized way to categorize and organize collected data. Consistent tagging practices ensure that all team members are on the same page and enable them to easily share and analyze data. Predetermining tags may limit flexibility and overlook emerging themes that were not anticipated during the initial planning stage.

Ad hoc tagging involves creating tags in real time based on the data as it is collected. This approach allows for greater flexibility and responsiveness to the nuances of the data, enabling researchers to capture unexpected or nuanced insights. However, ad hoc tagging may lead to inconsistency in how data is labeled and analyzed, making it more challenging to compare and synthesize findings across different sources or researchers. Ultimately, the choice between predetermined and ad hoc tagging depends on the research goals, the nature of the data, and the preferences of the researchers.

Identify Trends

After your data collection is complete, you should begin organizing your findings into groups. These groups will help you determine trends and themes that represent the characteristics of your personas.

Group Similar Findings with an Affinity Map

Affinity diagramming is a method used to organize and synthesize large amounts of unstructured or disparate information into meaningful groups or themes. A researcher uses data points on individual sticky notes or cards, which are grouped based on similarities or relationships.

CHAPTER 6   RESEARCHING YOUR PERSONAS

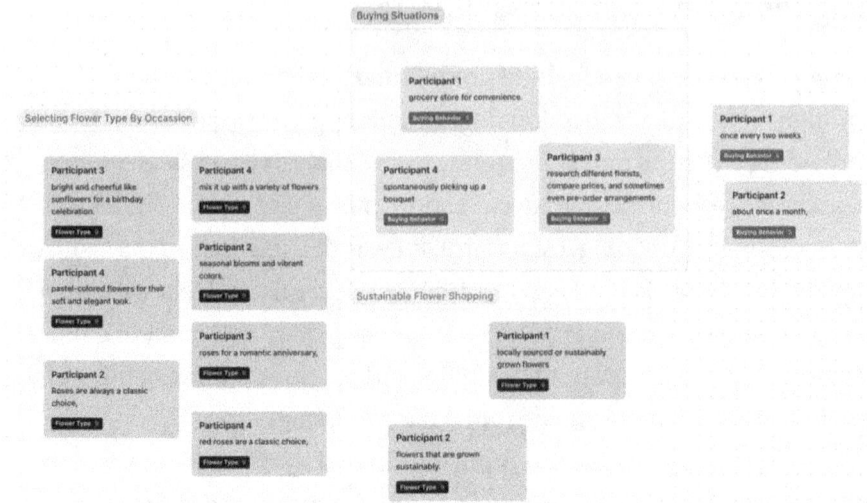

Perform Some Housekeeping Before Starting Your Affinity Map

You will likely have a large number of insights from your research that can feel overwhelming to categorize. Before starting your affinity mapping activity, you should attempt to consolidate the number of cards that you initially created. The easiest way to start is to pull together any findings that are exactly the same common across participants. You will likely find many of these 1:1 findings, and this will help to reduce the number of cards to sort through quickly. Your next pass should determine their applicability to the persona that you are planning to create. You may have identified many interesting facts about your participants during your research, but only some of them will be useful as insights for your personas.

Finding Relationships

After you perform an initial review and vetting of your findings, you can begin to sort them into logical groups. Your groups should be based on the relationship between findings. For example, Samantha's research about her retail customers contained lots of insights into how they select the flowers that they ultimately buy. Sorting is an iterative process; continuously review and refine your groupings as you progress. You may find that certain insights don't fit neatly into any existing group or that some groups need to be split into smaller subgroups.

Labeling Groups

Once you have a cluster of findings, you will generate a descriptive name that reflects the group's contents, such as "Deciding on what flowers to buy for an occasion." Make your descriptions as specific as possible so that they are easily distinguishable from other groups.

After you have organized your data into insights, you will begin to create themes that will inform your persona.

Key Takeaways

- **Planning User Research and Defining Objectives**: Before starting research, define clear objectives that are specific, relevant, and measurable. These objectives guide the selection of research methods and ensure focused data collection.

- **Choosing Research Methods**: Based on the defined objectives, select research methods such as surveys, interviews, and subject matter expert input. Utilize existing knowledge and diverse sources to gather insights efficiently.

- **Identifying Users**: Classify users based on demographic, geographic, and behavioral data to effectively understand their characteristics and behaviors.

- **Understanding Users**: Use methods like interviews to delve deep into users' experiences, needs, and perspectives. Employ techniques like the "3 P's" questioning method to ensure productive discussions and mitigate biases.

- **Analyzing Data**: Organize research findings using tags and affinity diagramming to identify trends and themes. This organized approach facilitates the synthesis of insights crucial for persona creation.

In the next chapter, we will focus on synthesizing your insights and translating them into components that will populate your personas.

CHAPTER 7

Synthesizing Data to Inform Your Personas

This chapter focuses on the essential process of data synthesis for persona development. We explore using Venn diagrams to analyze the shared traits and distinctions among personas, providing a clear understanding of their commonalities and differences. Additionally, we will examine various visualization techniques to plot persona characteristics, enabling a comprehensive view of your audience's attributes.

CHAPTER 7 SYNTHESIZING DATA TO INFORM YOUR PERSONAS

Creating Themes

In the last chapter, we focused on tagging and organizing your data to make it easier to understand and work with. This data housekeeping is necessary to identify clear trends that will ultimately become themes about your personas. Your research may yield many different kinds of themes relating to your users, including what they do, what their preferences are, and what they need to achieve. Themes represent the most salient attributes that will be incorporated into your personas. High altitude themes will be broad and all-encompassing, while others at a low altitude will only pertain to specific use cases.

Determining Which Themes to Inform Your Personas

Many themes can be generated about a user based on your research, but not all of them are equally important, and some may not be represented in a persona. When considering findings that may be included in a theme, make sure to first consider the following:

- **Strength of Evidence:** Is there enough data from your research to indicate a well-supported theme?
- **Relevancy:** Would this theme directly help to inform the creation of experiences for this type of user, or is it just nice to know?
- **Priority:** How important is the theme to the business and user goals?

Once you have a set of themes, you will begin to use them to examine the attributes and their relationship between personas.

Using Themes to Identify Similarities and Differences between Personas

Depending on where you are in your persona creation process, you may already have a preliminary persona tree and some proto personas from which to work. In this situation, the first step is to understand how your themes relate to these personas. Your personas likely share many themes that can highlight the key similarities and differences between them.

Take the example of Samantha, our flower shop business owner. Through her research she learned more about her current B2B customers and lots of new information about her prospective wholesale customers. She is trying to understand what common traits these two types of customers have and what makes them unique.

CHAPTER 7   SYNTHESIZING DATA TO INFORM YOUR PERSONAS

Examining Themes and Understanding the Differences

When comparing your personas, it is easiest to organize your themes in a table with separate columns for each persona and separate rows for each established theme. Then, you can populate the table with the information learned about each persona and each theme.

This table includes the major themes found during Samantha's research. The columns compare the attributes in each theme that relate to each persona.

B2B Business	Wholesale Business
Product Offering	
Offers specialized products or services tailored to a niche market.	Deals with a broad range of products.
Focusing on quality, uniqueness, and customization.	Prioritizes factors such as freshness, variety, and bulk purchasing options.
Customer Base	
Individual clients or smaller businesses seeking personalized solutions.	A diverse clientele including retail florists, event planners, supermarkets, and other businesses requiring large quantities of flowers for resale or use in their operations.
Sales Channels	
Relies heavily on direct sales, personalized consultations, and networking to attract clients.	Often utilizes online platforms, distribution networks, and trade shows to reach a broader market and facilitate bulk orders.

(continued)

B2B Business	Wholesale Business
Pricing and Margins	
May command higher prices for their specialized products or services, focusing on quality over quantity.	Operate on thinner margins due to the competitive nature of the floral industry and the need to offer competitive pricing to attract wholesale buyers.
Inventory Management	
Maintains a diverse but small amount of products at a time.	Maintains a highly diverse, everchanging and large amount of stock.
Marketing and Branding	
Often emphasizes storytelling, branding, and building personal relationships to differentiate themselves in the market and attract loyal clients.	Focuses more on showcasing the quality, variety, and reliability of their products, often through targeted marketing campaigns aimed at industry professionals.

Comparing identical themes to compare personas helps the organization understand how to support its users' unique needs.

Examining Themes and Understanding the Similarities

A table also helps clearly delineate established themes to identify similarities across your personas. Samantha's research yielded additional themes with attributes common to both her B2B and prospective wholesale customers.

Quality Standards

Both groups prioritize the quality of the flowers they purchase. They seek fresh, vibrant blooms that meet their standards for appearance, fragrance, and longevity.

Variety and Selection

Whether for retail sale or use in their own arrangements, both types of business owners value a wide variety of flower options. They look for suppliers that offer diverse selections to meet the preferences and needs of their customers.

Reliability and Consistency

Consistent supply and reliable delivery are essential for both B2B boutique owners and wholesale flower business owners. They rely on their suppliers to provide flowers on time and in the quantities requested to meet customer demand and maintain business operations.

Cost Effectiveness

While quality is important, both groups are also mindful of costs. They seek suppliers that offer competitive pricing without compromising on the quality of the flowers.

Customer Service

Good customer service is paramount for both types of business owners when purchasing flowers. They value suppliers who are responsive, communicative, and willing to address any issues or concerns promptly.

Flexibility

Both B2B boutique owners and wholesale flower business owners appreciate suppliers who are flexible and accommodating. They may have specific requirements or preferences regarding flower varieties, quantities, or delivery schedules, and they value suppliers who can adapt to meet their needs.

(continued)

CHAPTER 7 SYNTHESIZING DATA TO INFORM YOUR PERSONAS

Sustainability

Increasingly, both groups are concerned about the environmental impact of their business practices. They may seek out suppliers who prioritize sustainability and eco-friendly growing practices in the cultivation and sourcing of flowers.

As it turns out, these two personas share many common traits. Identifying these commonalities helps determine what capabilities and experiences remain consistent and what Samantha needs to invest in and customize for her customers.

Using Venn Diagrams to Visualize Similarities and Differences

Viewing the details associated with themes in a tabular format can be overwhelming and make it difficult to easily understand how they relate. Venn diagrams are simple and easy to understand, making them accessible to a wide audience. They present complex information in a visually intuitive format, making it easier to grasp the similarities and differences among personas at a glance.

CHAPTER 7   SYNTHESIZING DATA TO INFORM YOUR PERSONAS

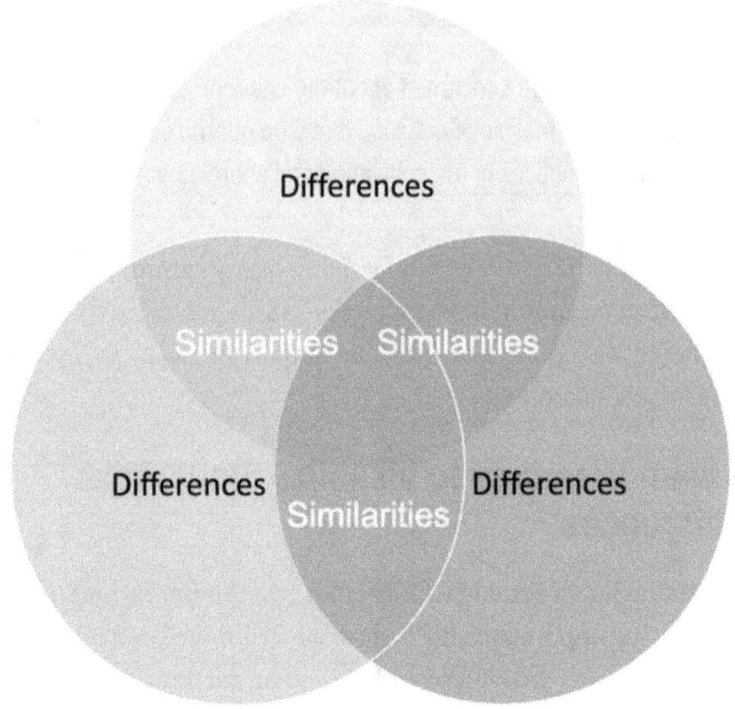

A Venn diagram is a useful visualization for examining a set of personas, where each circle represents a unique persona. By using overlapping circles, you can easily see which attributes are shared between personas and which are unique to each. We can combine the thematic tables and their information into a single Venn diagram to highlight each persona's themes and specific attributes. When compared using a Venn diagram, let's look at how Samantha's B2B and wholesale customer personas look.

B2B

- Specialized products tailored to a niche market
- Focused on uniqueness, and customization
- Individual clients or smaller businesses
- Focused on quality over quantity
- Maintains a diverse but small inventory.
- Sells by personal relationships and storytelling

Wholesale

- Broad range of products
- Prioritizes factors such as freshness, and variety
- Needs for large quantities for resale or in their operations
- Online platforms, distribution networks, and trade shows
- Thinner margins and bulk prices
- Highly diverse, everchanging and large amount of stock
- Targeted marketing campaigns aimed at industries

Shared
Quality Standards
Variety and Selection
Reliability and Consistency
Cost Effectiveness
Flexibility
Sustainability

This diagram highlights the common themes shared by both B2B and wholesale customers while identifying specific attributes unique to each persona from the themes.

Understanding Themes on a Spectrum

When analyzing the attributes within specific themes, it's important to consider that they often don't exist in a binary state. In other words, they cannot simply be categorized as present or absent. Instead, these attributes need to be evaluated on a spectrum, where they can exist in varying degrees or levels. This nuanced approach allows for a more accurate and comprehensive analysis, considering the complexity and diversity of the attributes under consideration.

Domain knowledge and experience are two common themes often represented on a spectrum. Domain knowledge refers to an individual's expertise and understanding within a specific field or subject area. On the other hand, experience is based on the situations and activities an individual has been involved in over time. It's important to note that domain knowledge and experience aren't always the same. For instance, after reading many books, a person can have extensive knowledge on the subject of aviation but may not have any actual experience flying a plane. Knowledge and experience are usually gained over time and can then help to classify users as novices or experts.

Plotting Domain Knowledge and Experience

Let's look at an example of two themes representing domain knowledge and experience. A cruise line company conducted research to better understand the unique backgrounds of those planning a cruise vacation. The cruise line identified technology savviness and cruise experience as two themes that would majorly impact its customer's booking experience. Let's break down these two themes into specific attributes and see how they fall within a spectrum.

Tech savviness

- Proficiency in using web and mobile applications
- Knowledge of common online purchasing workflows
- Adept at using search aggregation tools to find the best deals

Cruise booking experience

- Has taken cruises over a long period of time
- Experience with the cruise booking process
- Experiences interacting with cruise line company booking staff

These themes and their attributes can be separated into four quadrants representing the spectrum from least to most knowledgeable and experienced.

CHAPTER 7   SYNTHESIZING DATA TO INFORM YOUR PERSONAS

The Four Quadrant Diagram

A four quadrant diagram is useful for classifying attributes and identifying where each persona fits on a spectrum. It is most effective when used comparatively to show personas' positions relative to one another. You can use the size of the dots in the diagram to indicate the relative number of users represented by that type of persona. The diagram below illustrates five identified personas based on the themes of tech savviness and cruise booking experience.

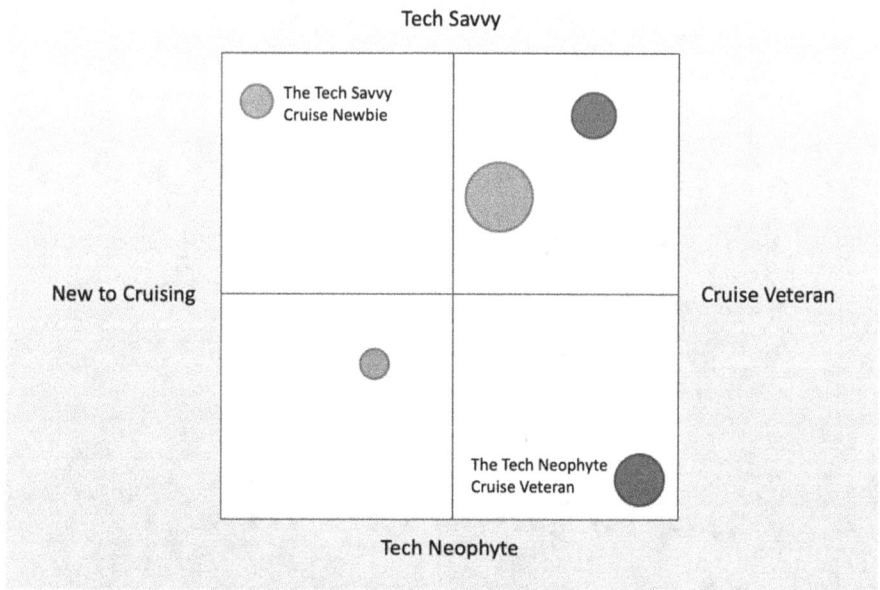

This four quadrant diagram has revealed two types of personas at opposite ends of the spectrum.

- **The Tech-Savvy Cruise Newbie** is a proficient technology user but lacks experience in booking and navigating the intricacies of a cruise vacation. This type of individual likely won't have any trouble using

119

a digital experience to book a trip, but they would not have expertise in the best times of year to sail, which ships have the best buffets, or where on the ship to book a cabin to minimize sea sickness.

- **The Tech Neophyte Cruise Veteran** is a seasoned cruiser with extensive experience booking cruise vacations, yet possesses a limited understanding of technology. This type of individual may rely on booking cruises over the phone or visiting their local travel agent. They may struggle with using anything beyond basic website features and may not understand newer mobile app paradigms.

In addition to these two extremes, many other personas can fit along the spectrum of technology knowledge and experience with cruising.

CHAPTER 7 SYNTHESIZING DATA TO INFORM YOUR PERSONAS

Using Data to Inform Your Diagram

Each plot representing a persona on your diagram should be based on primary and/or secondary research. Before constructing your diagram, make sure to

- **Determine What Type of Data You Will Use**: You can use qualitative, quantitative, or both data types to plot your personas.

- **Be Clear About Where Your Data Sources Came From:** You should identify which source(s) informed your diagram, such as attitudinal data from user interviews or behavioral data from analytics.

- **Standardize Your Approach**: Use visualization design patterns consistently to make your diagrams easy to understand and avoid confusion.

The type of data that you select will be used to inform where the persona fits on a spectrum.

Using Quantitative Insights

Quantitative data can inform the amount of knowledge and experience a persona has. Examples of numerically derived insights can include

- The average number of cruises taken per year
- The number of cruises taken over an individual's lifetime so far
- How frequently they make purchases online in an average month

CHAPTER 7   SYNTHESIZING DATA TO INFORM YOUR PERSONAS

Using Qualitative Insights

Qualitative insights can describe the types of knowledge and experiences the persona has. Examples of descriptive insights can include

- How well they understand the process for booking a cruise vacation
- Their preferences for booking travel (i.e., online, in-person, over the phone, etc.)
- How they find out information that helps them to make travel booking decisions

Using a Combination of Qualitative and Quantitative Insights

You can use both qualitative and quantitative data to chart where a persona fits on a spectrum. Here are examples of how both types of data can be combined to represent knowledge and experience in a range from low to high:

- **High Cruise Experience**: Has booked at least two cruises each year for the last five years and frequently reads cruise ship reviews.
- **Low Cruise Experience**: Has taken no more than two cruises before and has no one in their immediate social network who regularly cruises.
- **High Technology Knowledge**: Makes online purchases at least three times per month and uses social media to learn about the latest trends from people in their network.
- **Low Technology Knowledge**: Has made no more than two online purchases in the past year and relies on a flip phone primarily for phone calls.

CHAPTER 7   SYNTHESIZING DATA TO INFORM YOUR PERSONAS

Key Takeaways

- Themes derived from research data play a crucial role in informing the creation of personas. These themes encompass various aspects, such as user behaviors, preferences, and needs, essential for developing accurate and effective personas.

- When determining which themes to incorporate into personas, factors such as strength of evidence, relevancy to user experiences, and alignment with business goals should be considered.

- Themes serve as a framework for understanding the similarities and differences between different personas. Venn diagrams offer a visually intuitive way to depict these similarities and differences.

- Attributes within themes often exist on a spectrum rather than in binary states. Techniques like four-quadrant diagrams help classify personas based on attributes such as knowledge and experience, offering a nuanced understanding of user diversity.

In the next chapter, we will represent your established themes and attributes in a persona.

CHAPTER 8

Constructing Your Personas

Now that you've defined your personas, conducted research to inform them, and synthesized the themes shaping their attributes, it's time to build them out. This chapter focuses on the practical aspects of persona construction and guidance on assembling the necessary components to understand and support your users.

CHAPTER 8   CONSTRUCTING YOUR PERSONAS

Benefits of an Effective Persona

In Chapter two, you learned about ineffective personas and why fictitious characters like Sally fail to be supported by organizations. A properly constructed persona can

- **Give your team a central point of reference and a shared understanding of your users.** This will help you stay focused on relevant facts and avoid getting bogged down in meaningless details.
- **Make better decisions.** When stakeholders provide their assumptions and guesses, you can go back to your research-backed persona to point out what really matters. Personas help you to make decisions about populations, not individual users.
- **Help relate to and remember your users.** Your personas should help your organization feel more connected to your users and easily recall key information about them.

This chapter will provide you with a strategy and step-by-step guidance on how to construct your personas.

Persona Construction Strategy

An effective persona strategy starts with building empathy and establishing a framework for understanding the user and the implications for design.

Empathetic

Empathy is generated by making tangible connections and a true sense of understanding. Written and visual stories that present a holistic view of the user can evoke a feeling of connectedness. A persona should reinforce that there are actual people impacted by the experiences that we create.

Actionable

A persona should influence every part of your organization's decision-making. They should include concise, evidence-based insights to give teams a clear vision of how to apply knowledge of the user tactically and strategically. Personas should be directly tied to Key Performance Indicators (KPIs) set by an organization such as

- **Experiential**: Increase satisfaction and enjoyment
- **Operational**: Increase productivity and efficiency
- **Financial**: Save money and increase revenue

In Chapter 16, you will dive more deeply into how to identify and measure KPIs associated with your personas.

Contextual

Contextual factors help us understand not only what users need but also why they need it and how to best support them. A persona should provide information with the consistent level of detail and context needed to represent the persona at a specific altitude.

Scannable

A persona should be quick and easy to understand with a strong visual hierarchy to guide the reader to the most important information. Your design should use best practices in visual science, content strategy, and information architecture.

Building Out Your Persona

Your documentation should provide readers with a consistent structure and framework that helps them quickly and easily understand your persona. The first thing to create is a cover page that provides an orientation to your persona and key takeaways about who they represent.

Provide an Introduction to Your Persona with a Cover Page

The first page of your persona should help the reader understand

- **Who the User Is:** a description that provides information about the user's background and current situation.

- **What They Need:** a description of the highest priority goal that the user needs to achieve.

- **How They Are Different from Other Users:** a set of attributes that highlight the defining characteristics of this type of user.

Create a Descriptive Title to Define Your Persona

Using a catchy fictitious name to represent your persona might make it feel more relatable, but it does not help the reader understand who the persona represents. A descriptive title should only use words that help to identify the persona. Your title should be easily scannable and limited to a few words. Lower altitude personas may need additional words to help identify their unique attributes. Do not use abbreviations or lingo in your title that others might not understand. Here are sample titles that describe several personas at different altitudes:

Higher Altitude Persona

- Cruise Traveler
- Sales Employee
- Florist Customer

Mid Altitude Persona

- Newbie Cruise Traveler
- Remote-Based Sales Employee
- Wholesale Florist Customer

Lower Altitude Persona

- Brand Loyal Tech Neophyte Cruise Veteran
- Remote-based Small Business Sales Manager
- International Wholesale Florist Customer

Provide Useful Background Information

Ineffective personas often include a creatively written narrative that may be inspired by or loosely based on user research. While providing an entertaining story, these descriptions can mislead with false information and distract your team from details that will help them design for your users. To act as an effective persona, your description should include objective, research-based details that help the reader understand who the persona is, what they do, and the background of their situation. Make your descriptions quick to consume and easy to remember by using 100 words or less. Note that lower altitude personas will contain descriptions that contain more specific details and context. Let's look at a few examples of descriptions that define personas at three different altitudes:

High Altitude Persona

A **florist** crafts bouquets and compositions that reflect their clients' preferences and occasions. Their responsibilities encompass every facet of floral design, from selecting the freshest blooms to arranging them in visually appealing displays. Interacting closely with customers, the florist offers expert guidance to ensure client satisfaction while managing inventory, overseeing operations, and cultivating supplier relationships to maintain superior quality standards and drive the growth of their floral business.

Mid Altitude Persona

A **wedding florist** coordinates logistics, manages budgets, and provides creative input to bring a couple's vision to life. They oversee flower selection, vendor coordination, and budget management, ensuring the flower arrangements stay within the couple's financial limits while maintaining the desired aesthetic. The wedding florist directly assists in designing floral arrangements and décor elements to enhance the overall wedding experience, all while offering guidance and support to the couple throughout the planning process.

Low Altitude Persona

A **tech-savvy wedding florist** leverages digital tools and SaaS platforms to streamline logistics, manage budgets, and design arrangements to realize a couple's vision. They use social media sites such as Pinterest and Instagram for design inspiration. They communicate via text messages and video calls to keep the couple informed and involved every step of the way. The tech-savvy wedding florist takes and shares wedding photos on social media, showcasing their work to market to prospective clients.

Identifying the Primary Goal

A persona represents many goals that a user wants to achieve, but not all goals have the same level of significance or priority. The primary goal should articulate the defining aspect that would make this persona successful. It should be based on

- **Importance:** The most important thing that the user wants to achieve. Importance is based on what users have told you rank as their highest priority and what they most want to accomplish.

- **Impact:** Achieving this goal will make a major difference in this person's life. It likely has numerous benefits for the persona, such as financial, social, and professional benefits.

- **Longevity:** The primary goal should reflect a longer-term goal that the user will need to achieve. For example, a primary goal would not be to lose some weight for an upcoming event. Instead, it would be to reach and maintain a specific healthy weight.

The cover page focuses on what the persona most wants to achieve, and secondary goals are covered on additional pages in your document. Let's take a look at the primary goals for our previously defined personas:

High Altitude Persona

The **florist's** goal is to create floral arrangements that reflect their client's individual preferences and occasions.

Mid Altitude Persona

The **wedding florist's** goal is to create floral arrangements that match the couple's vision and budget.

Low Altitude Persona

The **tech-savvy wedding florist's** goal is to maximize the effectiveness and efficiency of digital tools to create floral arrangements that match the couple's vision and budget.

Keeping to a distilled and focused goal will help your team ensure that your products and services help the user achieve long-term success. In addition to the primary goal, your persona will represent other goals and tasks important to the user after the cover page. In Chapter 12, you will utilize these goals to build flight paths for your journey maps and represent them across different situations and contexts.

Select Identifiers

Identifiers provide a set of distinguishing characteristics that help to identify a persona. Your identifiers should be based on the attributes you have previously defined for your persona. You should select three to six attributes that most strongly identify this persona and use short phrases of one to three words. Let's take a look at a set of identifiers for our previously defined personas:

High Altitude Persona

Small Business Owner, Floral Designer, Personalized Service

Mid Altitude Persona

Wedding Occasions, Logistics Coordinator, Vendor Management, Client Management

Low Altitude Persona

SaaS Management Tools, Design Apps, Photo Editing Apps, Videoconferencing, Social Media Marketing, Online Research

Ensure that your identifiers extend to all the users that your persona represents. Never use traits that are unique to individuals such as personality, moods, or personal preferences. Keep in mind that your lower altitude personas will inherit the traits of your higher altitude personas.

Include Metadata

Your personas will be used by many individuals and shared across your organization over a long period of time. You should provide metadata such as the date created, last updated, version numbers, the name of the document creator, and the creator's contact information. You should also indicate where this persona fits into the greater persona hierarchy. You can represent these as breadcrumbs such as

> B2B Customer ➤ Florist ➤ Wedding Florist ➤ **Tech Savvy Wedding Florist**

You may also include references to research that informed the creation of the personas such as citing research reports or links to external sources. Indicate whether the persona is a proto persona. Proto personas should be used as preliminary and draft representations of your users and should be updated once your user research is completed.

CHAPTER 8   CONSTRUCTING YOUR PERSONAS

Let's look at a wireframe draft cover page for a persona of the Tech Savvy Wedding Florist.

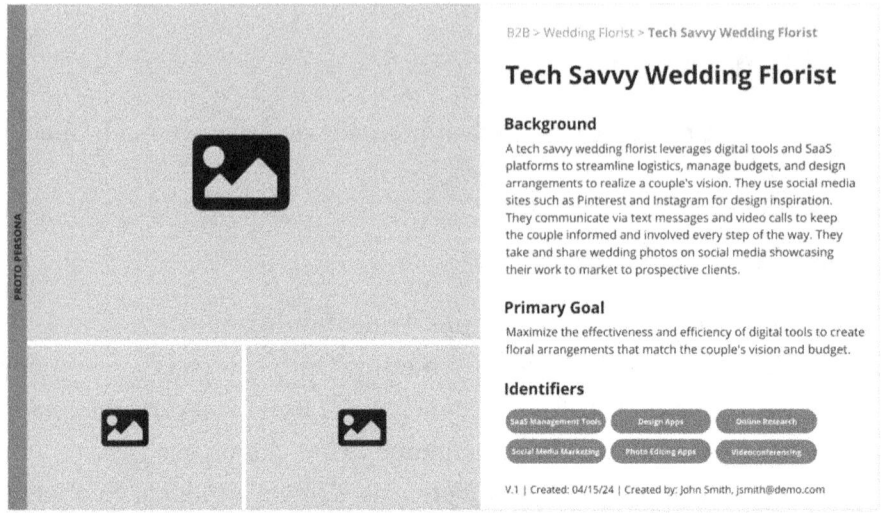

Getting into the Details of Goals and Tasks

Your cover page provides a snapshot of your persona with key takeaways. The additional sections will explore their needs, background, and situation more deeply.

Defining Goals

Now that you have established a primary goal, you will need to identify other goals that will support the success of your persona. These goals should be selected based on importance, impact, and persistence. Let's look at three goals that would support the success of our wedding florist persona:

- Create a shared vision of the couple's ideal wedding decor based on their preferences, budget, and the latest floral industry trends.

CHAPTER 8   CONSTRUCTING YOUR PERSONAS

- Keep to the client's budget while providing flower arrangements that meet or exceed the couple's expectations.

- Acquire new clients from referrals from satisfied couples and examples of previous work.

Your goals should be consistently defined at the same altitude as your persona. Higher altitude personas will contain broader goals, while lower altitude ones will be more narrow and contextual.

Defining Tasks

Tasks are specific actions that your users need to complete to achieve a goal. They should be selected based on importance, impact, and persistence toward a goal. Tasks should describe activities that explain how the user would perform them. Let's look at a wedding florist persona's goal and the tasks that would most support its success. The bolded phrases highlight specific parts of the goal that the tasks should address.

Goal #1: Create a **shared vision** of the couple's ideal wedding decor based on their **preferences**, **budget**, and the latest floral **industry trends**. The associated tasks to accomplish this goal include

- Review social media of wedding influencers for inspiration and magazines for seasonal trends.

- Create a questionnaire for clients to understand the vision for their wedding theme, likes/dislikes, and to provide examples of flower arrangements.

- Create a mood board to share with the client, showcasing recommended color palettes, flower species, floral arrangements, and other decorative elements.

Goal #2: Keep to the client's **budget** while providing flower arrangements that **meet or exceed the couple's expectations**. The associated tasks to accomplish this goal include

- Find flowers that are economical by using locally sourced flowers that are in season.
- Subscribe to flower and home decor reseller lists to find sales and clearance items that can be used for decorative elements.
- Keep track of all floral, decor, and vendor expenses.

Goal #3: Acquire **new clients** from **referrals** from satisfied couples and **examples** of previous work. The associated tasks to accomplish this goal include

- Take numerous photos and videos of flower arrangements to post on social media.
- Request written and video testimonials from clients to post on the business website.
- Request that clients leave online reviews about their experience working with the business and their satisfaction with the outcome.

Your persona should include any dependencies, constraints, and pain points that would prevent a persona from completing the tasks that they need to complete to reach their goal. These friction points will be used to identify opportunities to improve the experience for this persona.

Dependencies

All tasks have requirements that a user must meet to complete an activity. These prerequisites can include having a certain type of knowledge, experience, or aptitude. They can also include successfully completing a different task before the next task can be completed. Let's look at a few dependencies associated with the goal of finding inexpensive flowers by using locally sourced flowers that are in season.

- Knowledge of pricing fluctuations associated with seasonal inventories
- Contacts in local flower reseller community
- Relationships with local flower resellers

Constraints

Your users will always have limited resources to complete a task. Constraints can be limitations on time, money, tools, inventory, etc. Let's look at a few dependencies associated with taking numerous photos and videos of flower arrangements to post on social media.

- Time availability before, during, and after the wedding event to take photos and videos
- Editing software and the ability to compose high-quality images and videos
- A marketing budget to spend on promoting social media posts

Pain points

Pain points are barriers that prevent users from completing their tasks and jeopardize accomplishing their goals. Contextualizing pain points provides a deeper understanding of an issue and the consequences of not completing a task successfully. Understanding the root causes and severity of these issues can help teams identify opportunities to improve upon an experience or create new products and services to support a need.

Unaddressed pain points may prevent users from completing a task. Articulating the results of task failure can help stakeholders empathize with users and identify potential risks. For example, let's consider the consequences of not being able to take numerous photos and videos of flower arrangements to post on social media.

> There is a very narrow window of time to take photos before the wedding event, and the flower arrangements are often either damaged, rearranged, or removed after the event. This often results in only a few hastily and poorly composed photos or videos taken before the event that are often unsuitable to post to promote the business's best work.

Pain points are further contextualized in journey maps, pinpointed to specific steps within the user's journey, and covered in Chapter 11.

Going Deeper to Understand Contextual Factors

Deeper and more specific contextual factors will be incorporated into your lower altitude personas. These aspects of your persona will help your team understand what your users do, what they know, and what resources they have to aid in their goals.

Roles and Responsibilities

Everyone has both formal and informal roles that define what we do. These can include official job titles such as customer service manager or self-defined identities like bird watcher. Responsibilities can include aspects of a specific job, such as a barista's responsibility to take customer orders and make drinks. They can also relate to activities outside of work, such as an amateur photographer who takes photos and posts them on social media to gain more followers.

Keep in mind that your users may wear many hats. For example, the same individual could be a scientist who conducts research and is also a faculty member teaching classes at a university. Each persona should only reflect one "hat" as the others may constitute completely different personas with their own unique attributes and needs.

Knowledge and Experience

Domain knowledge refers to an individual's expertise and understanding within a specific field or subject area. Experience is based on the situations and activities an individual has been involved in over time. This section of your persona should reflect how these capabilities support the user's goals. Let's examine the knowledge and experience of a Tech-Savvy Cruise Travel Veteran:

- **Frequent Cruise Traveler**: Takes at least three cruises per year to travel to many destinations across the world.

- **High Status Customer**: Has top-tier customer recognition status and frequently receives perks and incentives for continuing to be a loyal cruiseline customer.

- **Expert Cruise Traveler**: Knows the best times of the year to sail, which ships have the best buffets, and where on the ship to book a cabin to minimize sea sickness.

- **Savvy Online Shopper**: Uses travel aggregator sites to compare pricing and signs up to receive notifications of cruise deals.

- **Heavy Social Media User**: Frequently reads posts from fellow cruise travelers and shares their experiences by regularly posting photos, videos, and other content about their cruise travels.

Tools and Resources

The tools and resources should be tangible artifacts that the persona would regularly have access to and use to achieve their goals. You should indicate why they are helpful and how this persona would typically use them. Let's look at tools and resources that our Tech-Savvy Cruise Travel Veteran would use.

- **Travel Aggregators**: Websites such as Kayak and Expedia to compare travel itineraries and pricing and sign up to receive notifications of promotional deals on specific cruises.

- **Social Media**: Cruise travel forums to read and share stories of past cruises and to provide reviews on ships, crews, and ports of call. Instagram to follow friends from past cruises and cruise travel influencers.

- **Travel Newsletters**: Subscriptions to email newsletters such as Cruise Critic, Lonely Planet, and member-exclusive messages from specific cruise lines.

Utilize your research to decide whether to include specific product names. Product utilization may vary over time, and each product has its own unique set of features.

People and Relationships

The people and relationships section is best suited for lower altitude personas, which are useful for highlighting how your persona would interact with certain types of individuals. These individuals can represent other personas in your persona family tree and can show up in service blueprint swimlanes (discussed further in Chapter 16). Let's examine several individuals and how they relate to the Tech Neophyte Cruise Veteran. This persona prefers a high-touch, human-centered experience.

- **Travel Agent**: This individual helps to plan, book, and coordinate all travel arrangements. They are called during the preliminary trip planning stages to discuss potential itineraries and travel preferences and then assist with all travel logistics.

- **Cruiseline Customer Support Representative**: This individual assists with any questions or concerns once a cruise has been booked. They are called when there are questions that the travel agent is unable to answer, often pertaining to the ship.

- **Travel Insurance Representative**: This individual answers questions regarding travel insurance policies and can help process any claims related to an insured trip. It is uncommon for this person to be called unless there are unusual events that may impact an upcoming trip or during travel.

Representing other individuals who support your persona can help you to understand their ecosystem, but be careful not to overgeneralize the types of people and their relationship to the persona. Make sure that you have strong evidence from your research to highlight a connection between these individuals and your persona.

A Caution When Using Demographics and Psychographics

Using demographics like gender, age, and race, or psychographics such as determined, loyal, and anxious to define your persona can trigger our brains to think in stereotypes and assumptions; it can even lead us to favor one persona over another. You should only use these attributes when they are a defining aspect of your persona, represent a majority of the population for this persona, and would have direct implications for designing for these users.

Implications and Considerations

Your personas are intended to help your team understand and empathize with your users. They are also used to guide decisions that will impact the user's experience. The final section of your persona should help connect key information about the persona with considerations for creating experiences for them.

Design Implications

Personas can have various implications for design, influencing decisions across different aspects of the human-centered design process.

- **Feature Prioritization**: Understanding the goals and preferences of different personas helps prioritize product features. Features useful to one persona may not be as valuable to another. Prioritizing features based on personas ensures that the most important functions are addressed first.

- **Content Strategy**: Personas can help to determine what information is most relevant and useful to each type of persona. Content can be personalized to resonate with their unique needs, interests, and level of knowledge.

- **User Flows and Navigation**: Personas can help to create intuitive user flows and navigation paths within an application that match the persona's mental model, preferences, and typical behaviors.

- **User Interface and Interaction Design**: Personas can inform how a user is intended to interact with a system based on their mental model and behaviors. This can include specific input methods, feedback mechanisms, and error handling tailored to the characteristics and behaviors of different personas.

- **Accessibility**: Personas can help identify accessibility needs and ensure the design is inclusive. Design decisions can be made to accommodate users with diverse abilities, ensuring that everyone can interact with the product effectively.

By considering these implications, designers can create more user-centered designs that effectively meet the needs and preferences of their target audience.

Business Implications

Personas have several implications for businesses, impacting various aspects of strategy, marketing, and operations.

- **Market Strategy**: Personas facilitate market segmentation by identifying distinct groups of users with similar characteristics, behaviors, and needs. This segmentation allows businesses to effectively target their marketing efforts and tailor products or services to specific segments.

- **Customer Acquisition and Retention**: Personas help businesses attract and retain customers by enabling them to offer personalized experiences and solutions.

By understanding the needs and preferences of different personas, businesses can better tailor their products, services, and customer support to meet customer expectations and build loyalty.

- **Revenue Generation**: Personas impact revenue generation by helping businesses identify opportunities for upselling, cross-selling, and pricing optimization. By understanding the value drivers and purchasing behavior of different personas, businesses can develop strategies to maximize revenue from existing customers and attract new ones.

- **Competitive Analysis**: Personas inform competitive analysis by highlighting competitors' strengths and weaknesses in meeting the needs of different user segments. This insight helps businesses identify opportunities for differentiation and competitive advantage.

- **Customer Service and Support**: Personas guide the development of customer service and support strategies by identifying the most common pain points and issues different user groups face. This enables businesses to allocate resources effectively and provide targeted assistance to users when needed.

By considering these implications, businesses can leverage personas to improve customer satisfaction, drive growth, and achieve their strategic objectives.

CHAPTER 8 CONSTRUCTING YOUR PERSONAS

Articulating Considerations

The considerations should have longevity and focus on strategic rather than tactical decisions. You should not provide detailed recommendations for your persona to address specific opportunities or pain points. Each organization, departmental unit, and individual team member must address the persona's needs differently. For example, for the same persona, a UX team may need to consider font sizes and tap targets for a mobile app, while the marketing team may need to design print brochures with prominent contact information.

Let's look at considerations for the Tech Neophyte Cruise Veteran persona and an organization undergoing a major digital transformation. This organization seeks opportunities to encourage users to adopt new technology solutions.

Hesitancy to Use Technology

The Tech Neophyte Cruise Veteran persona represents users reluctant to use technology due to a lack of knowledge and experience. These users primarily rely on traditional forms of information-seeking and interactions using phone and print publications. They have basic web browsing and email skills and are reluctant to download new apps to their smartphones without assistance. Considerations for this persona include

- **Gradual Introduction**: Introduce technology gradually, starting with simple functions and progressing to more complex features. This prevents them from being overwhelmed and builds confidence over time.
- **Personalized Guidance**: Determine a persona's initial knowledge and confidence with technology and

provide contextual help and step-by-step guidance for features these users access for the first time.

- **Provide Reassurance**: Address any fears or concerns about technology, such as privacy or security. Explain basic safety measures and provide reassurance that taking things at your own pace is okay.

- **Offer Continued Support**: Let these users know that support is always available whenever they have questions or encounter challenges. Knowing that they have someone to turn to can make the process less daunting. This could include tutorials, FAQs, and dedicated support channels staffed by knowledgeable representatives.

High-Touch, Human-Centered Experience

The Tech Neophyte Cruise Veteran strongly prefers to interact with humans and considers AI-based support channels to be an inferior experience. Considerations for this persona include

- **Hybrid Approach**: Blend traditional, in-person interactions with technology to create a seamless experience. For example, offer the option for customers to schedule appointments online and follow up with a personalized confirmation call.

- **Customized Solutions**: Offer customized solutions that cater to individual preferences and requirements. This could involve providing options for different levels of technology integration or allowing customers to choose the communication channels that work best for them.

- **Virtual Consultations**: Offer real-time virtual consultations via video conferencing platforms for those who prefer face-to-face interactions but may not be able to meet in person. Ensure these consultations are personalized and focused on addressing specific needs or concerns.

- **Emphasize Human Touchpoints**: While incorporating technology, emphasize the role of human touchpoints throughout the customer journey. Make it clear that behind every digital interaction, there are real people ready to provide assistance and support.

- **Feedback Loops**: Establish feedback loops to gather customer input about their experiences with technology integration. Use this feedback to continuously improve and refine your approach, ensuring it remains aligned with their preferences and needs.

Key Takeaways

- Personas should focus on empathy, ensuring a true understanding of user experiences. They should be actionable, influencing decision-making across the organization, contextual, providing information at the appropriate level of detail, and scannable, making it easy for teams to grasp key insights quickly.

- Start with a cover page introducing the persona. Use descriptive titles and objective descriptions to define the persona clearly. Identify the primary goal, ensuring it reflects the user's highest priority and ongoing need.

CHAPTER 8 CONSTRUCTING YOUR PERSONAS

- Establish primary and secondary goals that align with the persona's objectives. Define tasks that outline specific actions users must take to achieve their goals. Consider dependencies, constraints, and pain points to understand potential obstacles.

- Dive deeper into roles, responsibilities, knowledge, and experiences relevant to the persona. Identify tools, resources, people, and relationships that impact the persona's journey.

- Consider design and business implications based on what the user wants to achieve and any friction points that may prevent them from reaching their goals.

In the next chapter, you will learn a systematic, modular approach to persona design.

CHAPTER 9

Designing Your Personas

This chapter presents a systematic, modular approach to persona design. It breaks personas down into elemental components that can be assembled into reusable templates using atomic design patterns and visual design principles.

CHAPTER 9   DESIGNING YOUR PERSONAS

Creating a Template for Your Personas

Creating templates for personas is essential to ensure that they will be easily understood and utilized by various teams within an organization. Templates establish a common language and framework facilitating communication and collaboration across business units. They also streamline the creation of new personas by utilizing pre-formatted pages with standardized sections for content about the user.

Different Levels of Design Fidelity

There are two levels of design fidelity templates: low-fidelity and high-fidelity. Each plays a distinct role in the persona design process, allowing creators to differentiate between levels of detail and refinement to suit various stages of development.

Low-Fidelity Designs

Low-fidelity designs are used in the early stages of persona creation to generate initial drafts or concepts for a persona quickly. These templates prioritize simplicity and ease of use, providing a basic framework for capturing essential user attributes. They facilitate rapid exploration and iteration, allowing teams to efficiently generate ideas and concepts without getting bogged down in intricate design details. Low-fidelity designs often resemble wireframes and can use placeholders for images and visual design elements. Online collaboration tools such as Miro, Mural, and FigJam make it easy for anyone on the team to make real-time edits and comments on the document.

CHAPTER 9 DESIGNING YOUR PERSONAS

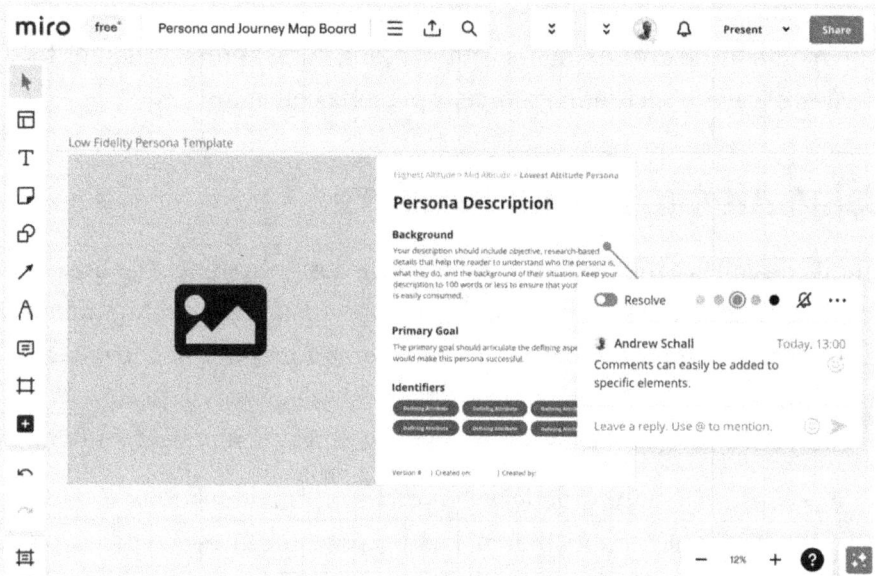

Low-fidelity templates are designed to be flexible, making it easy to incorporate feedback from stakeholders and insights gathered from research as the design evolves. These templates might be sufficient for your organization's needs without using high-fidelity designs for your personas.

High-Fidelity Designs

High-fidelity templates are used later in the creation process when more detailed and refined representations are needed and are typically used in presentations to stakeholders. These templates build upon the foundation laid by low-fidelity drafts by incorporating visual design elements to create a more polished and finalized portrayal of the intended users. They take more time and effort to create and modify compared to low-fidelity designs and may require specialized knowledge of design tools such as Figma, Illustrator, or Sketch.

151

CHAPTER 9   DESIGNING YOUR PERSONAS

You should consider who in your organization will need to create and update these documents as your persona library grows. Chapter 15 discusses ways to scale and grow your persona collection.

Using Atomic Design Patterns

Atomic design is a methodology for creating design systems that break down interfaces into smaller, reusable components. These components, ranging from atoms to molecules to organisms are assembled to create a complete system. When applying atomic design patterns to personas, you can think of each persona as a composite of these smaller components.

- **Atoms**: At the atomic level, you have individual traits or characteristics that make up a persona. These could include specific goals, attributes, or other descriptors. Each of these traits can be considered one of many "atoms" of the persona.

- **Molecules**: Just as molecules are formed by combining atoms, personas can be built by combining atomic traits. For example, a molecule can include sections like "Background," "Goals and Tasks," and "Domain Knowledge." This modular approach groups similar traits.

- **Organisms**: At the organism level, you have more complex structures that represent broader themes of the persona. This could include pages like "Introduction," "Contextual Factors," and "Considerations." Each of these pages is made up of molecules and atoms.

- **Systems**: Once you have defined the atoms, molecules, and organisms that make up your persona, you can assemble them into a cohesive whole. This would include a standardized layout or format that your team uses to create and document personas.

By using atomic design principles, you ensure consistency and scalability across all your persona templates. Let's look at several atomic design components that you can include in your persona.

Narratives

A narrative is a molecule composed in a sentence format and provides a deeper explanation of a focused topic. A narrative is best used to give a cohesive background explanation for your persona with interconnected details and additional context. Narratives may take many different forms, as discussed below, but whichever form you use, it is important to keep your narrative to a single paragraph and break it out into additional narratives if you need to include other unrelated topics. Here is an example of a narrative used to explain a global sales executive persona's domain knowledge and experience:

> A global sales executive is equipped with a nuanced understanding of diverse markets spanning multiple languages and cultures. Their domain knowledge includes a deep insight into the varying needs, preferences, and purchasing behaviors of customers worldwide. They adeptly navigate the complexities of global business landscapes, including regulatory frameworks, trade agreements, and cultural sensitivities, to develop tailored sales strategies that resonate across different regions. Drawing from extensive experience, they excel in building and nurturing relationships with stakeholders on

CHAPTER 9   DESIGNING YOUR PERSONAS

an international scale, driving sustainable revenue growth, and fostering cross-cultural collaboration to achieve organizational objectives.

Blocks

A block-style format is characterized by its simplicity, clarity, and ease of navigation, making it ideal for presenting information that can be quickly understood and absorbed. This format can best be used to provide a short description of each of your persona's key attributes. Each block starts with a succinct header as a handy reference point, aiding readers to grasp the block's content swiftly. A concise description of the topic follows the header, keeping the information streamlined and easily digestible.

By being self-contained, each block presents a complete unit of independent information. This ensures that readers focus on one specific topic without being burdened by unnecessary details. Related topics are grouped using a series of blocks, organized logically or thematically. This grouping allows readers to seamlessly navigate through the persona while maintaining a coherent understanding of the interconnected topics.

Trade Agreements	Regulatory Frameworks	Advanced Degree	Languages	Cultural Knowledge
Familiar with NAFTA and WTO agreements	Knowledge of import/export laws & tariffs	Has an MBA with international focus	Speaks several languages fluently	European, LATAM, and Asian cultures

Tables

A tabular format is a structured layout that organizes data into rows and columns as a table. This design is effective for presenting large amounts of information in a format that facilitates easy comparisons between attributes. Considerations for using a tabular format

- **Headers:** The top row contains headers for each column, providing labels that describe the content of the data within that column. These headers make it easy for readers to understand what each column represents.

- **Color and Formatting:** Color and formatting can be used strategically to highlight important data points, distinguish between categories, or draw attention to key insights. Use unique colors sparingly to avoid overwhelming the reader.

- **Whitespace:** Adequate whitespace should be incorporated to improve readability and prevent the table from appearing cluttered. Proper spacing between rows, columns, and individual cells helps readers navigate the information more easily.

Lists

A list format offers a streamlined and efficient way to convey key points without overwhelming the reader with unnecessary details. This format is characterized by presenting items in a sequential or bulleted list, making it easy for readers to quickly skim through. Considerations for using a list format:

- **Bulleted or Numbered Lists:** Bulleted lists are often used when the order of items is not important such as a list of tools that a persona uses. Numbered lists are used when the sequence or hierarchy of items matters, such as a set of prioritized needs or steps in a task process.

- **Concise Points:** Each item in the list consists of a brief, succinct point or piece of information. The goal is to provide just enough detail about the persona without overwhelming the reader with extraneous information.

- **Parallel Structure:** It's important to maintain a parallel structure, meaning that each item should be phrased in a consistent grammatical form. This enhances readability and makes it easier for readers to process the information.

- **Clear and Readable Formatting:** Lists should be formatted clearly and readable, with consistent spacing, indentation, and font styles. This helps ensure that the information is easy to scan and comprehend at a glance.

International Business Knowledge and Experience

- Knowledge of diverse markets, understands cultural nuances, and speaks multiple languages.

- Deep insights into the varying needs, preferences, and unique purchasing behaviors of customers worldwide.

- Experience managing the complexities of global business landscapes, including regulatory frameworks and trade agreements.

- Experience building and nurturing relationships with stakeholders on an international scale, fostering trust and collaboration consistently.

- Experience fostering cross-cultural collaboration, effectively utilizing diverse perspectives and expertise to achieve organizational objectives.

Creating a Visual Hierarchy

An effective visual hierarchy will highlight key information and create an engaging and readable persona. Designers can use visual hierarchy to organize elements, communicate their relative importance, direct users' attention, and enhance understanding. Design elements, including iconography, color and contrast, typography, white space, and alignment, contribute to the effective use of visual hierarchy. An important aspect of creating a visual hierarchy is using the concept of visual weight to influence what your readers pay the most attention to.

Visual Weight

Visual weight refers to the relative prominence of elements. It gauges how much attention an element draws compared to others, and more significant visual weight elements tend to captivate the viewer's attention more. Several factors contribute to an element's visual weight, including

- **Size:** Larger elements occupy more space and are more prominent, giving them greater visual weight.
- **Color:** Bright or saturated colors increase visual weight compared to muted or neutral colors.
- **Contrast:** Elements that stand out due to differences in color, value, or texture have greater visual weight.
- **Position:** Elements placed closer to the center or vital compositional points, such as intersections or focal points, have higher visual weight.
- **Complexity:** Intricate or detailed elements draw more attention and require more time to process, giving them greater visual weight.

Understanding visual weight is vital in design. It helps designers create balanced compositions that effectively guide the viewer's attention. By manipulating the visual weight of different elements, designers control the flow of information and direct the viewer's focus to key areas of the design.

Size

Larger elements occupy more space and are more prominent, giving them greater visual weight.

I'm a larger header
I'm a smaller header

Value

Darker and bolder elements have more visual weight than lighter elements.

I have a darker value
I have a lighter value

Color

Bright or saturated colors increase visual weight compared to muted or neutral colors.

This color attracts attention
This color does not

Localized White Space

Any element placed within a surrounding area of white space will stand out because of the empty space around it.

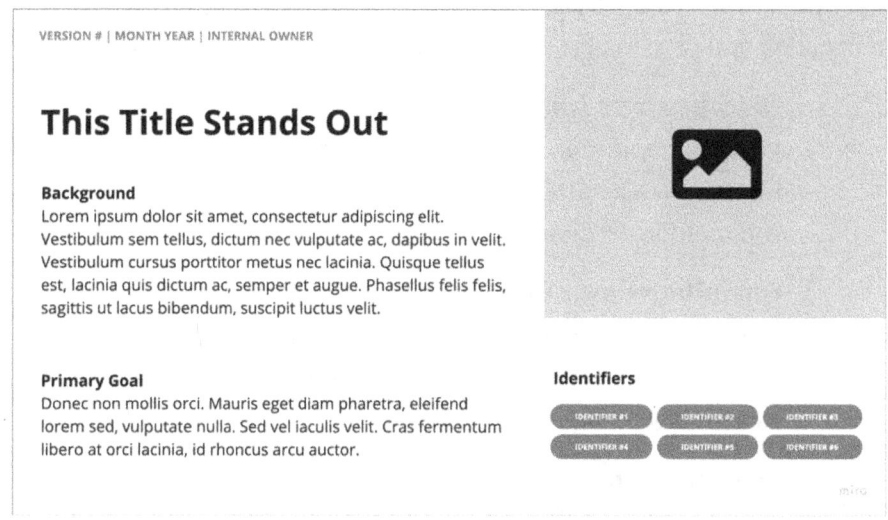

The example above illustrates how combining design techniques can create more or less visual weight to guide the reader's attention.

Iconography

Using icons can increase the scannability of content, enabling readers to easily identify pertinent details without having to sift through dense paragraphs of text. Icons are best used when there is a recurring need to highlight a certain element, such as a key insight or pain point. Whenever possible, use icons that are commonly used to represent these items. If you decide to use a unique icon, include it in a legend.

Information Visualizations

Information visualizations such as Venn diagrams and graphs greatly enhance the understanding and usability of personas by presenting complex data in a clear, intuitive manner. Consider what type of information you plan to represent before selecting a visualization.

- **Objective over Subjective:** Use data that represents facts over opinions. Objective data can include behaviors or available resources, while subjective data can include preferences or personal habits.

- **Quantitative over Qualitative:** Use numerical data representing quantities and percentages whenever possible. Scales without clearly defined measurements can be vague or easily misinterpreted.

- **Mainstream over Niche:** Use data that reflects the majority of users that the persona represents.

Venn Diagrams

Venn diagrams illustrate relationships and commonalities between different personas or user segments. They're useful for showing overlapping characteristics or interests among groups. For example, in a product design context, a Venn diagram can visually represent the shared needs and preferences between two distinct user segments, helping designers identify common design solutions that cater to both groups.

CHAPTER 9 DESIGNING YOUR PERSONAS

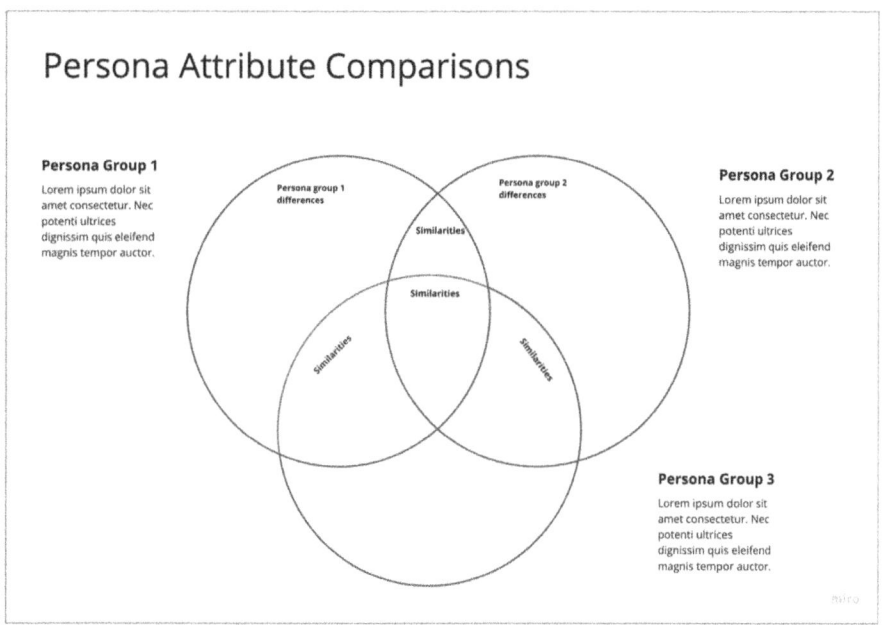

Radar (Spider) Maps

Radar or spider maps effectively show different attributes and how they relate. Plotting these attributes for each persona on a single radar chart allows you to quickly compare and contrast different personas, identifying patterns and outliers. This can aid in making informed design decisions that cater to diverse user needs.

CHAPTER 9   DESIGNING YOUR PERSONAS

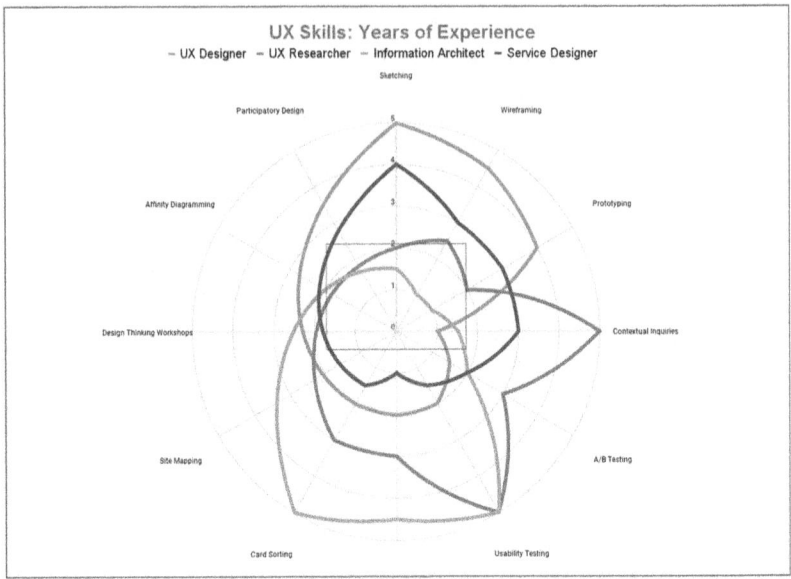

Bar Charts

Bar charts are best used to provide counts and totals for a set of attributes. They highlight attributes that represent significant high and low values.

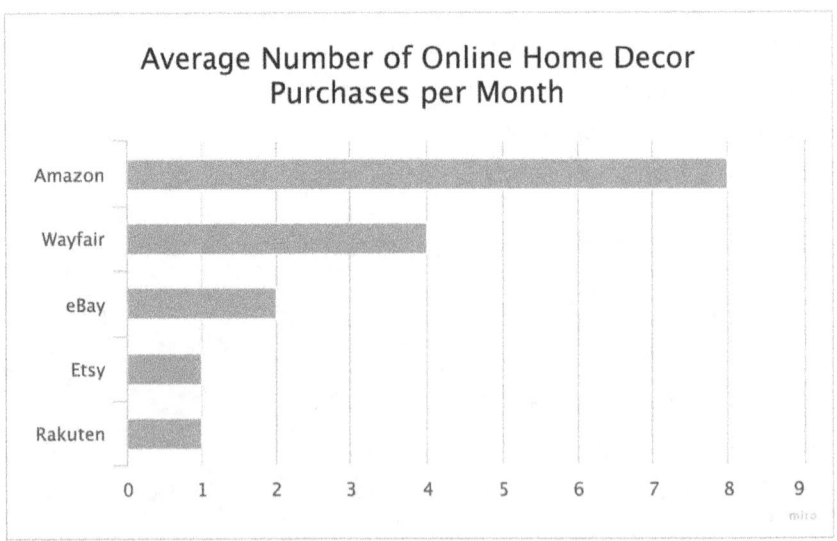

CHAPTER 9   DESIGNING YOUR PERSONAS

Pie Charts

Pie charts are effective in illustrating proportions and percentages within personas. They highlight the distribution of activities that a persona commonly performs. For example, a pie chart may be used to visually represent the percentage of time spent on daily tasks.

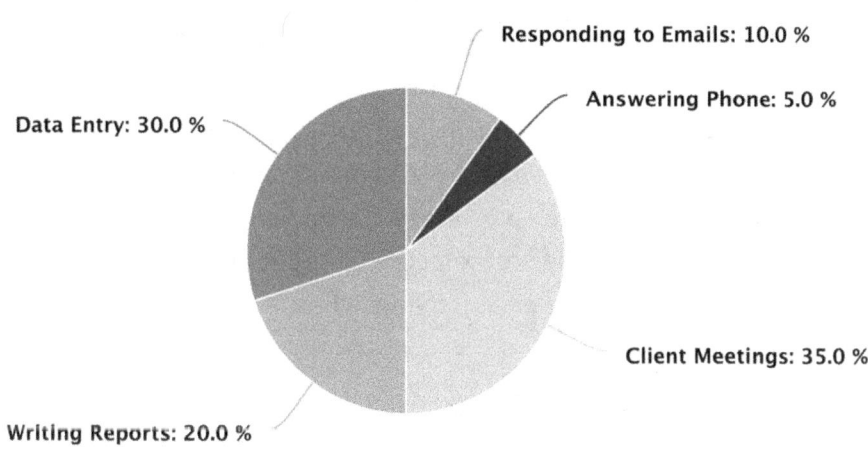

Using Photos to Represent the Persona

Photos can enhance the reader's understanding of a persona and should be chosen with this purpose in mind. Photos further help users empathize with personas. Proper photos may provide situational, artifact-based, or diverse information about their subjects.

CHAPTER 9   DESIGNING YOUR PERSONAS

Situational Photos

Situational photos depict scenarios or contexts relevant to the persona's characteristics, needs, or interests. Here are some types of situations that can be used in personas:

- **Everyday Life Scenes:** Images showing everyday life scenes will often depict typical daily activities related to the persona's lifestyle or profession. For example, a photo of someone working at a desk or a parent playing with their child.

- **Problem-Solving Scenarios:** Photos illustrating problem-solving scenarios will demonstrate challenges or problems that the persona might encounter. This could include images of someone troubleshooting a technical issue or a person trying to find their location on a map.

- **Social Interactions:** Images related to social interactions will portray social situations like networking events, family gatherings, or team meetings. These help to understand how the persona interacts with others in various settings.

- **Environmental Context:** Pictures reflecting environmental context will depict specific locations or environments relevant to the persona's activities. For instance, a photo of a bustling city street for an urban dweller persona or a serene natural landscape for an outdoor enthusiast persona.

- **Product or Service Usage:** Images of product or service usage demonstrate the persona using a particular product or service in their daily life. This helps teams to understand how users integrate a product or service in their routines and the benefits they derive from it.

- **Cultural Context:** Photos of cultural context reflect background elements that influence the persona's behavior or preferences. These may include images of traditions, customs, or symbols significant to the persona's cultural background.

Let's look at some situational photos appropriate for a barista working at a cafe.

CHAPTER 9 DESIGNING YOUR PERSONAS

Incorporating situational photos in a persona helps to humanize the profile and provide context for understanding the persona's behaviors, needs, and motivations in different situations.

Artifact Photos

Photos of artifacts should be used to reflect items that the persona uses to achieve goals and complete tasks. Examples of different types of artifacts can include

CHAPTER 9   DESIGNING YOUR PERSONAS

- **Tools of the Trade:** Images of tools or equipment crucial for the persona's work or hobbies, such as a graphic designer's tablet and stylus, a chef's kitchen utensils, or a carpenter's toolbox.

- **Productivity Aids:** Photos of items that facilitate organization and time management, such as planners, task boards, or productivity apps on a smartphone. These artifacts assist the persona in staying on track and meeting deadlines.

- **Technology Essentials:** Images showcasing gadgets and devices essential for communication, research, or productivity, such as a high-performance laptop, a smartphone with productivity apps, or noise-canceling headphones for focused work.

- **Learning Resources:** Pictures of books, online courses, or educational materials relevant to the persona's field or interests. These artifacts support their learning and skill development, helping them progress toward their objectives.

- **Networking and Collaboration Items:** Images of artifacts facilitating networking and collaboration, such as business cards, conference badges, or collaboration software.

By incorporating photos of artifacts that assist the persona in reaching their goals and completing tasks, you provide a visual representation of the tools and resources integral to their success and productivity.

CHAPTER 9   DESIGNING YOUR PERSONAS

Diversity

When choosing a set of photos for personas, creators should pay careful attention to diversity, ensuring that the photos used are inclusive and represent a wide range of individuals. Refrain from using a headshot of a single person to represent all of the users for your persona. Examples of considerations for inclusive and diverse photos include, but are not limited to, the following:

- **Ethnic Diversity:** Include photos of people from various ethnic backgrounds. This can encompass a wide range of skin tones, facial features, and cultural attire.

- **Age Diversity:** Feature individuals of different ages, from children to seniors. This demonstrates inclusivity across generations and acknowledges the unique perspectives and experiences that come with each stage of life.

- **Gender Diversity:** Represent a spectrum of gender identities, including cisgender, transgender, non-binary, and gender-fluid individuals. Avoid stereotypes and ensure that all gender identities are portrayed respectfully.

- **Ability Diversity:** Include people with diverse abilities and disabilities. This can include individuals using mobility aids, sign language, or assistive technologies and those with invisible disabilities.

- **Body Diversity:** Showcase a range of body types, sizes, and shapes. Avoid promoting unrealistic beauty standards and celebrate the beauty of diversity in physique.

- **Cultural Diversity:** Depict individuals from various cultural backgrounds, highlighting differences in clothing, customs, traditions, and languages.

- **Lifestyle Diversity:** Show people engaged in different activities and lifestyles, such as work, leisure, sports, hobbies, and family life. This reflects the diverse ways people live their lives and spend their time.

- **Intersectionality:** Recognize that individuals may embody multiple aspects of diversity simultaneously.

- **Authenticity:** Use genuine, candid photos that capture real people in natural settings. Avoid staged or tokenistic images that may come across as inauthentic or exploitative.

By incorporating diversity into photos of a persona, you can create a more inclusive and accurate portrayal of the users that persona represents, reflecting the richness and complexity of the human experience.

Key Takeaways

- **Modular Persona Design:** Breaking down personas into elemental components enhances stakeholder comprehension and simplifies development. Employing modular design principles fosters clarity and effectiveness in persona creation.

- **Template Creation:** Establishing standardized persona templates fosters universal understanding and collaboration across organizational teams. These templates provide a common framework and language, promoting consistency and efficiency in persona development.

- **Low-Fidelity vs. High-Fidelity Designs:** Low-fidelity designs aid in rapid concept generation, while high-fidelity designs offer refined representations for stakeholder presentations. Starting with low-fidelity designs allows quick iteration before transitioning to more polished versions.

- **Atomic Design Pattern Approach:** Applying atomic design principles ensures consistency and scalability in persona creation. Breaking personas into reusable components enhances cohesion and adaptability across all templates.

- **Visual Hierarchy and Design Elements:** Effective visual hierarchy enhances persona readability and engagement. Manipulating visual elements like size, color, and contrast guides the reader's attention. Incorporating icons, visualizations, and diverse photos improves scannability and inclusivity, creating engaging and informative personas.

In the next chapter, you will learn research strategies used to inform journey maps that reflect how users achieve their goals.

CHAPTER 10

Conducting Research to Understand Your User's Journey

This chapter explores the research methods used to create journey maps. It emphasizes behavioral user research techniques, including ethnographic methods, to understand how users go about achieving their goals.

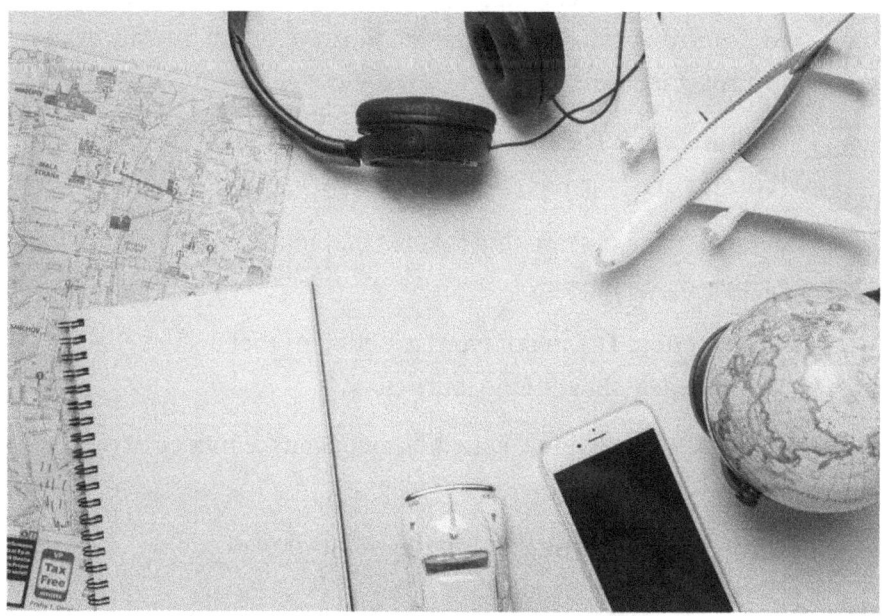

CHAPTER 10   CONDUCTING RESEARCH TO UNDERSTAND YOUR USER'S JOURNEY

Planning User Research

In this section, you will learn about the process of planning a successful journey map research strategy. This process includes

1. Defining your research objectives
2. Choosing research methods to gather the necessary insights
3. Gathering data about your persona's journey
4. Analyzing the collected data to identify patterns, trends, and key insights

Define Your Research Objectives

By understanding a user's goals, the major activities they engage in, and the barriers they face, you can create a comprehensive picture of their experience. Your research will be used to inform different aspects of your persona's journey, including

- **Flight Paths:** The user's goals as represented in the context of a journey.
- **Phases:** The overarching themes that represent the stages of the journey.
- **Milestones:** The major types of activities that occur within each phase of the journey.
- **Steps:** The individual activities that occur within each milestone.
- **Pain Points:** Barriers or friction points that occur during steps in the journey.

CHAPTER 10   CONDUCTING RESEARCH TO UNDERSTAND YOUR USER'S JOURNEY

Users associated with your persona will have many goals that they want to achieve; however, not all goals will need to be represented by a journey map. Your research plan should focus on understanding primary goals aligned to a specific altitude. Your decision on which journey maps to create first should be based on your organization's near-term decision-making needs. Chapter 17 will cover future state journey maps that inform longer-term organizational strategies.

Selecting Research Methods

Your approach to choosing research methods to inform a journey map will be similar to your persona research strategy:

- **Use Existing Knowledge:** Secondary research can jumpstart your discovery process and reduce the amount of time and resources needed to construct your journey maps.

- **Use Mixed Methods and Triangulate Your Data:** Take a mixed methods approach and use multiple data sources and research methods to validate findings and ensure the credibility of insights. This will include a mix of qualitative and quantitative data to inform behavioral and attitudinal insights.

- **Learn from Subject Matter Experts:** Interview subject matter experts (SMEs) as a valuable starting point for understanding a user's journey. SMEs often have direct experience with users, enabling them to provide nuanced perspectives and valuable context that can be used to identify typical user behaviors or challenges that users may encounter.

CHAPTER 10   CONDUCTING RESEARCH TO UNDERSTAND YOUR USER'S JOURNEY

Behavioral Data

Behavioral data provides a more objective measure of the user's experience rather than an individual's subjective impressions of it. These insights help you to understand what users do rather than how they feel or think. Many sources of data can help you to understand what your users do:

- Behavioral analytics
- User Action Logs (UALs)
- Session recordings
- Contextual inquiries

Behavioral data provides insights into how users interact with products and services, such as how long they spend on a particular page, what features they interact with, how long they have to wait in a queue, and what actions they perform to achieve their goals.

Identifying Behavior Patterns with Analytics

Behavioral analytics can reveal the actual paths users take as they interact with software, websites, or mobile apps. By analyzing data on user navigation, feature usage, and interactions, researchers can identify common user paths and touchpoints that provide valuable information for understanding the user's journey toward completing their goals.

CHAPTER 10   CONDUCTING RESEARCH TO UNDERSTAND YOUR USER'S JOURNEY

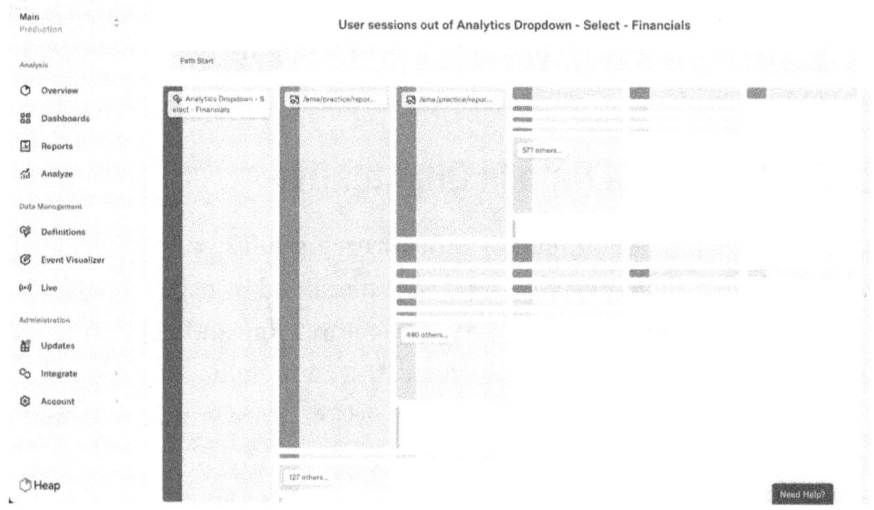

When analyzing behavioral workflow patterns using analytics, we look at aggregated behaviors in the context of a specific beginning and endpoint. Questions to consider when analyzing behavior patterns include

- What specific actions are users performing within the system?
- How often do users repeat certain actions or sequences of actions?
- What are the most common sequences of actions taken by users?
- How often do users repeat certain actions or sequences of actions?
- What features or areas of the system are users spending the most time on?
- When are users performing actions at certain times, days of the week, or on specific occasions?

175

This analysis focuses on understanding what your users are doing and looking for consistent behavior patterns that can inform the steps in your journey map.

Not All Behavioral Data Is Quantitative

Behavioral data is often thought of as being exclusively quantitative, but it doesn't have to be. Qualitative insights can be gained by using behavioral data to describe the actions that the user is performing and help to identify the root causes that drive their behaviors. Research methods that focus on qualitative behavioral insights include session replays and contextual inquiries.

Observing Users with Session Replays

Many behavior analytics platforms now offer the ability to watch recordings from each user session. These recordings can be replayed to see what interactions took place, including a screen capture of the page, mouse movements and clicks, scrolling behavior, and text entry.

CHAPTER 10   CONDUCTING RESEARCH TO UNDERSTAND YOUR USER'S JOURNEY

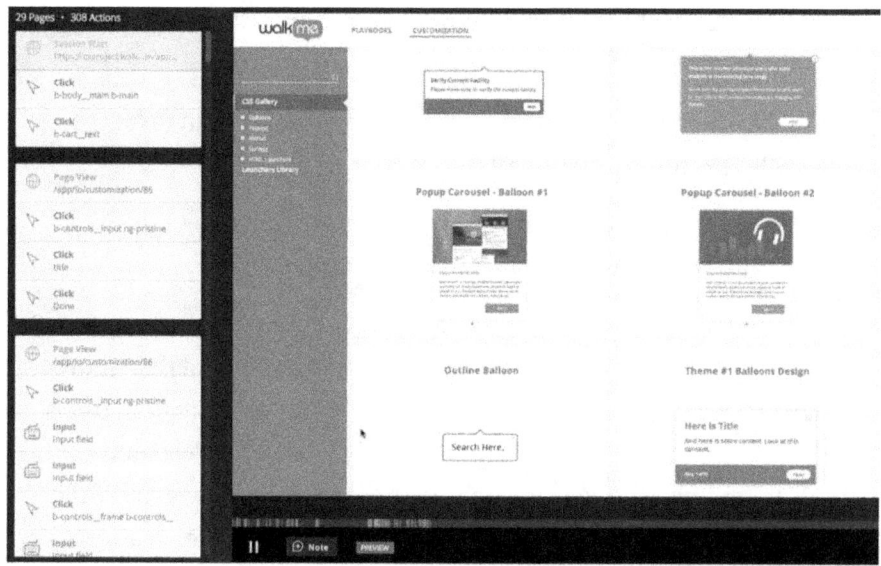

In the example above, a researcher can see a sequential set of actions taken by a user on the left panel, and in the center panel, they can play a recording to see these actions taking place.

Researchers can then analyze these behaviors to gain insight into what a user was doing as they were completing a task such as:

- Where does their mouse cursor go as they explore the page?

- Do they tend to quickly scroll down the page, or do they spend most of their time on certain content?

- Do they tend to scroll back up after reaching the bottom of the page, indicating a need to revisit certain content?

- Do they appear to change their actions in response to what is happening on the screen?

- Do they exhibit hesitation or uncertainty in cursor movements, suggesting indecision or confusion?
- Do they frequently delete or modify their input in text fields, indicating uncertainty or correction of mistakes?
- How do they respond when encountering errors or validation messages during task completion?

Session replays are like sitting next to an individual and observing as they interact with your product. They are a powerful tool that allows researchers to identify trending behaviors common to individual users. These behaviors can be explored more deeply with other research methods to uncover the reasons behind those actions. However, while extremely useful, session replays are not substitutes for user sessions because creators lack the ability to ask individuals questions about their experience.

Observing Users in Real Time

Contextual inquiry is a qualitative research method that delves into understanding users' behaviors, needs, and challenges within their natural environment. It stands apart from traditional research approaches by emphasizing observation in real-life settings, capturing the intricacies of user interactions with products, services, or systems as they complete tasks to achieve their goals. This method prioritizes participant engagement during observation sessions, fostering a dynamic dialogue between researchers and users. Researchers actively interact with participants, asking questions, seeking explanations for actions, and encouraging users to articulate their thoughts, thereby gaining deeper insights into user behaviors.

CHAPTER 10   CONDUCTING RESEARCH TO UNDERSTAND YOUR USER'S JOURNEY

One of the key principles of contextual inquiry is its holistic perspective. It not only focuses on users' actions but also considers the physical environment, social dynamics, and other contextual factors shaping user behavior. By observing users in their natural environment, researchers gain a comprehensive understanding of the user experience, uncovering underlying needs and motivations that may not be evident in controlled settings. This holistic view allows for a more nuanced understanding of user needs in the context of their environment and situation.

Conducting a Contextual Inquiry

Contextual inquiries require a substantial amount of planning and preparation to ensure they are effective and yield valuable insights.

- **Selection of Participants:** Participants should strongly represent the persona your journey map is intended to represent. Properly screen potential participants to ensure that they have the right background, knowledge, and experience to match your persona.

- **Selection of Observation Goals:** Your sessions should have a very specific focus based on the goals that your persona needs to achieve. Since you will have limited time with each participant, you should make sure to observe them conducting activities that help them accomplish their goals.

- **Observation:** Contextual inquiries are scheduled as one-on-one sessions where the researcher can observe the participant in the environment where they typically perform their tasks. Create a structured observation guide to ensure consistency during the inquiry. Include questions, prompts, and areas of focus relevant to the research goals.

- **Engagement:** During the observation, researchers engage with participants by asking questions and encouraging them to explain their actions, thought processes, and decision-making. This helps researchers gain deeper insights into the participants' behaviors and motivations.

- **Documentation:** Researchers document their observations, taking note of significant actions, behaviors, and patterns. They may also capture photos, videos, or audio recordings to supplement their notes.

By following these preparatory steps, researchers can enhance the quality and effectiveness of their contextual inquiries, resulting in valuable insights that can inform design, product development, and user experience improvements.

Tips for Conducting a Contextual Inquiry Session

Contextual inquiries work best when you can spend most of your time observing the participant and planning your questions strategically. Here are some recommendations for a successful session:

- Spend most of your time observing and documenting. This allows you to capture the natural flow of the work process without interrupting the participant. Take notes of what you see and hear, and make sketches or diagrams to help you remember important details.

- Take photos to document the environment and processes. Photos can provide a valuable record of the physical surroundings and the work activities that you observe. Be sure to get permission from the participant before taking any photos.

- Find an appropriate break in a process to ask clarifying questions. Interrupting a participant in the middle of a task can be disruptive and frustrating. Instead, wait for a natural break in the process, such as when the participant is transitioning between tasks or taking a break.

- Limit the number of questions during the contextual inquiry. Asking too many questions can overwhelm a participant and make it difficult for them to focus on their work. Instead, focus on asking a few key questions that will help you understand the most important aspects of the work process.

- **Schedule a follow-up call if you have more questions:** If you have additional questions after the contextual inquiry, schedule a follow-up call with the participant. This will allow you to ask more detailed questions and clarify any points that remain unclear.

Identifying People, Places, and Things

Contextual inquiries are all about understanding your users' actions in context. You should focus your attention on who your participants interact with, their environment, and the things they use to complete their tasks.

People

When observing participants during a contextual inquiry, observe their interactions with others and how they behave within their environment. These observations provide valuable insights into an organization's culture, including interpersonal dynamics, organizational structures, and power hierarchies. These observations involve noting how participants communicate with others both verbally and nonverbally. They also include identifying interaction patterns, such as who initiates conversations, who listens actively, and who dominates the discussions.

Observing organizational structures involves noting the formal and informal structures within the organization. This includes identifying who reports to whom and how decisions are made. Additionally, identifying cross-functional teams or project groups and observing their operations can provide insights into the organization's culture. Participants can also be observed in environments outside of a formal organization, where they may interact with family, friends, or the general public.

By observing these aspects of participant behavior, researchers can gain a deeper understanding of an organization's culture, including its shared values, beliefs, and norms. This information can be used to develop design solutions aligned with the organization's culture and working methods.

Places

A person's "place" or environment consists of many different facets that may impact their productivity and well-being. Physical features, technology, and spatial relationships all play crucial roles in shaping a person's experiences. Aspects such as room layout, lighting, noise levels, temperature, and availability of natural light also provide insights into their environment. Investigating spatial relationships, such as proximity to colleagues, customers, and access to shared resources, helps assess the effectiveness of an organization's efforts to facilitate teamwork, knowledge sharing, problem-solving, and task efficiency.

You may also observe participants transitioning from one environment to another. This can include sitting at an office desk to accomplish administrative tasks, moving to a conference room to meet with other employees, or working from a home office on certain days of the week. Each of these may have a unique impact on a person's productivity and/or effectiveness at completing tasks.

Things

The "things" that you observe your participants use will help you to understand how they accomplish their tasks. Observing an environment reveals artifacts such as projects, presentations, and reports—communication channels like email, messaging, and video conferencing shape workplace interaction. Productivity tools enhance efficiency, while automation and AI tools impact the workplace landscape. In other environments, you may observe participants utilizing personal devices such as smartphones, tablets, or other smart devices. They may also interact with analog devices. Your observations should focus not just on what artifacts participants use but also on how they use these items to achieve their goals.

Identifying the Steps in the Delivery Process

Let's look at an example from a contextual inquiry that identifies the people, places, and things for a food delivery person with the goal of delivering food to a residence. In this scenario, a researcher would have shadowed the delivery person for at least a day or two while that person delivered food.

Here are the steps in the food delivery task representing people, places, and things:

1. The food delivery person receives a notification on his phone of a new delivery order.

2. He reviews the order in the food delivery app and indicates that he accepts the job.

3. He uses the food delivery app to know when the food will be ready for pick up.

4. He uses his phone's navigation app to find the quickest route to the restaurant.

CHAPTER 10   CONDUCTING RESEARCH TO UNDERSTAND YOUR USER'S JOURNEY

5. Upon arrival at the restaurant, he uses the food delivery app to indicate the food has been picked up.

6. He uses his phone's navigation app to find the quickest route to the residence.

7. Upon arrival at the residence, he uses the food delivery app to contact the customer to let them know that he has arrived.

8. He uses the food delivery app to indicate that the customer accepted the delivery.

Understanding what users do and how they do it is the first step in defining the backbone that will create the end-to-end experience represented in your journey map.

For greater detail on how to plan, conduct, and analyze the results from contextual inquiries, I recommend reading the books *Observing the User Experience* by Elizabeth Goodman and Mike Kuniavsky and *Contextual Design* by Karen Holtzblatt and Hugh Beyer.

Attitudinal Data

Attitudinal insights help us to understand how users feel about an experience and why it makes them feel that way. In journey map creation, attitudinal data can help uncover the cause of positive and negative experiences in the journey. This can include experiences that result in delight, confidence, frustration, or confusion.

There are many sources of data that can help you to understand how your users feel:

- Voice of the Customer (VoC) surveys
- User interviews
- Customer support case logs

Attitudinal data can be represented qualitatively and quantitatively. Open-ended customer survey responses or user interview discussions can yield qualitative descriptions of an experience. Quantitative insights by indicating how often users report feeling a certain way and rating scores that indicate the intensity of their feelings. It's important to contextualize attitudinal data. This can include when, where, and what the user was trying to accomplish at the time they self-reported their experience.

Key Takeaways

- Define clear research objectives focusing on understanding the persona's goals, activities, and barriers. Select appropriate research methods, combining secondary research, mixed methods, and subject matter expert insights to gather comprehensive data.

- Use behavioral data sources such as analytics, user action logs, and session recordings to objectively measure user actions. Identify patterns and common user paths through detailed analysis of user interactions with products and services.

CHAPTER 10   CONDUCTING RESEARCH TO UNDERSTAND YOUR USER'S JOURNEY

- Conduct contextual inquiries to observe users in their natural environments, focusing on actions, interactions, and environmental factors.

- Gather attitudinal insights through Voice of the Customer surveys, user interviews, and customer support logs. Use qualitative and quantitative data to understand and quantify user feelings and identify causes of positive and negative experiences in the user journey.

In the next chapter, you will learn how to synthesize data related to behaviors, mental models, pain points, and other common themes across the journey.

CHAPTER 11

Synthesizing Data to Inform Your Journey Map

In this chapter, we will explore the process of synthesizing data to inform your journey map. We will begin by discussing the different types of data that can be used to create a journey map, including qualitative and quantitative data. We will then discuss the process of organizing and analyzing data to identify key themes and trends. Finally, we will explore how to use data to create a visual representation of the customer journey that can be used to identify opportunities for improvement.

CHAPTER 11 SYNTHESIZING DATA TO INFORM YOUR JOURNEY MAP

Using Data to Understand the User's Behaviors in Context

To fully comprehend user behavior in its context, it is essential to go beyond mere data collection and engage in the process of synthesis. This involves transforming raw data into meaningful insights that can inform a comprehensive journey map. Synthesis is a critical step in contextual inquiry research, allowing researchers to connect the dots between various data points, reveal underlying patterns, and provide a nuanced understanding of the user's experiences, motivations, and challenges. By distilling complex information into clear and actionable insights, synthesis helps in creating a more accurate and empathetic representation of the user's journey.

CHAPTER 11   SYNTHESIZING DATA TO INFORM YOUR JOURNEY MAP

Data Organization

Data organization is the first step in this process, setting the stage for effective synthesis. By formatting and categorizing your research findings, you create a clear and accessible framework that facilitates deeper insights. This step ensures that all relevant data is readily available and comprehensible, allowing you to draw accurate conclusions and identify key patterns. Proper data organization is essential for transforming raw data into actionable insights

Recording, Transcription, and Compilation

Recording your contextual inquiries and interviews is helpful for gathering accurate and comprehensive data for your analysis. It ensures that every word, nuance, and tone is captured, preventing misinterpretation or omission of critical details that might occur with reliance on memory or handwritten notes. Recording also allows you to focus fully on engaging with participants, asking follow-up questions, and responding to cues, leading to richer data collection. The recorded conversations are then transcribed into text using transcription tools, providing a textual resource for analysis that is easier to review, tag, and reference. This transcribed data can be annotated with tags or codes to highlight significant themes, concepts, or patterns, a crucial step in qualitative analysis.

All notes, photos, sketches, recordings, and other artifacts are compiled in one centralized location, ensuring a comprehensive view of the data and making all relevant information accessible. Annotations and descriptions are added to these artifacts, providing context such as who was observed, the date, time, and setting of the session, and the purpose of each artifact. This metadata is essential for understanding the context in which the data was collected and for future reference. Qualitative analysis tools like Dovetail, EnjoyHQ, or NVivo are then used to store, organize, and analyze all the artifacts. These tools offer features for coding, categorizing, and visualizing data, helping researchers draw insights and conclusions from their findings. By following these steps, you ensure that your data is well-documented, organized, and systematically analyzed.

Data Tagging and Categorization

Tagging is an important part of making sense of the large amount of qualitative data that you will capture and can then help to track and organize findings. You start the process by performing an initial coding of the data, tagging segments with descriptive phrases. These codes can relate to actions, emotions, pain points, or needs observed. Depending on the complexity of your findings, you may develop a hierarchical coding scheme where codes are grouped into broader categories. The example below illustrates how a researcher has tagged findings from a contextual inquiry observing the activities of a nurse.

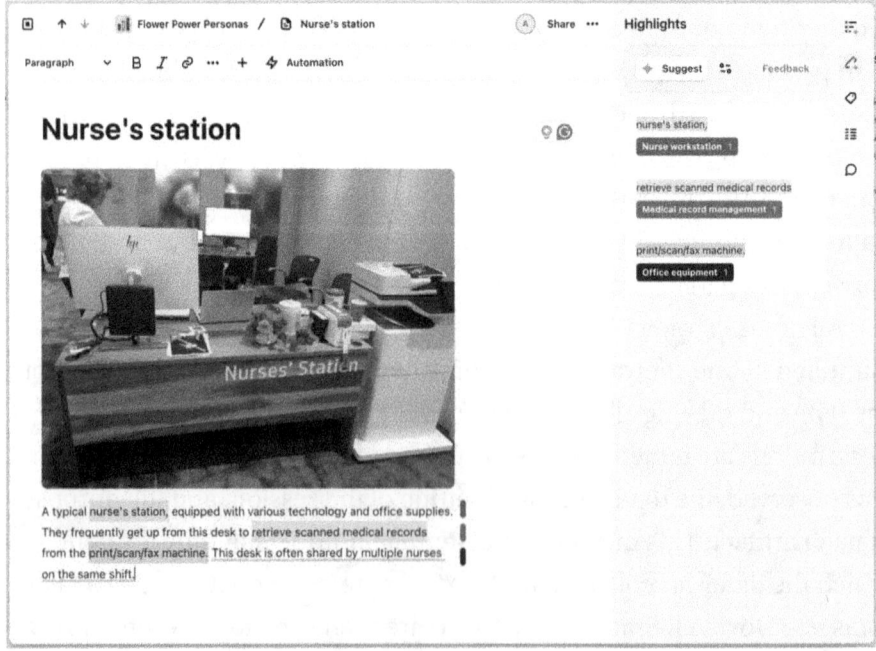

CHAPTER 11   SYNTHESIZING DATA TO INFORM YOUR JOURNEY MAP

Once you have tagged and categorized your data, it will be easier to identify trends that will ultimately become themes in the creation of your journey map.

Sketching Out Each Participant's Journey

When sketching out a research participant's journey, you will engage in a detailed process to better understand their interactions as they complete tasks to achieve their goals. This involves mapping out each step of their experience to capture their behaviors, challenges, and needs. You will examine moments in the journey by considering each participant's knowledge and experience, expectations, and the systems and processes they interact with.

CHAPTER 11   SYNTHESIZING DATA TO INFORM YOUR JOURNEY MAP

The goal of this activity is to document each participant's journey, with the ultimate goal of synthesizing their journey with that of all the other participants. It is crucial not to worry about formatting or presentation during this activity. You can quickly assemble a sketch of a journey using a physical or digital whiteboard or even a sheet of paper. The materials

CHAPTER 11 SYNTHESIZING DATA TO INFORM YOUR JOURNEY MAP

used are not as important as the process of documenting the journey. The focus is on capturing the essence of each individual's journey and then combining them to create a comprehensive overview.

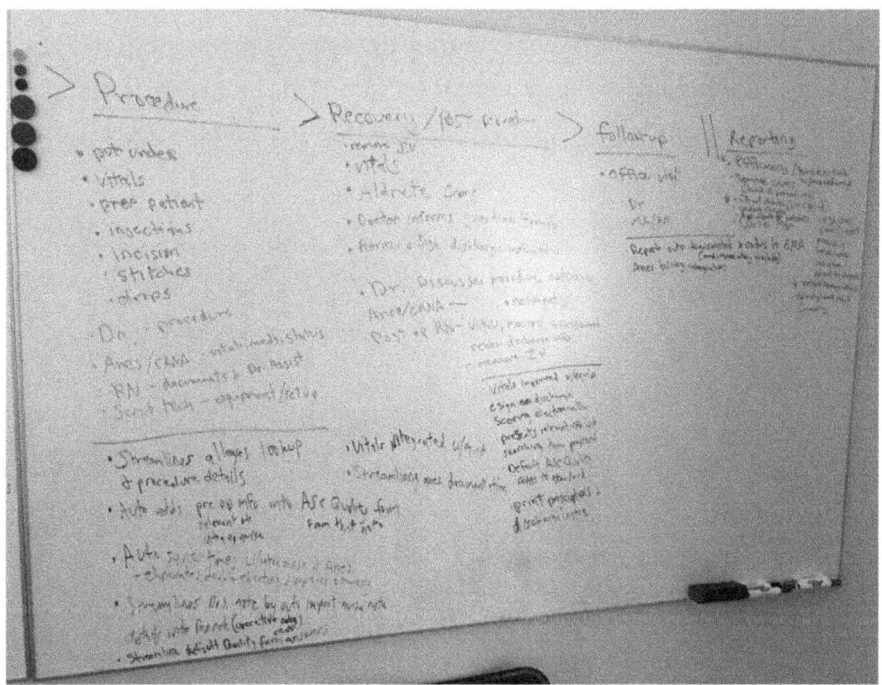

Identify the Parts of the Journey

You should break down your observations into phases, milestones, touchpoints, and behaviors for each participant's journey. Phases represent broad themes in the journey. For example, a customer journey for a retail purchase might have phases such as "Pre-purchase," "Purchase," and "Post-purchase."

Milestones are smaller steps within each phase. For example, in the "Pre-purchase" phase, milestones might include "Researching products," "Comparing prices," and "Making a decision."

Touchpoints are the places where participants interact with the product, service, or organization. This can include physical touchpoints, such as a store, or digital touchpoints, such as a website or a mobile app. For each touchpoint, it is important to detail the specific actions and behaviors of the customer. What are they doing at each touchpoint? How are they interacting with the system or service? This information can help you understand the customer's experience and identify areas for improvement.

Integrate Contextual Insights

When creating a journey map, it's important to embed real quotes and stories from contextual inquiries to add depth and authenticity. These anecdotes can highlight specific pain points or moments of delight. For example, you could include a quote from a user saying, "I was so frustrated

CHAPTER 11 SYNTHESIZING DATA TO INFORM YOUR JOURNEY MAP

trying to find the return policy information I needed on this website." This quote illustrates the user's pain point of not being able to find the information they were looking for.

In addition to quotes and stories, you can also include artifacts such as photos, sketches, or screenshots gathered during the inquiries to provide visual context and enhance understanding. For example, you could include a screenshot of the user's screen to show where they were having trouble finding the information they needed.

It is also helpful to create narratives for each journey. You can use storytelling techniques to make the narratives compelling and relatable. For example, you could highlight critical moments and turning points in the user's journey. This can be created entirely with text or incorporated into a storyboard format.

It's important to highlight key findings from the contextual inquiries. These key findings can be transitional moments between different phases of a journey or moments that significantly impact the user's experience. You can use a star or different colored markers to draw attention to critical pain points, needs, and opportunities.

CHAPTER 11 SYNTHESIZING DATA TO INFORM YOUR JOURNEY MAP

As you assemble journey maps for each participant, make sure that they are written as much as possible at the same altitude and detail level. This will make it much easier to compare the journeys of different participants.

Identifying Common Journey Experiences

Your research will likely yield experiences that vary from participant to participant. By identifying and synthesizing common components among all of your participants that represent a single journey, you will be able to gain an aligned understanding of how users typically achieve their goals.

CHAPTER 11 SYNTHESIZING DATA TO INFORM YOUR JOURNEY MAP

To create a single journey map that synthesizes individual journeys from various participants, start by defining the overarching phases common to all journeys. A journey map begins when participants initiate the first task and ends when they have completed the final task to achieve the goal represented in the journey. Group activities within each phase to identify common patterns, such as identifying the problem, researching options, selecting a solution, implementing it, and evaluating the results. Assess the consistency of these activities across different participants to highlight shared experiences while noting variations due to personal preferences or contexts.

Next, determine if these activities follow a specific sequence or can occur in varying orders, as well as whether they are one-time events or recurring processes. Identify common challenges associated with each activity, such as information overload in the Awareness phase, overwhelming options in the Consideration phase, decision uncertainty in the Decision phase, implementation difficulties in the Action phase, and assessment issues in the Reflection phase.

Your single synthesized journey should only include phases, milestones, and activities that are common to your study participants. Create a simple chart or use a spreadsheet to visually compare the components of each participant's journey. This will help to highlight the commonalities and differences. You will need to reconcile differences where certain participants perform activities, and others do not, as well as activities that happen in a different order or only in certain circumstances.

CHAPTER 11 SYNTHESIZING DATA TO INFORM YOUR JOURNEY MAP

In rare cases, it may be necessary to represent major divergences in a single journey. This should only be used when it is critical to show how a significant portion of the intended journey's population experiences a separate path that has a major impact on their experience. Creating too many branches will make the journey difficult to follow and will create a disconnect between the steps in the journey and the experiences that occur in each step. Once you have defined *what* happens in a unified journey, you will need to synthesize *why* these experiences occur and *how* they impact the user's experience.

Identifying Common Themes

Once you have defined a common framework for your journey map, themes help you understand the user's journey. Themes represent the most salient findings that will be incorporated into your journey map. High altitude themes will be broad and all-encompassing, while themes at a low altitude will pertain only to narrow use cases.

Determining Which Themes Inform a Journey Map

Many themes can be generated about a user's journey based on your research, but not all of them are equally important, and some may not be represented in a journey map. When considering findings that may be included in a theme, make sure to consider the following:

- **Strength of Evidence:** Is there enough data from your research to indicate a well-supported theme?

- **Relevancy:** Would this theme directly help to inform the creation of experiences for this type of user, or is it just nice to know?

- **Priority:** How important is the theme to the business and user goals?

Themes generated by your research will populate each aspect of your journey map with insights to understand the motivations, friction points, and root causes of behaviors.

Integrating Other Data Sources into Your Journey Map Research

Contextual inquiries provide a powerful combination of behavioral and attitudinal insights, often from a relatively small sample size. These research activities offer a great start to provide foundational information that can then be augmented and validated using methods with larger sample sizes and quantitative and qualitative data to represent the journey of a population of users. Quantitative data can inform behaviors associated with how frequently and how long users perform certain activities. It can also be used to determine if users perform tasks optimally or if they take workarounds or make errors while attempting to achieve their goals. Qualitative data can inform why they are taking certain actions and how they respond and feel at moments in the journey.

CHAPTER 11   SYNTHESIZING DATA TO INFORM YOUR JOURNEY MAP

Let's take an example of research conducted to better understand the experiences of a Budget-Conscious, Seasoned Cruise Traveler persona. The goal of this research was to identify the phases and understand the steps of the cruise vacation booking journey. This research included data from several quantitative and qualitative sources, including customer interviews, behavioral and search analytics from the cruise line website, customer support logs, and website intercept surveys prompted during different phases of the booking experience. Here are the synthesized insights and themes from this research broken out into three phases of the journey: research, evaluation, and booking.

Cruise Research Phase

During the research phase, budget-conscious, savvy travelers browse multiple travel websites and cruise line platforms, subscribe to newsletters, and follow social media accounts to stay updated on the latest deals. They join online forums and communities to read reviews and gather tips from fellow travelers, utilizing price comparison tools and apps to find the best value. However, they often feel overwhelmed by the sheer volume of information and options available. Consistent and reliable reviews are difficult to find, and hidden fees not disclosed up-front add to their frustration.

Cruise Evaluation Phase

The traveler compiles a shortlist of potential cruises in the evaluation phase based on budget, desired destinations, and preferred amenities. They read detailed reviews and ratings from past travelers and check loyalty program benefits and potential discounts. Engaging in forums, they seek advice and compare experiences with other travelers. During this phase, they encounter inconsistent information across different sources and struggle to compare amenities and services offered by various cruise lines. The benefits of the loyalty program are sometimes unclear or underwhelming.

Cruise Booking Phase

In the booking phase, the traveler selects the cruise and finalizes the booking process. They choose additional packages such as dining, drinks, and excursions, complete the payment, and receive confirmation. They may also engage with customer service for any queries or clarifications. The booking interface is often complicated, with too many steps, and there is confusion around additional package costs and benefits. Additionally, they sometimes face long wait times or unhelpful customer service.

Keeping Track of Unanswered Questions

After completing your research synthesis, it's common to find that some questions remain unanswered. These unresolved questions can indicate areas where further exploration is needed. It's important to keep track of these questions, as they can guide future research efforts and help you gain deeper insights into the journey. By revisiting these questions in subsequent studies, you can continue to refine your understanding and address any gaps in the data, ultimately leading to a more comprehensive and nuanced view of the user experience. Here are some example questions from each phase that could be further explored in future research initiatives.

Research Phase Follow-Up Questions

- What pages or sections of the website do travelers spend the most time on during their initial research?
- Which price comparison tools or features are used most frequently?
- What is the drop-off rate at various stages of the research process?

- Which sources (e.g., newsletters, social media, forums) drive the most traffic to the website?
- What search terms or filters are most commonly used when researching cruises?
- What percent of those who booked a cruise had previously signed up to receive cruise deal newsletters?
- What are the common topics of confusion that lead travelers to seek help from customer service during their research?

Evaluation Phase Follow-Up Questions

- How frequently do they revisit their shortlist of potential cruises on the website?
- Which cruise features or amenities are most commonly compared?
- What review or rating sections are viewed the most?
- How often do travelers access loyalty program information during the evaluation phase?
- What are the most common navigation paths taken when comparing different cruises?
- What specific features or amenities do travelers inquire about most frequently?
- What are the main reasons travelers contact support when evaluating cruises?
- What feedback is provided about the clarity and completeness of the information available for comparison?

Book Phase Follow-Up Questions

- What is the average time taken to complete the booking process?
- Where do travelers most frequently abandon the booking process?
- How frequently do travelers revisit the booking page before finalizing their purchase?
- What are the most common issues or questions raised during the booking process?
- What are the main reasons for booking abandonment reported by travelers?
- How satisfied are travelers with the customer service experience during the booking phase?
- What feedback is provided about the clarity and ease of the booking interface?

Taking a Collaborative Approach to Research Synthesis

A collaborative approach to research synthesis engages the entire team and makes it more likely that the team will consider a diverse range of perspectives. Each individual involved in observing the research brings his or her own unique background, experiences, and expertise to the table, thereby enriching the synthesis process with varied insights. Collaboration facilitates the identification of different aspects of the research data, leading to a more comprehensive understanding of user behaviors, pain points, and motivations. The journey map paints a more nuanced picture of the user experience by pooling these observations.

Collaborative synthesis helps mitigate individual biases that could influence the interpretation of the research findings. When multiple people are involved in the process, they can challenge each other's assumptions and interpretations, leading to a more objective representation of the data. This, in turn, enhances the accuracy of the journey map by more effectively addressing inconsistencies or inaccuracies in the data interpretation. The journey map can more closely reflect the true user experience through cross-referencing observations and insights among team members.

Collaboration fosters a shared understanding among team members about the user journey. Through discussions and debates, team members align on key insights and conclusions drawn from the research, ensuring that everyone is on the same page regarding the user experience.

Conducting a Research Synthesis Group Activity

Preparation

To begin a research synthesis group activity, gather all necessary materials, including research data from contextual inquiries, interview notes, observations, and other qualitative data. Ensure you have tools ready like sticky notes, markers, whiteboards, large paper, and digital tools (e.g., Miro, Mural) for remote collaboration. Prepare templates for journey maps and synthesis frameworks such as affinity diagrams. Set up a physical or virtual space conducive to collaboration, ensuring all materials and tools are accessible. Clearly define the objectives, outlining the goals of the synthesis activity and the purpose of creating a journey map, ensuring all team members understand its impact.

Introduction

Start with a welcome and overview session, briefing the team on the day's agenda, objectives, and expected outcomes. Then, provide a high-level summary of the research conducted, highlighting key insights and themes. This introduction should take about 15 minutes and set the stage for the day's activities.

Data Familiarization

Allow time for individuals to review and familiarize themselves with the research data. Each team member should jot down key points, quotes, and observations on sticky notes. Following this, hold a session where each team member shares his or her key findings, adding them to a common area such as a whiteboard or virtual board. This process helps the team familiarize themselves with the data collectively.

Affinity Diagramming

Spend 60–90 minutes on affinity diagramming. By working collaboratively, the team will group the sticky notes by theme or category, looking for patterns, similarities, and relationships between data points. Someone from the team can then label each group with a descriptive title that captures the essence of the clustered insights. This step is crucial for organizing the data into meaningful themes.

CHAPTER 11   SYNTHESIZING DATA TO INFORM YOUR JOURNEY MAP

Identify Phases of the Journey

In the next 30–45 minutes, someone will need to define the key phases of the customer journey based on the identified themes. The themes should be placed in the appropriate phase of the journey, ensuring a logical flow.

Detail the Journey

Over 60–90 minutes, the team will create personas, if not already done, which represent typical users based on the research. Identify and map out touchpoints, actions, thoughts, and emotions for each phase of the journey for the personas. Highlight significant pain points, barriers, and opportunities for improvement at each touchpoint.

Synthesize and Visualize

Spend another 60–90 minutes creating the journey map, ensuring that it is visually clear and logically organized. Use the collected data to fill in details for each phase. Collaboratively review and refine the map, making necessary adjustments to ensure it accurately reflects the research insights.

Debrief and Next Steps

Conclude with a 30-minute debrief session to review and reflect on the completed journey map, fostering consensus and addressing any team member's remaining questions or concerns. Outline the next steps for finalizing the journey map and assigning responsibilities for follow-up tasks.

Follow-Up

After the session, digitize (if using physical media) the journey map and any supporting materials. Share these documents with all team members and relevant stakeholders. Plan validation sessions to ensure the journey map is accurate, incorporating feedback and adjusting as needed. Integrate the journey map into design decisions, strategy development, and other relevant organizational processes.

Tips for Success

Ensure a skilled facilitator guides the group to keep the team focused and productive. Encourage active participation and ensure that all voices feel heard. Be open to adjusting the plan based on the group's needs and the flow of the session. This structured approach will help the team effectively synthesize research findings into a detailed and actionable journey map, providing valuable insights for user-centered design and strategic decisions.

Validate and Iterate Your Preliminary Journey Concept

Before creating your journey map, validating and iterating on your preliminary themes and concepts is essential. This involves sharing your ideas with stakeholders such as team members, executives, and individuals that represent the persona. Gathering feedback from these individuals helps ensure that the journey map accurately reflects the user's experience. Based on the feedback received, necessary adjustments should be made to ensure the journey map remains a dynamic tool that evolves as more insights are gained.

Incorporating feedback from those representing the persona is crucial to validating the synthesized findings. Conducting follow-up interviews or surveys with actual users helps confirm the accuracy of the insights. Any necessary adjustments based on user feedback should then be made to ensure that the findings genuinely represent user experiences.

Key Takeaways

- **Synthesizing Data for Journey Mapping:** The chapter emphasizes the importance of synthesizing data gathered from contextual inquiries and interviews to create meaningful insights. This involves organizing, transcribing, tagging, and categorizing data to identify trends and common themes across the user journey.

- **Mapping Individual Journeys:** To understand user interactions comprehensively, it's essential to sketch out each participant's journey, documenting their behaviors, challenges, and needs. This process helps capture the essence of each individual's experience before combining them to create a comprehensive overview.

- **Identifying Common Journey Experiences:** Synthesis identifies common components consistent across all participants' journeys. These commonalities are then used to create a single journey map that provides an aligned understanding of how users achieve their goals.

- **Creating Themes to Inform Journey Mapping:** Themes derived from research findings populate the journey map with insights. These themes, ranging from broad to narrow, help understand motivations, friction points, and root causes of behaviors, thereby effectively informing the design process.

- **Collaborative Research Synthesis:** Collaborative synthesis involves pooling together varied observations from team members to paint a nuanced picture of the user experience. By engaging in activities like affinity diagramming and detailing the journey collectively, the team ensures a shared understanding and accurate representation of the data.

In the next chapter, we will begin constructing your final journey map and creating a template to standardize your organization's approach to journey map creation.

CHAPTER 12

Creating a Flight Path for Your Journey Map

This chapter uses the concept of flight paths to help structure your journey maps. It focuses on determining the right level of detail, setting clear waypoints, and creating meaningful milestones. Charting a user's journey involves identifying the starting point, understanding the destination, and plotting the steps in between. By adopting this approach, you can develop a consistent, clear, and effective structure for your journey map.

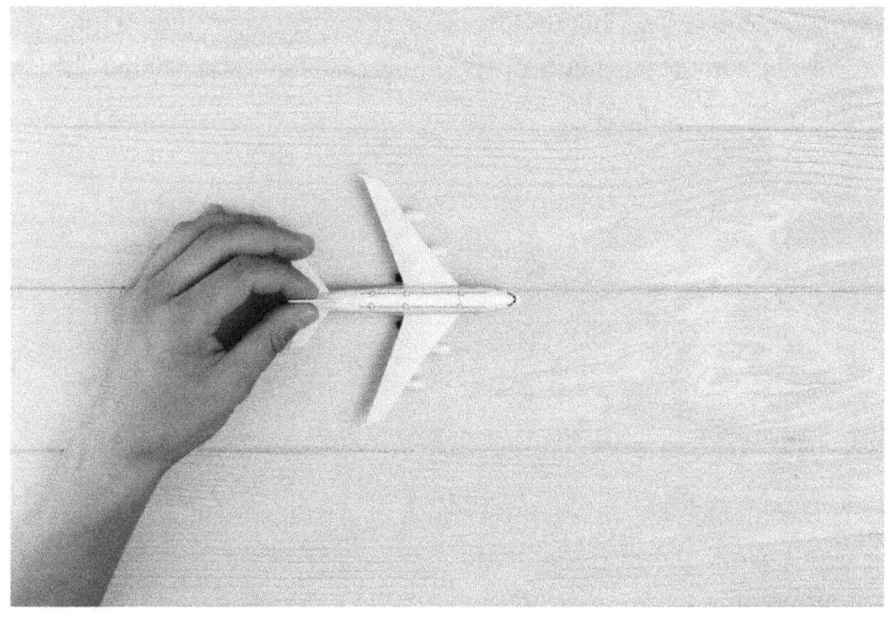

CHAPTER 12 CREATING A FLIGHT PATH FOR YOUR JOURNEY MAP

Charting the Course for the Journey Ahead

Understanding flight paths is crucial to designing an effective journey map. Just like a pilot considers the optimal altitude and navigates various waypoints, you must consider the overall structure and critical points that lead a user to their end goal. This approach ensures that users have a coherent and engaging experience, free from unnecessary turbulence and confusion.

Mapping a user's journey begins with a clear understanding of where they need to go. Charting this course involves several key steps, similar to planning a flight. These include identifying the starting point, understanding the desired destination, and plotting the intermediate steps that the user takes along the way.

A persona's goal is fundamentally linked to the concept of a flight path in journey mapping, as it serves as the destination that guides the entire journey. Just as a pilot plans a flight path with a specific endpoint in mind, you will map out a user's journey with the persona's goal as the final objective. This alignment ensures that every step, interaction, and waypoint in the journey is purposefully directed toward helping the persona achieve their goal.

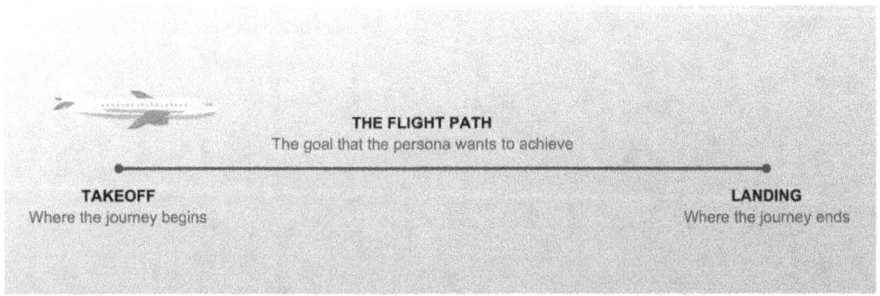

In the last chapter, you learned how to make sense of all of the data as the first step to building out your journey map. You synthesized your data to identify components of the journey and to understand the activities that users perform to reach their goals. Creating a well-defined flight path is the critical step to finalizing the structure of your journey map from beginning to end with all of the phases, milestones, and actions.

Finding the Right Altitude

Journeys can begin and end at any point in the user's experience. A journey map should represent a window of time focusing on a specific set of tasks that conclude in the successful completion of a goal.

Finding the right altitude involves determining the level of detail and context that will best serve an organization's needs to understand and make decisions based on the journey. Too much detail can overwhelm, while too little lacks sufficient value. Striking the right balance is essential for maintaining engagement, clarity, and focus. Your journey map strategy should include a combination of higher altitude and lower altitude flight paths to understand both the big picture and the finer details. Higher altitude flight paths provide a broad overview of key milestones and overall trends, giving a sense of direction and strategic goals. Lower altitude flight paths dive into specific touchpoints and customer interactions, uncovering insights that can drive tactical improvements. By balancing these perspectives, organizations can ensure that they are both visionary and actionable, enabling them to respond to immediate needs while also planning for the future.

High Altitude Flight Paths

Your initial flight path should be at a high altitude to provide an orientation and overview of all the activities the persona needs to complete to reach their goals. High altitude flight paths represent broad journeys that cover a long distance.

CHAPTER 12   CREATING A FLIGHT PATH FOR YOUR JOURNEY MAP

Your flight path should consist of a persona that matches the altitude of your journey map, the primary goal that the persona needs to accomplish, and the end-to-end scope of the journey ending with completing the goal. Examples of high altitude flight paths:

- The journey of a florist, providing floral arrangements for a customer's event, from initial consultation to execution and post-event follow-up.

- The journey of a salesperson, acquiring a new client, from initial outreach to sale completion and post-sale follow-up.

- The journey of a vacation traveler, planning and embarking on a vacation, from booking to returning home from the trip.

CHAPTER 12   CREATING A FLIGHT PATH FOR YOUR JOURNEY MAP

Each of these flight paths can be broken down into lower altitude flight paths representing more specific activities that will make this persona successful in achieving its goals.

Low Altitude Flight Paths

Low altitude flight paths represent narrower and deeper journeys that typically cover shorter distances.

These flight paths are based on the previous higher altitude examples and incorporate more details and context. Examples of low altitude flight paths:

- The journey of a tech-savvy wedding florist taking, editing, and posting photos and videos from their client's weddings to promote their business on social media.

- The journey of a remote-based salesperson scheduling, conducting, and following up on initial consultation video calls with prospective clients.

- The journey of a tech neophyte traveler planning, researching, and booking a cruise vacation with their travel agent.

Each flight path would contain phases representing a subset of a higher altitude flight path with more specific details about the actions that occur in each phase.

Aligning Your Persona and Flight Path to the Same Altitude

Journeys are based on the experiences represented by your personas. A journey can include very different experiences depending on the persona it is associated with. For example, let's look at a flight path for a user who wants to order a meal at a fast-casual restaurant.

CHAPTER 12   CREATING A FLIGHT PATH FOR YOUR JOURNEY MAP

A high altitude flight path for this journey would move through three phases: Review, Evaluate, and Order. Sample activities along this flight path would include

- Finding out what food and drink options are available
- Deciding on what to purchase
- Selecting and paying for their order

A high altitude persona associated with this flight path would represent any customer who wants to achieve this goal. It would include information that represents the audience's most common experiences. A flight path at this altitude helps to understand the common milestones and actions that all personas of this type would take to achieve their goal.

A low altitude flight path for this journey would move through the same three phases, but the milestones and actions would be much more specific to the needs of a low altitude persona.

A low altitude persona may have attributes that could significantly augment and change a flight path. Example attributes and their implications include

- Do they have allergies or other dietary restrictions that require them to find out about specific ingredients before placing an order?
- Do they prefer digital experiences over interacting with employees when ordering?
- Do they have specific ways they want to pay (i.e., cash, contactless payment, Apple Wallet, etc.)?

These attributes can introduce additional steps into a flight path and may alter how this persona achieves their goal. A flight path at this altitude helps understand how these unique attributes would shape this persona's journey and provide a deeper context for their experience.

Identifying a Place to Take Off

The takeoff point in your user's journey is where the experience begins. Identifying the right place to take off involves understanding your user's needs and expectations and the organization's goals. This can start at the user's first interaction with an organization, any activity they perform daily as part of their job, or at any moment before the completion of their goal.

CHAPTER 12   CREATING A FLIGHT PATH FOR YOUR JOURNEY MAP

Your flight path can start at any phase. For example, a vacationer's journey could start as early as the consideration phase, where they decide what type of trip to take, or a much later phase, where they are all set to book their vacation. The starting point should also take into consideration the goals of the organization. For example, if a team has been tasked with improving the online checkout experience, the flight path should be mid to low altitude with a phase that begins right before or when the user is checking out.

Identifying a Place to Land

Just as every flight has a destination, every flight path should have a clear endpoint. Identifying the right place to land ensures that you have represented all of the activities that lead up to a user's goal being accomplished. An endpoint should be very specific and conclude at the end of the last phase.

CHAPTER 12   CREATING A FLIGHT PATH FOR YOUR JOURNEY MAP

The endpoint should also take into consideration the goals of the organization. For example, the flight path for the team tasked with improving the online checkout experience may end when the user has successfully completed their transaction. This endpoint should be something that an organization can measure as a Key Performance Indicator (KPI). Measuring KPIs associated with your journey maps will be covered in detail in Chapter 15. Remember that a flight path's endpoint is not necessarily the end of your user's ultimate journey. For example, your flight path may conclude when a product has shipped, but the experience continues while the package is in transit before it reaches the customer's home.

Using Milestones to Break Down Phases

As you define flight paths for lower altitude journeys, breaking down your phases into milestones will become necessary. Milestones help to make each phase into more manageable segments and define the types of actions that occur within a phase.

Each milestone represents a set of related events or experiences that contribute to moving from one phase of the journey to the next. Milestones typically follow a logical sequence within each phase, often building on the completion of previous milestones. In the flight path for ordering a meal, milestones in the ordering phase include food selection and order customization.

Using Actions as Progress Markers in the Flight Path

Actions represent the individual activities that occur through the experience, highlighting the steps toward reaching a goal. Actions should be represented sequentially within each milestone.

An action should be a specific activity that the persona performs. These actions should be exclusively focused on and represented from the persona's point of view. Other individuals that this persona may interact with or activities performed by a system (such as an AI bot) in the journey are best articulated in a service blueprint. They are covered more extensively in Chapter 16.

Addressing Nonsequential Actions

Journey maps represent a linear progression toward a goal; however, your research may indicate that certain actions do not always occur in the same order. The purpose of a journey map is to provide a consistent and clear understanding of the most common user's journey. Complex actions

CHAPTER 12 CREATING A FLIGHT PATH FOR YOUR JOURNEY MAP

involving many branches, exceptions, dependencies, and decisions can make a journey map extremely difficult to read and cause confusion. These scenarios should be addressed and expanded in a workflow or system diagram covered in Chapter 16.

Using Actions to Indicate Transitions in the Flight Path

Transition points represent actions that are crucial to the user's progress. They signify the user's movement from one phase or milestones of their journey to the next. For example, in our flight path for the food ordering journey, a transition action would be when a user decides what food they want at the end of the evaluation phase and then begins the order phase when they select and pay for their meal.

These transition points should be a focus in your journey map when identifying pain points that may make it difficult for your users to move from one part of their journey to the next.

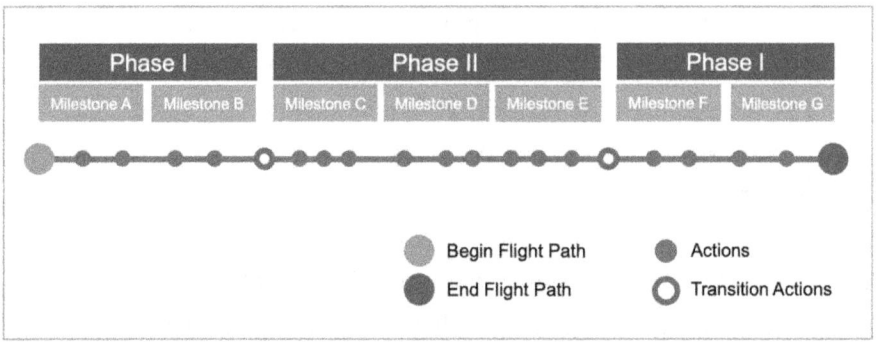

The flight path will become the backbone of your persona's journey and is the first step in assembling your journey map.

Key Takeaways

- **Structure Journey Maps Using Flight Paths**: The concept of flight paths is utilized to structure journey maps by determining the right level of detail, setting clear waypoints, and creating meaningful milestones. This approach ensures a consistent, clear, and effective journey map from the starting point to the destination.

- **High Altitude vs. Low Altitude Flight Paths**: High altitude flight paths provide a broad overview of the entire journey, covering long distances and general phases. Low altitude flight paths delve into more detailed, specific segments of the journey, covering shorter distances and more granular actions.

- **Align Personas with Flight Paths**: Personas' goals guide the journey mapping process, similar to how the destination guides a pilot's flight path. Aligning personas and flight paths ensures that each step and interaction is purposefully directed toward achieving the persona's goals, considering different user experiences at varying altitudes.

- **Identify Takeoff and Landing Points**: The takeoff point marks the beginning of the user's journey, influenced by their needs and the organization's goals. The landing point represents the clear endpoint where the user's goal is accomplished. These points are critical for structuring the journey and measuring success.

- **Use Milestones and Actions to Define Phases**: Milestones break down phases into manageable segments, representing related events that move the journey forward. Actions are the specific activities the persona performs, which should be sequenced logically within milestones. Transition actions are crucial points that indicate movement between phases, helping to identify pain points and streamline the user experience.

In the next chapter, we will utilize the flight path to layer in the behavioral and attitudinal insights to provide a more holistic understanding of your user's experience.

CHAPTER 13

Adding Contextual Layers to Your Journey Map

This chapter delves into building your journey map through various layers that provide context and understanding. It introduces the concept of the experience quality score, quantifying users' experiences as they progress through the journey. The root causes of positive and negative experiences are explored by representing mental models encompassing users' knowledge, expectations, and interactions with systems and processes.

CHAPTER 13 ADDING CONTEXTUAL LAYERS TO YOUR JOURNEY MAP

Representing the Quality of the Experience

The fundamental challenge for teams lies in comprehending the answer to the complex question, "How are we performing?" The quality of an experience reveals emotional and perceptual facets of the customer's journey, highlighting pain points and improvement opportunities that are not evident from the sequence of events alone. This customer-centered approach fosters empathy, improves personalization, and leads to designing experiences that are not only effective but also enjoyable and memorable. By understanding the quality of the experience, organizations can make strategic decisions, prioritize actions, and ultimately build customer loyalty.

Quantifying the Experience with an Experience Quality Score

An experience quality score is a numerical metric representing the relative quality of the experience occurring at specific touchpoints in the journey. The recommended scale ranges from -5 (extremely negative) to +5 (extremely positive), with 0 as the baseline for neutral experiences. Utilizing this type of scoring metric in your journey map has several benefits:

- **Gauges an Experience Quickly**: The score's simplicity makes it easily understandable and interpretable by stakeholders and team members. The straightforward range from -5 to +5 enables quick identification of positive and negative touchpoints.

- **Benchmarks and Tracks Progress**: It allows tracking changes in user experience over time, making monitoring the impact of improvements and interventions easier.

- **Ability to Use Cross-Functionally and Across Journeys**: It creates a common language and framework for understanding and assessing user experiences across the organization.

Determining the Score

Creating a composite experience quality score involves integrating data from multiple sources to assess the customer journey comprehensively. Each data source offers unique insights that, when combined, form a

CHAPTER 13 ADDING CONTEXTUAL LAYERS TO YOUR JOURNEY MAP

detailed and accurate picture of overall experience quality. Example sources and uses include:

- Customer surveys capture subjective opinions and attitudes.
- Customer support interactions highlight common pain points and the effectiveness of support services.
- Web and mobile analytics track user behavior, identifying usability issues and areas needing enhancement.
- Social media monitoring provides real-time public perception and emerging trends.
- Transaction and purchase data offer insights into customer preferences and spending behaviors.
- Voice of the Customer (VoC), Net Promoter Scores (NPS), and Customer Satisfaction (CSAT) scores quantify loyalty and satisfaction.
- Usability testing satisfaction ratings identify pain points in product interaction.

Many factors can contribute to your experience scores, but not all have the same impact and importance. Scores can be weighted based on the number of responses, tagged observations, and the relative strength of evidence through data triangulation. Your initial experience score serves as a preliminary assessment based on current data, offering a starting point for understanding the user's experience.

Once a journey map is established, your organization should develop a standardized approach to weighing and calculating its score as part of a continual measurement and improvement program. This approach should include meaningful KPIs that matter most to the organization and its users, ensuring the score accurately reflects the user experience.

Utilizing multiple data sources and a standardized scoring method enables organizations to make informed decisions, prioritize actions, and improve customer satisfaction and loyalty.

Establishing a Baseline

A baseline score provides a neutral reference point (set at 0) against which all touchpoint experiences can be measured. Every touchpoint in the journey can be determined if it is a positive or negative experience relative to the baseline.

Initially assign a baseline score of 0, assuming neutrality, until specific data is gathered to indicate a positive or negative experience. This serves as the starting point for measuring deviations.

For example, a journey map includes reviewing items in an online shopping cart. A consistent sentiment from users is represented in the quote, "The cart review process is straightforward and works the same way on all of the other sites that I visit." Survey ratings related to this step were slightly positive and users commented that it met their expectations. This action would receive a score slightly higher (+1 or +2) relative to the baseline on the experience quality scale based on the available evidence.

Applying Scores to Actions

Once you understand your baseline experience, you can analyze user behavior through analytics, transaction logs, and other user interaction data to identify any actions that cause friction throughout the journey. You can then correlate user behavior (such as time spent on a page, drop-off rates, and user errors) with attitudinal feedback. Frustration during an action might show high drop-off rates and correlate with negative survey ratings. Combining behavioral and attitudinal insights can help you identify an appropriate experience quality score for each touchpoint.

For example, let's say a journey map includes the action of accessing order history on a shopping website. A consistent sentiment from users

CHAPTER 13   ADDING CONTEXTUAL LAYERS TO YOUR JOURNEY MAP

is represented in the quote, "The website immediately shows items that I frequently purchase and even anticipates when I might be running low on certain items. It feels like the site really knows me and what I want!" Survey responses and usability test results related to this step were extremely positive and exceeded user expectations. This action would receive a 5 score on the experience quality scale based on the available evidence.

Adjusting Scores over Time

Your initial experience quality scores will be a measurement based on a composite of qualitative and quantitative data representing the overall user experience at the time your journey map is created.

One of the major benefits of using an experience quality score is the ability to track progress over time after your journey map has been created. You will learn how to continually infuse data into your journey maps and introduce the concept of dynamic scoring in Chapter 15.

Additional Considerations

Leaving a specific action unscored is better than guessing or arbitrarily assigning a score. Doing so can mislead your team into false assumptions about the user's experience. Do not provide scores for actions that you do not have sufficient research to support.

It is common for actions in a journey map to have a relatively neutral score. This typically means that the experience matches users' expectations. Do not feel compelled to adjust your scores to show wide variances in your journey map.

Keep in mind that your initial journey map represents the current state of your experience, which can change over time. Your journey map does not need to represent temporary states such as seasonal variations, changes in user expectations, policy changes, system upgrades, or external events that might influence user sentiment.

Example Journey Map with Experience Quality Scores

Let's take a look at experience quality scores applied to an example journey map.

Persona: The Frequent Online Shopper

A tech-savvy shopper who prioritizes convenience, speed, and reliability in their online shopping experience. They frequently reorder the same household essentials online and are loyal to a particular online shopping website.

Journey: Reordering Items

The user's goal is to be able to reorder a previously purchased item with minimal effort quickly.

Login Process

- **Action**: Logging into the website
- **Experience Quality Score**: 3
- **Representative Feedback**: "Logging in is quick and easy, especially with saved login details."

The moderately positive score indicates that the login process is generally effective, particularly with saved login details. Users find it quick and easy, contributing to a convenient start to their shopping experience.

Accessing Order History

- **Action**: Finding past orders
- **Experience Quality Score**: 5

- **Representative Feedback**: "The website immediately shows items that I frequently purchase and even anticipates when I might be running low on certain items. It feels like the site really knows me and what I want!"

The high score reflects exceptional performance in this area. The website excels at showing frequently purchased items and even anticipates when users might need to reorder, creating a personalized and user-friendly experience.

Selecting Previous Orders

- **Action**: Selecting an item from past orders
- **Experience Quality Score**: 3
- **Representative Feedback**: "It's very convenient to reorder items directly from my past purchases list."

A positive score suggests that reordering items from past purchases is convenient. Users appreciate the ease of accessing their previous orders, though there is potential for further enhancement in speed and responsiveness.

Adding Item to Cart

- **Action**: Adding the item to the cart from the order history
- **Experience Quality Score**: 3
- **Representative Feedback**: "Adding items to the cart is seamless and instant."

CHAPTER 13   ADDING CONTEXTUAL LAYERS TO YOUR JOURNEY MAP

The positive score indicates a seamless and instant process for adding items to the cart. This step meets user expectations and contributes positively to the overall shopping experience.

Reviewing Cart

- **Action**: Reviewing items in the cart
- **Experience Quality Score**: 1
- **Representative Feedback**: "The cart review process is straightforward and works the same way on all of the other sites that I visit."

A slightly positive score shows that the cart review process is straightforward but unremarkable. While functional, it provides no standout features compared to other sites.

Checkout Process

- **Action**: Completing the checkout
- **Experience Quality Score**: -2
- **Representative Feedback**: "The payment method doesn't save correctly, and I have to re-enter my details each time."

The negative score highlights significant issues with the checkout process, specifically with saving payment methods. Users are frustrated by having to re-enter their details each time, which detracts from the convenience of the shopping experience.

Order Confirmation

- **Action**: Receiving order confirmation
- **Experience Quality Score**: 1
- **Representative Feedback**: "The confirmation email is prompt and includes all necessary details."

A slightly positive score indicates that the confirmation email is prompt and includes all necessary details. However, there is room for enhancement to provide a more detailed and informative summary.

Delivery Tracking

- **Action**: Tracking delivery status
- **Experience Quality Score**: -1
- **Representative Feedback**: "Tracking updates are timely, but the interface is confusing and difficult to navigate."

The negative score reflects timely updates but a confusing and difficult-to-navigate interface. Users find the tracking process frustrating, which can negatively impact their overall satisfaction with the service.

Receiving the Order

- **Action**: Delivery of the order
- **Experience Quality Score**: -5
- **Representative Feedback**: "The delivery was late, and the packaging was damaged, causing some items to be unusable."

The highly negative score indicates severe issues with the delivery process, such as lateness and damaged packaging. These problems significantly impact user satisfaction and need immediate attention.

By addressing these specific touchpoints, especially the more negative ones, the business can significantly improve the reordering process for frequent shoppers like this persona, enhancing overall satisfaction and loyalty.

Using a quantitative scoring technique such as an experience quality score helps standardize your assessment of each moment within a journey, but it does not explain why they scored that way. In the next section, we will cover how to represent the root causes of the experiences driving the experience score.

Representing Root Causes of an Experience

Root cause analysis is a systematic process used to identify the underlying reasons for positive and negative experiences and to understand why certain experiences delight and exceed expectations. This analysis will help your organization understand the drivers behind your users' experiences and why certain touchpoints were notably high or low.

Using the "5 Whys" Analysis Technique

This technique has been credited to Taiichi Ohno at Toyota Motor Corporation and involves asking "why" repeatedly (typically five times) until the root cause is identified. For example, if users abandon their online shopping carts, you might ask:

- Why are users abandoning their carts? Because they find the checkout process too complicated.

- Why is the checkout process complicated? Because it requires too many steps.
- Why does it require too many steps? Because users need to enter information multiple times.
- Why do they need to enter information multiple times? Because the form does not save previously entered data.
- Why does the form not save data? Because of a lack of auto-save feature.

Using the "5 Whys" technique throughout your analysis is the best way to ensure that you have sufficiently unpacked the drivers behind an experience.

Alignment with Mental Models

Mental models represent how each person experiences the world. Your journey map should represent a composite view of mental models, with significant overlap for users represented by a particular persona. The aspects of a user's mental model that have the most impact on their experience are their existing relevant knowledge, prior experiences, and expectations for an experience.

Relevant Knowledge

Knowledgeable individuals have a clear and accurate understanding of the concepts, procedures, and standards related to their tasks. With a strong grasp of the subject matter, individuals can correctly apply techniques, methodologies, and best practices. Familiarity with the subject matter reduces the time spent on learning and understanding basic concepts.

CHAPTER 13 ADDING CONTEXTUAL LAYERS TO YOUR JOURNEY MAP

With relevant knowledge, users can make informed decisions based on a deep understanding of the subject. They can evaluate options more effectively, anticipate potential outcomes, and choose the best course of action.

They are more likely to be aware of and utilize advanced features of a product or system. This maximizes the value they get from the tools at their disposal, enabling them to accomplish tasks that might be difficult or impossible for less experienced users.

Depending on the type of persona associated with a journey, an organization may need to provide additional instructions and information for those who lack the knowledge to complete their tasks. For example, Carnival provides an extensive glossary of cruise ship lingo on its website for those who aren't familiar with these terms.

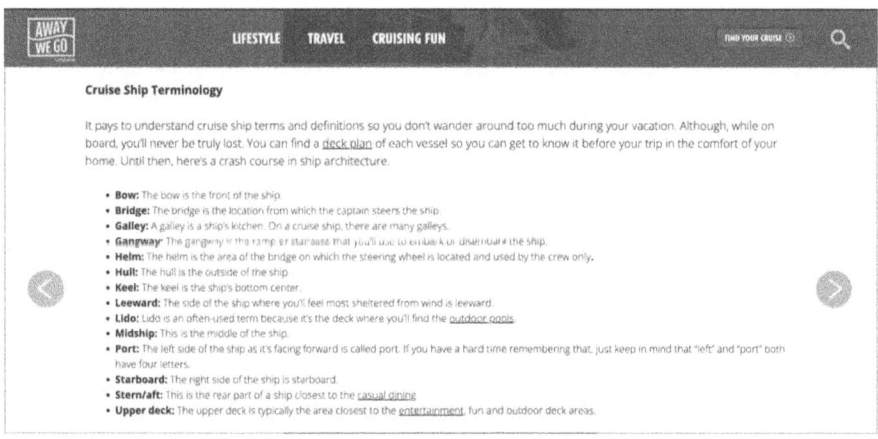

Knowing what your users know at each touchpoint in their journey can help identify opportunities to be informed and choose the best course of action.

Relevant Prior Experiences

Experienced users are better equipped to troubleshoot issues. They can draw from previous experiences to identify and resolve problems that might arise, often without needing additional support or guidance.

They are more adept at anticipating what resources or information they need at each process step. This foresight allows them to prepare in advance, ensuring they have everything required to achieve their goals without unnecessary delays.

For example, Intuit's TurboTax software does an excellent job of understanding users' existing knowledge, experience, and comfort with doing their taxes. Based on this information, the system tailors its workflows, level of support, and type of guidance to the user.

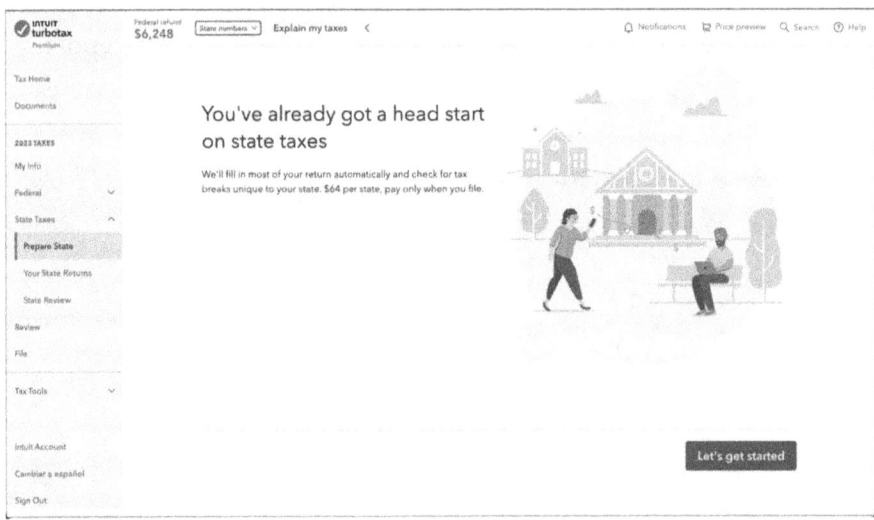

Understanding what your users have experienced before can identify opportunities in the journey to provide extra guidance for unfamiliar situations or streamline familiar processes.

Expectations

Expectations are people's beliefs or anticipations about how an experience should work. These can include beliefs on perceptions of quality, efficiency, or value. Organizations do not always have direct control over setting their users' expectations. Expectations may or may not be based

CHAPTER 13   ADDING CONTEXTUAL LAYERS TO YOUR JOURNEY MAP

on prior experiences that individuals have had. They can be set by friends, family, or influencers on social media. For example, those who have never taken a cruise before or have not cruised with a specific line or on a specific ship can watch candid reviews of experienced cruise travelers such as the social media influencers Ben and David. These individuals have expectations based on their prior experiences and compare each cruise experience against those.

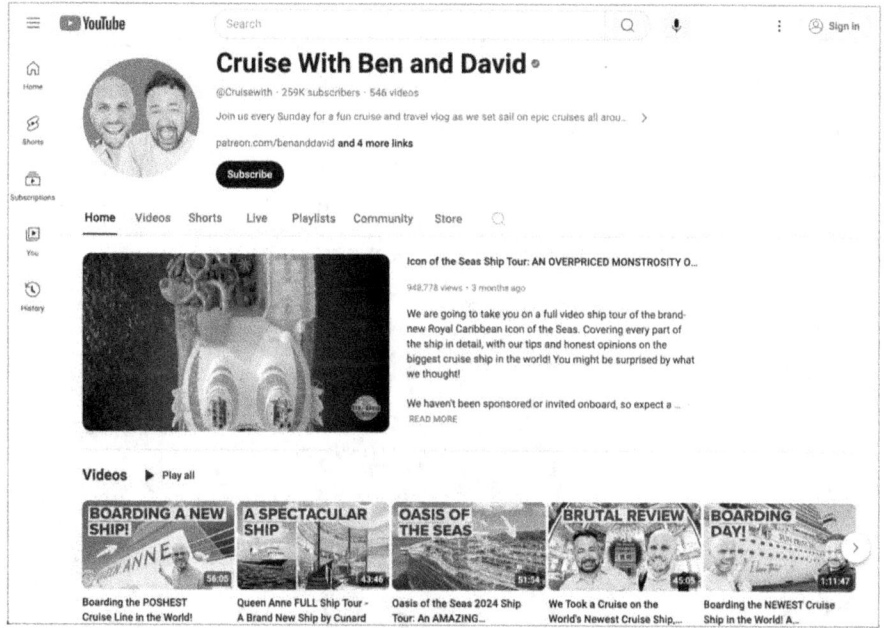

Understanding how users expect a system to behave can help identify why certain problems occur. For instance, users might expect a speedy single-click checkout based on experiences on other websites, but another website requires multiple steps, leading to frustration.

When an experience does not measure up to what a person expected, whether in terms of quality, completeness, speed, or other factors, it can have several implications on both the individual's perception and the broader context. Let's explore these implications from various perspectives.

CHAPTER 13   ADDING CONTEXTUAL LAYERS TO YOUR JOURNEY MAP

When expectations are not met, the most immediate impact is often disappointment. This emotional response can vary in intensity depending on how important the expectation is to the individual. For example, if someone expects premium service at a luxury hotel but receives subpar service, the discrepancy between expectation and reality can lead to significant dissatisfaction. Consistently unmet expectations can erode the trust and perceived reliability of a brand.

There are situations where organizations can introduce experiences that can inform their users and manage their expectations. For example, riders can become stressed when they don't know if their train will be on time or late or if they can expect a packed train car. The updated MTA TrainTime app and in-station digital displays provide real-time information to help riders know ahead of time if their train is delayed and how full they should anticipate certain train cars to be.

Understanding user expectations is critical to shaping their experiences. Exceeding expectations is very difficult if you don't know what your users expect. To understand the customer experience comprehensively, you should examine expectations within a journey at a high and a lower altitude.

At a high altitude, it is essential to consider the holistic, end-to-end experiences that encompass the entire customer journey. This perspective allows you to see how various touchpoints and interactions cumulatively impact the user's perception of the brand. Understanding these broad expectations will enable you to identify overarching themes and patterns influencing user satisfaction and loyalty. This high-level analysis helps to ensure that the brand consistently meets or exceeds user expectations across the entire journey, fostering a positive overall impression and strengthening the brand reputation.

Examining the more granular expectations associated with specific actions and interactions within the journey is equally important at a lower altitude. These detailed expectations can include the ease of navigating a website, the responsiveness of customer support, or the simplicity of a checkout process. By focusing on these individual touchpoints, you can identify specific areas where users may encounter friction or delight. Understanding and addressing these micro-expectations can significantly enhance the user experience at critical moments, contributing to a smoother and more satisfying journey.

Integrating insights from both high altitude and lower altitude analyses can create a more cohesive and user-centric journey. This comprehensive approach allows you to meet and exceed user expectations at every stage, driving greater engagement, satisfaction, and loyalty. Consistently positive experiences build a strong foundation for lasting customer relationships and a favorable market reputation, which can majorly impact the brand.

CHAPTER 13 ADDING CONTEXTUAL LAYERS TO YOUR JOURNEY MAP

Usability

Usability is a fundamental part of any experience and a significant factor in the performance of actions and user satisfaction within a journey. Analyzing usability aspects will help identify why specific touchpoints contribute positively or negatively to an experience.

Learnability

Learnability measures the ease with which new users can achieve proficiency with a system or process. It involves the initial learning curve and how intuitive it is for first-time users. A highly learnable process allows users to quickly grasp how to act without extensive training or a steep learning curve. Duolingo's interface is simple and intuitive, with clear instructions and easily navigable menus. Users can quickly understand how to access lessons, practice exercises, and track their progress. The app guides users through a structured learning path, starting with basic vocabulary and grammar concepts and gradually increasing in complexity as users advance. Each lesson builds upon previous knowledge, ensuring a smooth learning curve.

Effectiveness

Effectiveness refers to the accuracy and completeness with which users achieve their goals. In a journey map, this means each touchpoint should enable users to accomplish their tasks. Kayak provides a compelling user experience for finding and comparing flights through its comprehensive filters and robust sorting options. Users can quickly refine their search by price, flight duration, number of stops, airlines, departure/arrival times, and airport preferences. The platform's sorting capabilities allow users to organize results by best value, lowest price, shortest duration, and departure times. Kayak's fare alert feature also notifies users of price drops for specific routes, enabling them to book at the best possible rates.

Efficiency

Efficiency refers to how quickly and with what level of effort users can complete their tasks. The Google search engine is an example of a digital experience with a high degree of efficiency. When users enter a query, Google delivers relevant results almost instantaneously, often providing the desired information on the first page of results.

Error Handling

Error tolerance refers to the design's ability to prevent errors and help users recover from them when they occur. In a journey map, each touchpoint should minimize the risk of user errors and provide recovery options. Design steps and touchpoints that reduce the likelihood of user errors. TurboTax excels at user error prevention in its online tax filing process. It employs real-time data validation, provides contextual help, performs automatic calculations, and conducts comprehensive reviews for errors before submission.

Other Factors That Can Impact an Experience

Research insights from contextual inquiries and other qualitative methods will reveal challenges that your users have while completing their tasks. These findings can be categorized into situations within touchpoints in your journey map. These situations often have direct implications for how your users behave to complete their goals. Here are some of the most common situations your users can encounter and example scenarios demonstrating how it impacts their experience.

Constraints

Constraints are limitations that can be tied to resources or time. For instance, having limited time, resources, or budget can impede the smooth flow of a task. Unrealistic deadlines and expectations can result in stress, burnout, and inefficiencies. The absence of needed product features can slow or impede progress toward a goal.

A tech startup project manager oversees the launch of a new personal finance app and faces several constraints. With a tight budget that prioritizes marketing and operations, their small team of three engineers and one designer is stretched thin. The fixed launch date driven by market research allows no flexibility for delays, even though the team is behind schedule. Additionally, limited APIs from third-party financial services hinder the app's development, complicating integration and further straining the project.

Inconsistencies

Inconsistencies occur when different processes lead to confusion, inefficiencies, or errors. For instance, varying procedures and standards followed by different individuals or teams can cause delays and confusion. Variations in work processes may result in errors and the need for rework. Unclear or inconsistent communication can lead to misunderstandings and misinterpretations.

An IT manager at a mid-sized corporation that recently merged with another company faces significant challenges due to inconsistent processes. The two companies followed different IT policies and security standards, leading to confusion and inefficiencies as the combined team struggled to align their practices. Additionally, varying communication methods—one team preferring email and the other instant messaging—result in missed messages and misunderstandings. These inconsistencies cause delays in routine maintenance and error resolution, increase the risk of vulnerabilities, and complicate the integration process, ultimately affecting overall productivity.

Bottlenecks

Bottlenecks occur when too many activities occur simultaneously. Inadequate infrastructure, such as slow Internet or outdated software, can also hinder productivity. These obstacles can have a ripple effect, slowing down processes and causing inefficiencies.

At a busy cafe, a barista faces a bottleneck as they juggle numerous online orders and a long line of in-store customers. Due to a recent promotion, the surge in online orders requires careful preparation, while the growing queue at the counter leads to frustration and delays. Overwhelmed by the dual demands, the barista struggles to keep up, resulting in longer wait times, potential errors, and decreased customer satisfaction.

Disruptions

Unexpected events such as equipment failures, software crashes, or power outages can disrupt workflows. Emergencies or urgent requests can also lead to interruptions and delays, requiring immediate attention. Additionally, priorities or project requirements changes can necessitate adjustments and disruptions, further complicating task completion. These disruptions can have a significant impact on productivity and overall efficiency, making it challenging to maintain a smooth and consistent workflow.

Employees who log into a company's HR portal to update their beneficiary information encounter technical glitches with the online system. Error messages pop up, preventing them from completing the necessary changes smoothly and requiring repeated attempts to access the system.

Distractions

Distractions can significantly impact an individual's ability to focus and concentrate. Phone calls, notification alerts, and noisy environments can disrupt a person's train of thought and break their focus, leading to mistakes and inefficiencies. It becomes challenging to complete tasks accurately and efficiently when the mind is constantly being pulled in different directions.

As a nurse rushes to attend to a patient with a severe injury, he is repeatedly interrupted by overhead paging announcements, phone calls from other departments seeking updates on patient statuses, and colleagues asking for assistance with non-urgent tasks. Despite his best efforts to remain focused, the barrage of distractions disrupts his workflow and increases his stress levels, impacting the quality of care they can deliver.

Dependencies

Dependencies occur when reliance on external factors, such as specific information or approvals, is required for a task's successful completion. Interdependencies between different tasks or processes further complicate the situation. Delays or issues in one area can create a domino effect, affecting subsequent steps.

A project manager at a software development company finds herself significantly impacted by dependencies while overseeing the launch of a new mobile app. As the deadline approaches, they realize that crucial design approvals from the client are still pending, delaying the development process. Moreover, the development team's progress is contingent on receiving timely feedback and assets from the graphic design department, which is overwhelmed with other projects. These interdependencies result in a domino effect, causing delays in coding, testing, and, ultimately, the app's release.

Workarounds

Individuals may turn to workarounds to accomplish tasks when ideal processes are unavailable or impractical. Workarounds can have inherent drawbacks. They can introduce inefficiencies, potentially leading to wasted time and resources. They may also increase the risk of errors and create deviations from standard ways of performing a task.

An HR manager grapples with outdated software for employee performance evaluations. Faced with the system's limitations, they implement a workaround by creating a complex series of spreadsheets to track employee performance metrics and feedback. However, this makeshift solution leads to inconsistencies and data discrepancies, as multiple versions of the spreadsheets circulate among team members, making it challenging to maintain accurate records.

Emotion Classification

Emotions can be a powerful driver that influences how we feel in situations, why we feel that way, and why we act in certain ways. Emotions play a critical role in this process, as they deeply influence user perceptions, actions, and overall satisfaction.

Create a standard vocabulary for emotional terms and ensure they are used consistently throughout the journey map. Limit the number of nuanced and unique emotional terms to keep the journey map clear and focused. Avoid using words with subtle differences that might be interpreted. For example, instead of using both "content" and "pleased," choose one term that broadly captures the intended emotion.

The intensity of the emotions represented should map directly to the experience score. For example, a score of +5 would indicate that a user is extremely satisfied with their experience, and -5 is extremely negative for that moment in the journey. The Arousal Valence Model, developed by James Russell and Lisa Feldman Barrett, is an example of an approach to standardize the type of emotion and its intensity.

CHAPTER 13   ADDING CONTEXTUAL LAYERS TO YOUR JOURNEY MAP

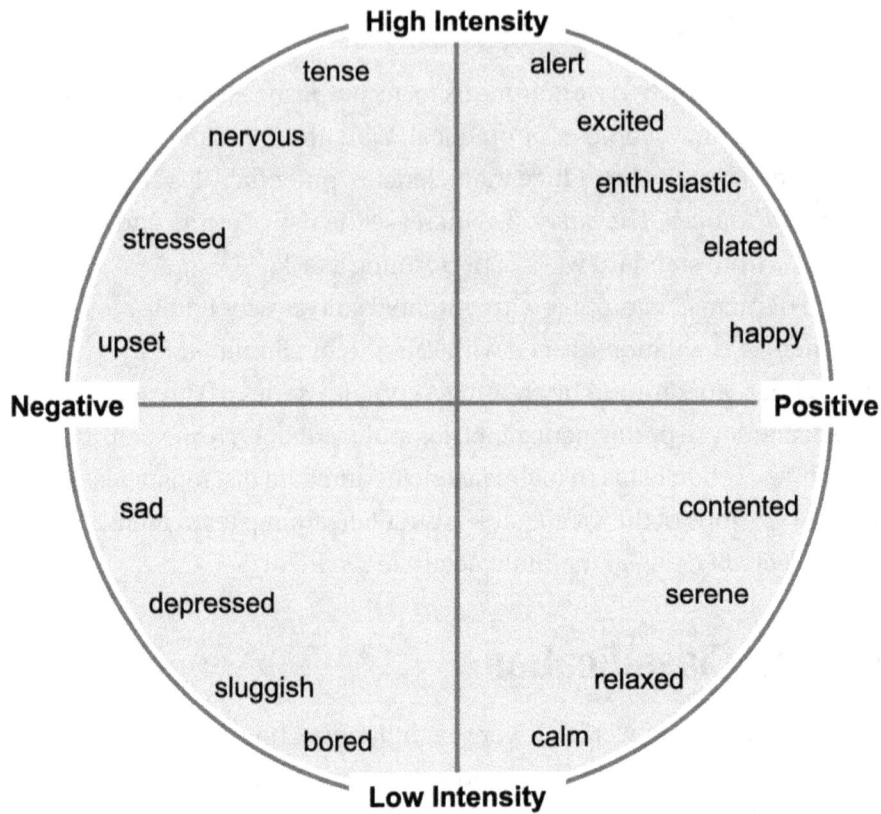

Adapted Arousal Valence Model by James Russell and Lisa Feldman Barrett

Be cautious when representing specific emotions in your journey map. It's crucial to consider whether all users would experience these emotions in the same circumstances, as their feelings may vary. Recognize that users' reactions can differ, and it is important to account for this variability, acknowledging that the journey map reflects common or average experiences rather than universal truths.

CHAPTER 13   ADDING CONTEXTUAL LAYERS TO YOUR JOURNEY MAP

Minimizing Turbulence in Your Journey Map

As you assemble all of the numerous insights that will be represented in your journey map, it can be challenging to consistently align all of these details to a specific altitude. Just as turbulence when flying creates an unstable and bumpy experience, turbulence in a journey map leads to confusion, misalignment, and a disjointed understanding among stakeholders. To maintain a consistent altitude in this metaphor means ensuring that your journeys are created and maintained with a uniform level of detail, clarity, and relevance.

The causes of this turbulence often stem from inconsistent data sources, varying levels of detail, and a lack of standardization. When different team members use varied and unaligned data sources or include varying levels of detail, the result is often a set of imbalanced and conflicting personas and journeys.

Creating smoother air involves several key practices. Clear guidelines should be established regarding the level of detail required for each journey map. If a touchpoint is written at an altitude that is too high, you can add more specific details that are contextually relevant to that action in the journey. Conversely, if a touchpoint is overly detailed and complex compared with the rest of the journey, removing non-essential details that do not contribute to the core understanding of user needs and behaviors can help to elevate the altitude level.

Establishing a common ontology and taxonomy is essential for maintaining consistency in how information is represented in your journey map. A common ontology involves developing a shared understanding of key concepts and terms, ensuring everyone interprets them uniformly. A common taxonomy creates a standardized classification system for categorizing user needs, behaviors, and attributes, helping maintain consistency within and across journey maps.

By addressing the causes of turbulence and actively working to create smoother air, teams can ensure that journey maps are consistently written at the right altitude, leading to a more coherent and unified understanding of users and their experiences.

CHAPTER 13   ADDING CONTEXTUAL LAYERS TO YOUR JOURNEY MAP

Key Takeaways

- **Utilize Experience Quality Scores**: Implement a numerical scale (-5 to +5) to quantify emotional sentiment at each touchpoint in your journey map. This allows for objective evaluation, prioritization of improvements, and tracking of progress over time.

- **Use the "5 Whys" Technique**: Employ the "5 Whys" technique and align with users' mental models to identify underlying reasons for their experiences.

- **Include Usability Attributes**: Incorporate usability issues, including the attributes of learnability, effectiveness, efficiency, and error handling, into your root cause analysis.

- **Include Situational Factors**: Identify and articulate constraints, inconsistencies, bottlenecks, disruptions, distractions, and dependencies that may impact users' ability to complete activities in their journey.

- **Adjust Altitudes to Minimize Turbulence**: Regularly review and adjust the level of detail within the journey map, ensuring it effectively balances granularity and clarity. By adding relevant details for specific touchpoints and removing non-essential information, teams can maintain a smooth and coherent understanding of user experiences, minimizing confusion and ensuring stakeholder alignment.

In the next chapter, you will integrate all of the journey's components into a cohesive journey map.

CHAPTER 14

Designing Your Journey Map

Now that you have gathered all the content for your journey map, this chapter introduces a structured, modular approach to journey map design. It decomposes journey maps into fundamental building blocks that can be combined to create reusable templates based on atomic design patterns and visual design principles.

Journey Map Construction Strategy

The core principles of an effective journey map strategy are the same as those of personas; it starts with building empathy and establishing a framework for understanding the user and its implications for design.

Contextual Framing

It should provide information at a consistent level of detail and context needed to represent the journey at a specific altitude. Contextual factors help us to understand how and why a user feels and acts in a certain way at specific touchpoints in their journey.

Scannable

It should be quick and easy to understand, with a clear visual hierarchy to guide the reader to the most useful information. An effective journey map design makes it easy for a reader to read horizontally to understand the progression through a journey and vertically to dig deeper into experiences associated with specific touchpoints.

Actionable

It should influence every part of your organization's decision-making. It should include concise, evidence-based insights to give teams a clear vision of how to apply knowledge of the user's journey tactically and strategically. A journey map should be directly tied to your organization's Key Performance Indicators (KPIs).

CHAPTER 14   DESIGNING YOUR JOURNEY MAP

Empathetic

It should reinforce that the experiences we create impact actual people. A journey map should connect our understanding of the user with the experiences that support them in achieving their goals.

Creating a Structure for Your Journey Map

Your journey map strategy should include establishing core components that provide a standard look and feel and that represent content in a consistent way.

Designing Components and Templates

Creating templates for journey maps is essential for ensuring that various teams within an organization can easily understand and utilize them. Templates establish a common language and framework facilitating communication and collaboration across business units. They can streamline the creation of new journey maps using a preformatted structure with standardized sections. Like designing personas, low and high-fidelity templates play distinct roles in the journey map design process, offering different levels of detail and refinement to suit various stages of development.

Low-fidelity templates are used in the early stages of journey map creation to quickly generate drafts of a journey. They facilitate rapid iteration, allowing teams to create ideas and concepts efficiently without getting bogged down in intricate design details. Low-fidelity templates are designed to be flexible, making it easy to incorporate feedback from stakeholders and insights gathered from research as the design evolves. These templates might be sufficient for your organization's needs without creating higher-fidelity designs for your journey map.

CHAPTER 14   DESIGNING YOUR JOURNEY MAP

High-fidelity templates are used later in the creation process when more detailed and refined representations are needed and are typically used in presentations to stakeholders. These templates build upon the foundation of low-fidelity versions by incorporating visual design elements to create a more polished and finalized portrayal of the journey. They take more time and effort to create and modify than low-fidelity designs and may require specialized knowledge of design tools such as Figma, Illustrator, or Sketch.

Using an atomic design approach with your templates efficiently creates design systems that break down your journey map into smaller, reusable components. This approach ensures consistency and scalability across all your journey maps.

Setting the Stage

Your readers should understand what your journey map is about before diving deep into its contents. Setting the stage helps inform the reader about who the journey is about and defines the goals of the journey map from a user and business perspective.

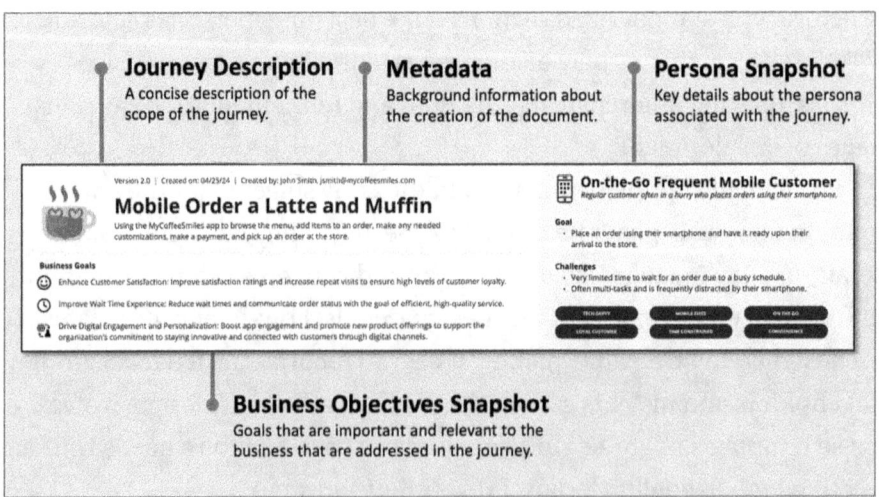

Aligning with Business Objectives

One of the top reasons journey maps fail is the lack of a direct connection to what the organization most cares about. The business objectives snapshot addresses this issue by ensuring that every aspect of the journey is aligned with and contributes to the organization's goals. This alignment helps prevent wasted efforts and resources on initiatives that do not drive the desired outcomes. The components of a business objective snapshot should

- **Connect with the Organization's Mission**: This should articulate how the journey map connects with the organization's greater mission. For example, a mission statement for a home insurance company could be "to provide comprehensive, reliable, and personalized insurance solutions that protect homes and cherished belongings, delivering exceptional service, peace of mind, and financial security with integrity and trust." The business goals reflected in the journey map should include one or more aspects of the mission.

- **Connect with the Current State Goals**: These represent what the organization is trying to achieve. It could include increasing revenue, improving customer satisfaction, enhancing operational efficiency, or expanding market share.

- **Identify Business Success Metrics**: This includes metrics that tell how well the experience meets business goals.

The business objectives snapshot needs to be at the same altitude level as the rest of the journey map. A high altitude journey map would have business objectives that represent the broader goals of the organization. A lower altitude version would be more narrow and focused on objectives to meet a specific goal.

Example of a Business Objectives Snapshot

Let's take the example of a large-scale coffee shop chain with the mission to "create a welcoming community hub by serving high-quality, sustainably sourced coffee and providing exceptional customer experiences in every cup." The organization's primary goals are to drive customer satisfaction, operational efficiency, and innovation, with measurable outcomes to track progress. The focus of this organization's journey map in this scenario is to highlight the journey of a frequent customer's experience, from purchasing to receiving their order.

Here is an example business objectives snapshot based on this organization's goals:

1. **Enhance Customer Satisfaction**: Enhancing customer satisfaction and repeat visits ensures the company maintains high customer loyalty and positive experiences.
   Measured By: Customer satisfaction scores on post-purchase email surveys.

2. **Improve Wait Time Experience**: Reducing order wait times and communicating order status aligns with the company's goal of efficient, high-quality service.
   Measured By: Average transaction time between the point-of-sale and completion of an order.

3. **Drive Digital Engagement and Innovation**: Boosting app downloads and promoting new product trials support the organization's commitment to staying innovative and connected with customers through digital channels.
   Measured By: Mobile app downloads, app engagement, and the number of customers trying new featured products.

Concentrating on these goals will allow this organization to align the journey with its broader business objectives, ensuring measurable success and continuous improvement.

Aligning with User Objectives: The Persona Snapshot

Journey maps aren't useful or relevant unless they are associated with a specific type of user. Your readers need a quick and easy way to understand the persona the journey map is associated with and key information that directly impacts this type of user's experience in the journey.

A persona snapshot is not intended to replicate all the information related to that type of user. Its primary purpose is to clarify the primary goals and expectations of the persona. This snapshot helps stakeholders understand what the persona aims to achieve, aligning everyone's understanding and focus as they review the journey map. The snapshot should also include any significant challenges this persona has that would significantly impact their ability to achieve the goals outlined in the journey map.

Identifiers provide a set of distinguishing characteristics that help to quickly and easily identify a persona. These should be the same identifiers from your complete persona document. Your readers should keep these aspects in mind as they review the journey map from the perspective of the user's experience.

Metadata

Many teams will use your journey maps and share them across your organization over a long period of time. You should provide metadata such as the date created, last updated, version numbers, the document creator, and their contact information. This approach ensures that the journey map can be referenced accurately in the future and clarifies who to contact with questions or for more details.

Visualizing the Journey
Laying Out the Flight Path

In the previous chapters, you learned how to create a flight path for your journey containing the phases, milestones, and actions that occur throughout the journey map. The flight path runs the entire width of the journey and can often be very wide. Your template should support scaling a variable width so that all components remain proportionate as you build

CHAPTER 14   DESIGNING YOUR JOURNEY MAP

out the rest of the journey map. You should also consider how individuals will view the journey map, whether on a large conference room monitor, a laptop screen, or a mobile device.

Phases

The journey phases should be the most prominent feature in the flight path to highlight the scope of the journey. The labels should be no more than one or two words that reflect the scope of the activities represented by that phase.

Milestones

The journey's milestones should be the next visible component in the hierarchy. They represent the next level of specificity and context for what is occurring in the journey. The labels used for each milestone should be no more than a few words and accurately summarize the actions they represent. If additional clarification is necessary for a reader to understand the milestone, you can add a subtitle with a single sentence that describes the actions represented by that milestone.

261

CHAPTER 14   DESIGNING YOUR JOURNEY MAP

Actions

The actions of the journey should be the least visually prominent component in the hierarchy. They represent the most specific and contextual details of what is occurring in the journey. The descriptions used for each action should be concise but sufficiently detailed to describe what happens in that step of the journey.

Visualizing Experience Quality Scores

Experience quality scores are used to understand the relative quality of a user's experience across the entire journey and within specific touchpoints. Not every action needs a score. Focus on key actions that significantly impact the user experience. For each action with an experience quality score, assign a number representing the quality of the experience. Color code each unique value using a hue corresponding to your numerical scale. When using a color gradient for your scale, ensure clear differences between colors to make it easy to distinguish between different scores. Lastly, lines visually connect the scores, showing the journey's progression from one touchpoint to the next.

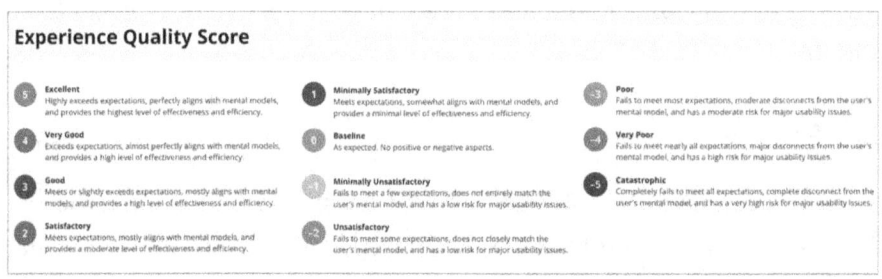

In this example, each touchpoint's color provides an immediate visual cue about the quality of the experience at that moment. The legend helps interpret the scores, making the journey map a powerful tool for identifying pain points and moments of delight.

CHAPTER 14   DESIGNING YOUR JOURNEY MAP

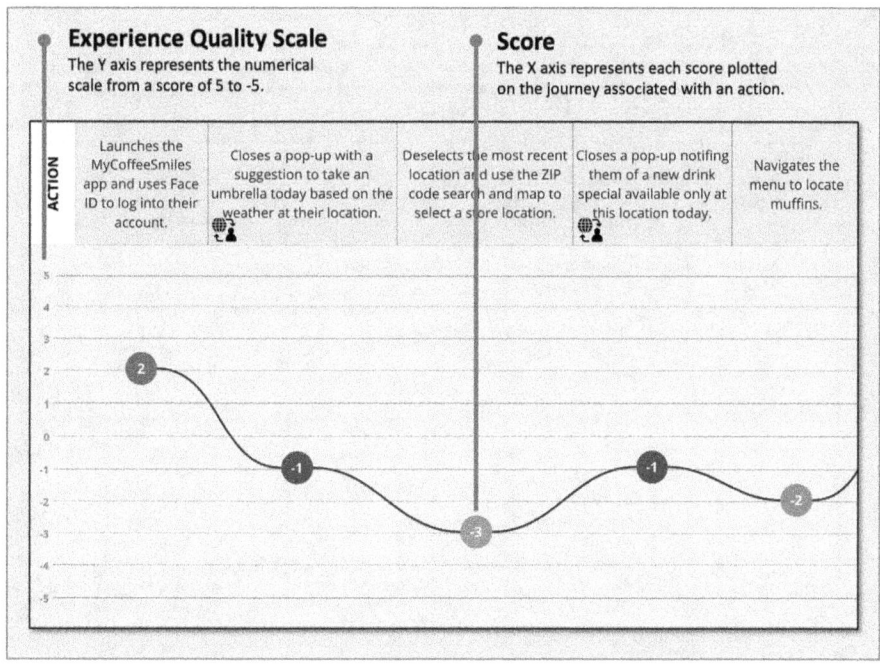

Insights Track: Highlighting Root Causes and Effects

The insights track follows the journey's path. It explains why certain actions occur in a specific way, how they impact the user's experience, and how the user responds. Any action with sufficient data to support an experience quality score should have content within that section of the insights track.

CHAPTER 14 DESIGNING YOUR JOURNEY MAP

Insights
Provides keywords and a description that characterizes the experience to explain why it is happening within a step in the journey.

Effects
Provides keywords and a description of what may result from the experience.

INSIGHTS	**Effective, Efficient and Intuitive** Very familiar with logging in using FaceID and likes that it is one step and doesn't require tapping.[1]	**Ineffective** Does not find this information helpful. **Does Not Match Expectations** Confused why a cafe ordering app would try to give advice related to the weather.[2]	**Ineffective and Inefficient** Prefers to select from a list of most frequented locations instead of having to first enter a ZIP and then locate the store on a map.[2,3]	**Ineffective** Not interested in seeing promotions unrelated to their favorite drinks or past order history.[2]
EFFECTS		**Disruption** Unnecessarily diverts their attention, and requires them to perform an action to dismiss this content before continuing with their task.[2]	**Error Potential** May accidentally order from the wrong store if they do not check which store has been preselected.[2,3]	**Disruption** Unnecessarily diverts their attention, and requires them to perform an action to dismiss this content before continuing with their task.[2]

Research Footnotes
Each number corresponds to a footnote referencing research that supports this insight.

Describe the Root Causes

To articulate the root causes of user experiences at a specific touchpoint in a journey, it's important to focus on several key themes:

- **Expectations**: Analyze why the experience met, exceeded, or failed to meet the user's expectations. This involves understanding what the user anticipated and how the actual experience aligned with those anticipations.

CHAPTER 14 DESIGNING YOUR JOURNEY MAP

- **Mental Models**: Examine how the experience aligned or conflicted with the user's mental models—their understanding of the concept or process. Consider whether the user had adequate knowledge and expertise to complete the task successfully.

- **Usability**: Evaluate the efficiency and effectiveness of the experience. Assess whether the touchpoint was easy or difficult to use and if it facilitated or hindered task completion.

- **Other Contextual Factors**: Identify specific situations or conditions that impacted the user experience at this touchpoint. These could include environmental, emotional, or situational factors unique to that moment in the journey.

By investigating these areas, you can uncover why a touchpoint succeeded or failed from the user's perspective, providing insights to improve the overall user journey.

Categorize Insights

Categorizing your insights helps readers quickly identify what the insight relates to. You should classify an insight as having a positive or negative impact on the experience. For example, an expectation-related insight might indicate whether the experience met, exceeded, or failed to meet user expectations. Insights related to mental models assess whether the experience aligned with or differed from users' understanding of a concept or process. Usability insights focus on whether the experience was efficient or inefficient, easy or difficult to use, and effective or ineffective. A bold font style helps to highlight categories within the journey map. Use consistent terminology for your categories throughout the journey map to ensure clarity.

CHAPTER 14   DESIGNING YOUR JOURNEY MAP

Describe the Effects on the User's Experience

Think about the last time you had a poor experience when trying to accomplish a task. How did you react, and what did you do? One of the most impactful aspects of a journey map is describing the effects on the user's experience. This aspect highlights the successes that result from a positive experience and the consequences of failing to meet user needs. After establishing what happens in the journey, the last step is identifying the effects of these events on the user's experience.

Consider what happens when

- A user's expectations aren't met.
- An experience closely matches a user's mental model.
- An experience creates inefficiencies in a process.

Let's look at two examples of the effects of expectations, mental models, usability, and other contextual factors on an experience.

Phase: Corporate Account Setup

Milestone: Creating a Login

Action: Setting a Password

- **Expectation**: The welcome screen says the account setup process will be quick and easy. Users expect to be able to create a password that will be easy for them to remember.

- **Reality**: Due to security requirements, users must create a password with at least 15 characters and include upper- and lowercase letters, special characters, letters, and numbers. The password cannot include any common words or phrases that can be found in the dictionary.

- **Inefficient**: Users make numerous attempts before creating a sufficiently complex password that the system considers acceptable.

- **Ineffective**: The new password requirements are complex and unintuitive, which makes it challenging for many users to create and remember strong passwords.

- **Workaround**: Users write their password down on a sticky note and place it on the side of their computer monitor or send an email to their personal email address with their new password.

Phase: Operations

Milestone: Message Management

Action: Addressing Important Messages

- **Expectation**: Users expect to be notified of important messages requiring attention and action.

- **Reality**: The system frequently sends out automated messages that are irrelevant to the user.

- **Lack of Knowledge**: The system uses iconography to represent important messages that require immediate attention, but users do not recognize it because it differs from other messaging systems they regularly use.

- **Distraction**: The system triggers a pop-up with an alert every time a new message is available.

- **Disruption**: The user must stop what they are doing and click to close the pop-up notification.
- **Workaround**: Users change their browser settings to disable all pop-ups from the system, regardless of what they are related to.
- **Bottleneck**: Many critical items are not promptly addressed because users do not regularly check the system's messages.

These examples illustrated how to break down the various insights associated with a touchpoint and how to identify the types of effects that can result from this experience.

Insights and Effects Must Be Evidence-Based

The insights and effects described in your journey map should be entirely based on your research and are not intended to be speculative. Do not include effects for a touchpoint if you do not have sufficient evidence to support it.

Here is an example of an insight and effects on an experience with sufficient supporting evidence:

> A contextual inquiry has clear and consistent evidence that a system is inefficient because many participants were observed clicking numerous times to navigate through an extensive menu each time they had to access frequently needed features. These actions were also validated by behavior analytics that identified click paths related to specific tasks and self-reported feedback from users in intercept surveys within the system. Rather than continually

encountering this pain point, many users were observed performing a workaround by bookmarking all of these pages in their web browser.

Provide Supporting Research Footnotes

All of the insights provided in your journey map should reference the research on which it is based. To establish credibility and to help readers delve deeper into a topic, give information on when the research was conducted and where the detailed findings can be found. Include a direct link to the research whenever possible and indicate if permission settings are needed to access the document.

> **1:** Usability test of the MyCoffeeSmiles app version #3.4 conducted on 3/21/24. UTFinalReportV3.pptx
> **2:** User interviews conducted on 2/23/24. IDIhighlights.pptx
> **3:** Behavioral analytics from MyCoffeeSmiles app data from 12/1/13 to 2/1/24. WorkflowAnalyticsReport22324.xlsx
> **4:** Contextual inquiry conducted on 10/21/23. CIReport.xlsx
> **5:** Intercept survey from MyCoffeeSmiles app results from 6/1/23 to 10/1/22. SurveyResults.xlsx

Description Writing Best Practices

Here are some best practices for writing effective descriptions to avoid readers missing or misunderstanding the information represented in your journey map.

Write consistently:

- **Start with a Key Point or Insight**: Ensure each bullet begins with the main idea.

- **Provide Supporting Details**: Add brief context or evidence to back up the key point.

- **Minimize Turbulence**: Based on the journey map's altitude, provide the same amount of detail and context for each touchpoint.

- **Keep a Similar Format**: Use parallel structure (e.g., start each bullet with a verb or noun phrase).
- Use consistent punctuation (e.g., decide to end bullets with periods and stick with it).

Concise:

- Each insight should be a single sentence with sufficient background, context, and explanation.
- **Use Simple and Direct Language**: Avoid unnecessary words.
- **Limit Each Bullet to One Main Idea**: Focus on a single insight per bullet.

Relevant:

- **Prioritize Information**: Place the most important or impactful insights first.
- **Stay Focused on the Action**: Only include insights directly related to the touchpoint's action and persona.
- **Tailor to Your Audience**: Consider the most relevant to the reader's interests and needs.

Bringing It All Together: The Complete Journey Map

Now that all of the necessary components are assembled for the coffee chain's mobile ordering customer journey example let's look at the complete journey map.

CHAPTER 14 DESIGNING YOUR JOURNEY MAP

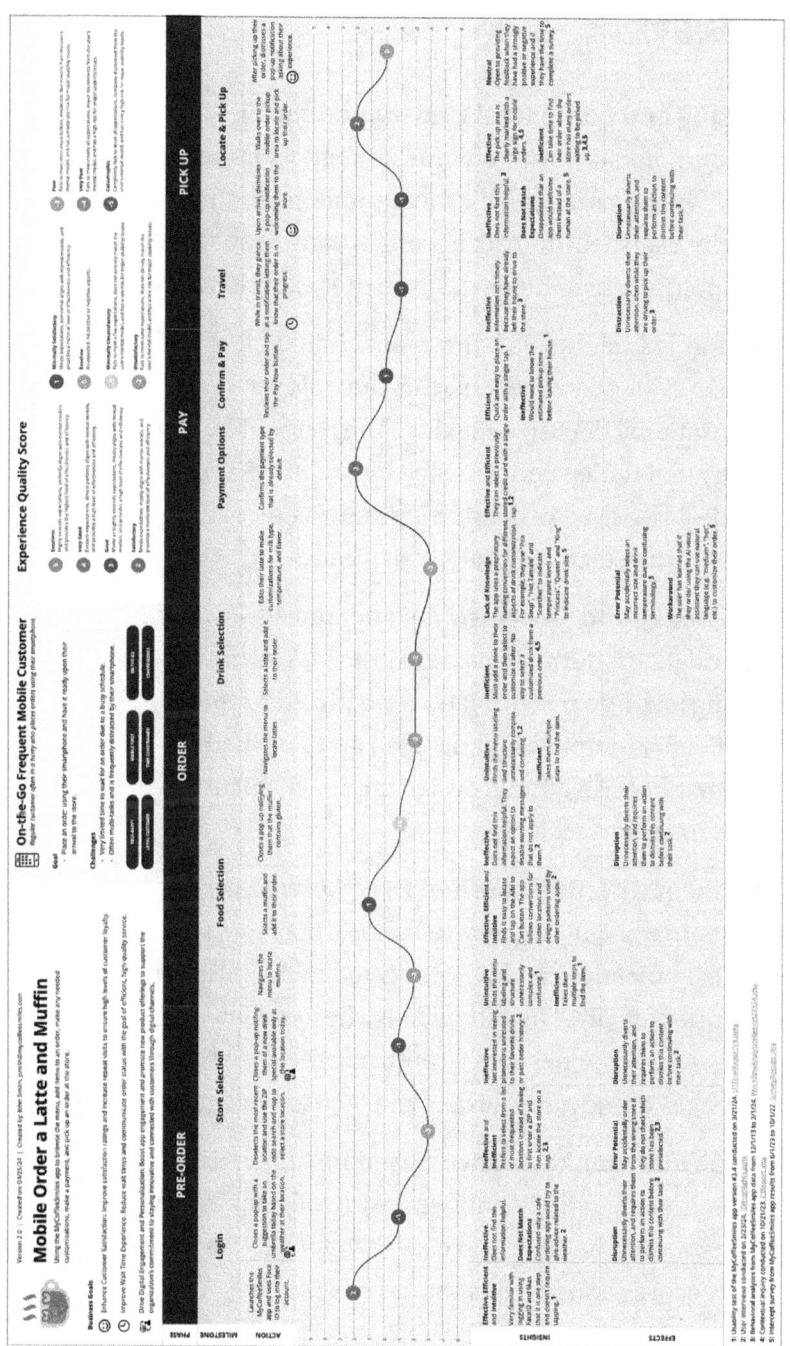

CHAPTER 14   DESIGNING YOUR JOURNEY MAP

Key Takeaways

- **Empathy and Contextual Understanding**: Effective journey maps start with building empathy for the user and providing context. This means understanding how and why users feel and act in certain ways at specific touchpoints, which helps design better experiences.

- **Actionable Insights**: Journey maps should offer concise, evidence-based insights that inform organizational decision-making. They should be directly tied to Key Performance Indicators (KPIs) to provide a clear vision of applying knowledge of the user's journey tactically and strategically.

- **Consistency and Structure**: A standardized structure and design for journey maps are crucial. This includes creating low-fidelity templates for early drafts and high-fidelity templates for detailed and polished presentations. An atomic design approach ensures consistency and scalability.

- **Alignment with Business and User Objectives**: Journey maps must align with the organization's business objectives and be connected to the mission and current goals. They should also be associated with specific user personas, capturing their goals and challenges to provide relevant and focused insights.

- **Visualization and Evidence-based Insights**: Visual elements such as flight paths, phases, milestones, and actions should be clear and easy to follow. Experience quality scores and insights should be visually

CHAPTER 14 DESIGNING YOUR JOURNEY MAP

represented, categorizing root causes and effects. All insights and effects must be supported by research, with appropriate metadata and references included to ensure accuracy and credibility.

In the next chapter, you will learn techniques to ensure that personas and journey maps remain relevant and integral to an organization's short-, medium-, and long-term strategies.

CHAPTER 15

Keeping Your Personas and Journey Maps in the Air

This chapter explores techniques to ensure that your personas and journey maps remain dynamic, relevant, and integral to an organization's strategy. You will learn about the importance of utilizing research insights across a persona family tree by integrating them into a research repository and knowledge system. You will also learn about the evolution of personas over time and the impact of disruptors like COVID-19, underscoring the need for organizations to adapt their strategies in response to changing user behaviors.

CHAPTER 15 KEEPING YOUR PERSONAS AND JOURNEY MAPS IN THE AIR

One of the most important lessons to be learned from the demise of the Sally persona is that she was created as a static representation of the user without any plan to make sure that she is constantly top of mind for the organization. Personas and journey maps need to be tightly integrated into how an organization aligns on who they are designing for, how decisions are made, and ultimately what is measured to determine if goals are met for the organization's success.

Measuring the Impact

The best way to ensure that your personas and journey maps have longevity and relevance is to tie in directly to their impact on the organization. Leaders at all levels are accountable for making the organization successful and rely on data to report this information to their stakeholders. Personas help the organization connect its success with the success of its customers, and journey maps provide context for how successful they are at each phase of their experience.

Key Performance Indicators

Key Performance Indicators (KPIs) are quantifiable metrics used to evaluate the success of an organization in meeting key objectives. They are critical benchmarks for measuring progress, performance, and effectiveness in achieving goals. KPIs can vary widely depending on the context, encompassing financial metrics like revenue growth, customer-focused measures like satisfaction scores, or operational benchmarks like production efficiency. By tracking KPIs, organizations can gain insights into their performance, identify areas for improvement, and make informed decisions to drive strategic growth and success.

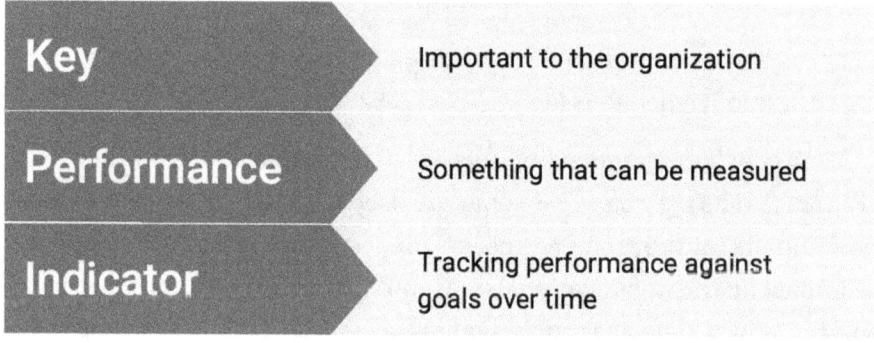

Defining Your Key Players and Their Goals

The key players are those who set the strategic direction and goals for the organization. They are ultimately held accountable for achieving these goals and are keenly interested in outcomes. These individuals can include C-level executives, department heads, or others responsible for setting organizational goals. These goals include objectives such as:

- Saving time
- Saving money

CHAPTER 15 KEEPING YOUR PERSONAS AND JOURNEY MAPS IN THE AIR

- Making money
- Saving lives

Return on investment is when organizational goals are associated with utilizing resources with an anticipated positive outcome such as:

- Saving each user 2.5 hours a week by completing admin tasks using macros
- Saving $2.5 million by replacing call center staff with conversational UI
- Making $25 million by upselling users before checking out
- Saving 2.5 million lives by using an app to alert patients about a health issue

Each goal your organization sets has direct implications for the business and its user base. Personas are used to classify a specific group of users and the journey map represents the resulting experience and reflects the impact on the organization. For example, saving a customer service representative's time at a touchpoint in the journey results in saving the organization money in hourly wages.

Measuring Performance

Performance metrics provide a concrete, objective method to assess whether goals are being met. They can be used to measure different aspects of an organization's operations.

CHAPTER 15   KEEPING YOUR PERSONAS AND JOURNEY MAPS IN THE AIR

Efficiency Metrics

Efficiency metrics measure how quickly and with how much effort users can achieve their goals. The number of clicks, taps, or scrolling percentage required to complete a task measures its efficiency. The number of steps needed and the time it takes to complete a task also helps identify bottlenecks in a process.

Utilization and Effectiveness Metrics

Utilization metrics assess how users interact with a product to measure user engagement. Metrics such as the number of users who enable a feature in administrator settings indicate feature popularity and usefulness. The aggregated number of clicks and total time spent within a feature shows the engagement level within that feature. Other metrics include the number of user accounts created, which measures user acquisition; the ratio of new to returning users, which tracks user retention and loyalty; and the number of app installs and uninstalls, which can indicate the app's effectiveness.

Learnability and Ease of Use Metrics

Ease of use metrics focus on usability issues such as the number of mistakes or errors that users make while completing a task. The number of times a user abandons a task can reflect task difficulty and user frustration. Learnability can be assessed by the frequency of users clicking on tooltips or accessing walkthroughs or other help content.

Satisfaction Metrics

Satisfaction metrics gauge how satisfied the user is with specific product features or the experience as a whole. Overall experience satisfaction is a general measure of user contentment. These metrics can come from post-experience usability test surveys, standardized experience surveys such as the Questionnaire for User Interaction Satisfaction (QUIS), or Net Promoter Scores (NPS). Context-specific satisfaction provides targeted feedback on specific features or tasks. These metrics can come from intercept surveys presented on specific screens or satisfaction questions presented at the end of a task in a usability test.

Considerations for Collecting and Analyzing Metrics

Evaluating these metrics involves understanding their capabilities and limitations. Metrics can provide insights into efficiency, usability, engagement, and satisfaction, and can identify areas for improvement while validating successful features or processes. However, they may not capture qualitative nuances and can be affected by external factors such as user mood and environment. Collecting significant data is often necessary for meaningful analysis. Data can be collected continuously through real-time analytics and in-app feedback or periodically through post-release surveys and usability tests. Analyzing this data involves statistical analysis for quantitative data and thematic analysis for qualitative data.

Your metrics should be associated with specific personas and journeys. This requires users to self-identify or be classified based on their behaviors and characteristics. For example, an intercept survey on a website may ask a user several questions about their job role, responsibilities, and the number of years at the company to associate them with a specific persona. A user's journey may be classified based on their click path behavior within an app to determine the beginning, middle, and end of a task related to a defined journey.

Indicators

Indicators are specific metrics that provide insight into an organization's performance and progress relative to its goals and objectives. They are selected based on their relevance and ability to reflect critical aspects of performance. These can include financial indicators (e.g., return on investment), operational indicators (e.g., production efficiency), customer indicators (e.g., customer retention rate), and employee indicators (e.g., employee turnover rate).

Multiple metrics can be examined to provide a composite view of how well a goal is being achieved and as a predictor of future outcomes. For example, let's say that an organization's goal is to reduce employee turnover rate. The organization has conducted research that strongly indicates that performance metrics related to employees' time spent completing specific tasks, how often they work overtime hours, and employee job satisfaction scores are directly correlated to employee turnover. These performance metrics are tracked over time to provide indications as to whether employee turnover is likely to increase, decrease, or stay the same.

Indicators That Performance Is Improving, Unchanged, or Getting Worse

Evaluating performance over time involves tracking KPIs at regular intervals (e.g., weekly, monthly, quarterly, annually) and comparing these data points to historical performance. This longitudinal analysis helps identify trends, seasonal patterns, and the impact of specific initiatives or changes. Tools like trend analysis, moving averages, and year-over-year comparisons are commonly used to understand long-term performance. You can also examine key moments in a product and service life cycle, such as launching a new product or making a major change in a workflow.

CHAPTER 15   KEEPING YOUR PERSONAS AND JOURNEY MAPS IN THE AIR

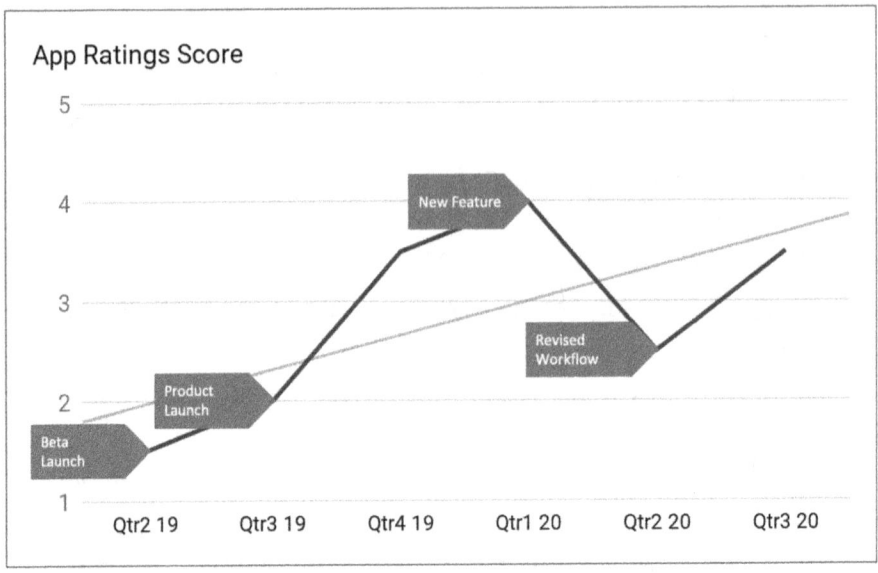

To determine if performance is improving, unchanged, or getting worse, you would regularly measure and analyze KPIs against established benchmarks or historical data. Improvements would be indicated by positive trends, such as increased sales, higher customer satisfaction scores, or reduced costs over time. If the KPIs remain consistent with no significant changes, performance is considered unchanged. Conversely, negative trends, such as declining sales, lower satisfaction scores, or increased costs, indicate worsening performance.

Articulating Goals with Solutions

Identifying solutions within the user's journey involves a structured approach where goals, solutions, actions, and targets are clearly defined. Goals represent the desired outcomes for both the organization and the user. For example, an organization might aim to save time by automating routine admin tasks, save lives by alerting patients about health issues, save money by replacing call center staff with a conversational UI, or make money by upselling users before they check out. These goals provide a clear direction for what needs to be achieved.

Solutions are the specific designs or processes implemented to achieve these goals. For instance, macros can automate admin tasks, while timely notifications can alert patients about health issues. Similarly, a conversational UI can be developed to manage customer interactions, and upselling opportunities can be integrated into the checkout process to boost revenue.

Actions are the precise steps that users take to accomplish these goals. For example, users might save time by clicking on the "Quick Workflows" tab and selecting a workflow to automate, or a business can generate additional revenue when a user selects "Upgrade Now" before checking out. These actions ensure that the users' behavior aligns with the intended goals.

Targets are the specific outcomes that measure the success or failure of a goal within a given time frame. For example, an organization might aim to save five minutes per user per month for each admin task completed with macros, save one million lives annually through a new health monitor alert app, decrease expenses by $3 million by the third quarter by replacing 25% of call center staff with a conversational UI, or make an additional $5 million in revenue by the first quarter through upselling users. These targets provide measurable benchmarks to evaluate progress and effectiveness.

Develop a Hypothesis Statement

Hypothesis statements should be generated once your organization has established a solid understanding of its personas and how *specific* actions will help the user and the business achieve *specific* goals. The statement should be structured so that the hypothesis can be validated based on a set of metrics. Here is a format that you can use to set up your hypothesis statement:

CHAPTER 15   KEEPING YOUR PERSONAS AND JOURNEY MAPS IN THE AIR

We believe [doing this/building this feature/creating this experience] for [a persona] will achieve [this outcome] to achieve [the organizational goal].

We will know we're right when we see the following:

An [increase/decrease] in [qualitative performance metrics] and/or [quantitative performance metrics]

Let's look at two examples demonstrating how to structure a hypothesis statement.

Example Hypothesis Statement #1

This example is for a healthcare clinic seeking to improve clinician and patient satisfaction as part of a major digital transformation initiative.

We believe that providing self-scheduling appointments for telehealth patients using their smartphones will reduce the number of appointments made by calling the office to address the organizational goal of reducing front desk staff burnout.

We will know we're right when we see the following:

- An increase in downloads for our patient portal app
- An increase in self-scheduled appointments using the app
- A decrease in appointments by call for those who use the app
- An increase in self-scheduled appointments using the app
- An increase in in-app ratings using the app attributed to ease of use related to self-scheduling

Example Hypothesis Statement #2

This example is for an e-commerce company seeking to enhance customer loyalty and boost revenue from repeat buyers through a series of AI-powered initiatives.

We believe that introducing an AI-powered chat assistant for our online store will enhance the shopping experience for the tech-savvy young adult frequent customers, leading to increased customer satisfaction and higher sales conversions. This will support the organizational goal of boosting overall revenue and improving customer retention.

We will know we're right when we see the following:

- A decrease in the average response time for customer inquiries

- An increase in the number of completed purchases following interactions with the chat assistant

- Higher customer satisfaction scores in post-purchase surveys

- An increase in repeat purchases from users who interacted with the chat assistant

- Positive feedback and higher ratings for the chat assistant feature in customer reviews

Your organization should regularly review its hypothesis statements to determine if they are still relevant or need to be modified to reflect changes in a product roadmap and/or shifts in user and business goals.

CHAPTER 15   KEEPING YOUR PERSONAS AND JOURNEY MAPS IN THE AIR

Representing KPIs in Personas and Journey Maps

There can be challenges connecting your organization's KPIs to personas and journey maps. Personas and journey maps are often created in silos across an organization without coordination. There are often no processes to update these documents and ensure that they represent the current state of users. Data that provides insights into how well an organization is supporting users is highly fragmented and does not offer a clear picture of how well initiatives are supporting users.

Despite these challenges, there are several important benefits of integrating KPIs into personas and journey maps:

- **Benchmarkable metrics** are used to provide consistent measurements to track progress toward meeting the needs of your users.

- **Integrated quantitative and (the "what") qualitative (the "why") insights** provide a deeper understanding in the context of a specific type of user and where they are in their journey.

- **Highlighting progress** using visualizations that help stakeholders understand how well investments are supporting the needs of our users through specific product experiences at key moments in their journey.

By infusing the latest KPI data, your stakeholders will view personas and journey maps as primary indicators of how well the organization meets its goals.

CHAPTER 15   KEEPING YOUR PERSONAS AND JOURNEY MAPS IN THE AIR

Create an Action Plan for Infusing KPIs into Personas and Journey Maps

One of the most challenging aspects of keeping your personas and journey maps relevant is regularly infusing them with the latest performance metrics. This effort requires coordination and resources across several parts of an organization.

1. Start by aligning with design, product, engineering, support, and data teams to define the metrics most relevant to the organization's personas and journey maps.

2. Identify where these metrics live (i.e., behavioral analytics platform, customer support case system, etc.) and who owns them.

3. Determine how frequently this data can be collected, ensuring that the schedule aligns with your organization's specific needs and the dynamics of your user interactions. This might include daily, weekly, or monthly data collection cycles, with clearly defined periods for data aggregation, such as quarterly reviews or annual summaries.

4. Define milestones for your KPIs that align with significant events in your product life cycle, such as product launches, major new feature releases, and key periods like the holiday season or other major events.

5. To get stakeholder buy-in, create a proof of concept to demonstrate how these various data streams can be visually represented to indicate your personas' current "health" and how well they are being supported to achieve goals along their journey.

6. Establish a plan for sharing this data with stakeholders at regular intervals, fostering transparency and informed decision-making across your organization. Create a template to standardize reporting on the status of each persona and what each team is doing to make progress on specific milestones within a user's journey.

Launching a metrics program associated with your personas and journey maps may seem daunting. It is best to start small, focusing on just a few KPIs that can easily be tracked consistently. Over time, you can continue to integrate additional metrics that provide a more holistic understanding.

The second part of this chapter focuses on creating a strategy to grow and scale your organization's knowledge about its users.

Growing Organizational Knowledge

Growing organizational knowledge is crucial for businesses aiming to leverage their collective expertise and insights for better decision-making, innovation, and competitive advantage. Insights related to your personas and their journeys should be an integral part of your organization's knowledge strategy.

CHAPTER 15   KEEPING YOUR PERSONAS AND JOURNEY MAPS IN THE AIR

Knowledge Systems

Developing a centralized repository for all research data, findings, and insights is crucial for growing organizational knowledge. This repository should be easily accessible and searchable, allowing team members to quickly find relevant information from user research studies, internal data sources, and external research reports. By having a single source of truth, organizations can enhance the usability and relevance of their data, ensuring that insights are readily available for decision-making and innovation. Your knowledge should be kept in a system designed for storing information. You may already have access to a platform your organization uses to store information, such as Sharepoint or Confluence. These systems provide the basic capabilities to keep your information but do a poor job of helping to make any sense of it. Newer platforms such as Dovetail and EnjoyHQ were created with user research insights as the focus and help to showcase content that can be valuable to the organization.

CHAPTER 15   KEEPING YOUR PERSONAS AND JOURNEY MAPS IN THE AIR

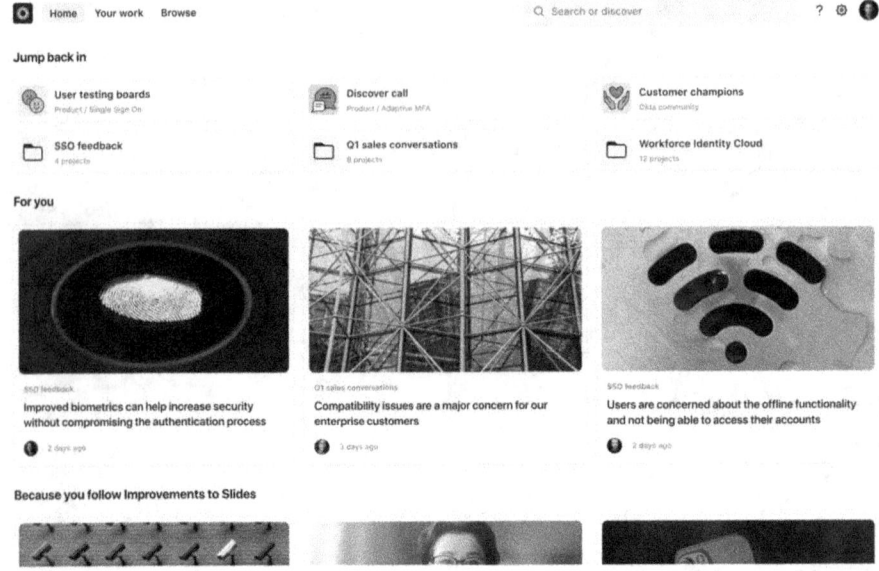

An example of a Dovetail dashboard displaying research insights from across the organization.

Integrating Personas and Journey Maps into a Knowledge System

Many organizations default to structuring their knowledge around products and services. This automatically creates silos that add to the organizational fog discussed in Chapter 3. A properly designed knowledge system takes a persona and journey-first approach where all insights are centered around the user and their needs. Linking research insights directly to relevant personas helps provide context and applicability to the findings. This integration allows for easy cross-referencing between personas and specific research studies. By making connections between insights and personas, organizations can enhance the practical utility of their research data.

Tagging Information

Tags are unique identifiers that can be used to associate with specific knowledge components. Information can be tagged to help identify

- Characteristics: personas and their attributes
- Behaviors: aspects of an experience
- Attitudes: perceptions of an experience

Consistently applied tags help organize and access the data efficiently, making the research repository more user-friendly and effective. Developing a comprehensive taxonomy of tags that covers all possible categories relevant to the organization's research is a fundamental step. Involving stakeholders from various departments in this process ensures that the taxonomy is inclusive and representative of their needs. Establishing a governance model to manage and update the tagging system as new categories and needs arise is crucial. Plan to regularly review and refine the tagging taxonomy to ensure that it remains relevant and effective.

Curated Collections of Knowledge

Imagine a vast warehouse filled with countless boxes of information piled high and stretching into the shadows. Within this chaotic labyrinth, finding a single piece of information is like searching for a needle in a haystack. The potential for insight is buried under heaps of disorganized data, rendering it nearly inaccessible.

CHAPTER 15   KEEPING YOUR PERSONAS AND JOURNEY MAPS IN THE AIR

In stark contrast, consider a curated museum collection. Here, knowledge is meticulously organized and thoughtfully displayed, each exhibit carefully crafted to tell a story. Information is not only easy to find but is also presented in context, allowing visitors to gain meaningful insights. Each display is tailored around specific personas, guiding viewers through a coherent narrative that brings clarity and understanding. The museum exemplifies the power of curation, transforming a mere collection of facts into a rich tapestry of knowledge that is both accessible and enlightening.

CHAPTER 15   KEEPING YOUR PERSONAS AND JOURNEY MAPS IN THE AIR

Collections can help teams to more deeply understand and make decisions based on knowledge that can help them achieve their goals. Examples of the types of collections can include

- Trends relate to user behaviors of a particular product in certain situations.

- Common frustrations users face while using a product.

- How specific features have been adopted and their impact on users' lives or workflows.

There can also be collections providing in-depth profiles of different personas, detailing their specific needs, preferences, and how they interact with the product to achieve their goals.

Adding Persona and Journey Insights to a Collection

Aggregating insights from various research studies and organizing them into curated collections focused on specific personas and their journeys can highlight key findings, trends, and actionable recommendations. These curated collections make it easier for stakeholders to access and apply relevant insights in their work. A collection can comprise contextual insights specific to personas and journeys instead of traditional, holistic, stand-alone artifacts. Your tagging system can pull together insights into a collection based on specific persona identifiers and the phases, milestones, or individual actions from a journey map. Collections should always reference where the insight came from and allow users to expand and collapse to see more or less details.

CHAPTER 15   KEEPING YOUR PERSONAS AND JOURNEY MAPS IN THE AIR

Let's look at sample content related to order customization from a collection for the large-scale coffee shop chain discussed in the previous chapter.

Mobile App Experience for Order Customization

Overview

This collection focuses on insights specifically related to order customization within the mobile app for primary mobile app users who are highly technologically proficient.

Pertains to:

- **Demographics:** Ages 18–35, students and young professionals, tech-savvy
- **Technological Proficiency:** Very high
- **Motivations:** Convenience, speed, and the ability to manage and extensively customize orders on the go

CHAPTER 15   KEEPING YOUR PERSONAS AND JOURNEY MAPS IN THE AIR

[Expanded] Insight: Intuitive and fast navigation to customization options is critical.

User Expectations:

- **Efficiency**: Users expect to navigate to customization options within a few taps.
- **Simplicity**: The customization process should be straightforward, with minimal steps and clear guidance.
- **Consistency**: The design and layout should be consistent with the rest of the app to avoid any learning curve.

Common Pain Points:

- **Complex Menus**: Overly complex or nested menus can frustrate users, leading to the abandonment of the customization process.
- **Hidden Features**: Important customization options buried within sub-menus can be missed by users.
- **Slow Load Times**: Any delays in loading customization options can deter users from using these features.

References:

- "Customization Trends in Mobile Apps," ACME Research, November 2023.
  - This research highlights the growing trend of extensive customization options in mobile apps and their impact on user satisfaction.
- "User Preferences for Order Customization," Coffee Chain Customer Insights, March 2024.

- A customer insights report focusing on users' preferences regarding order customization in the coffee shop's mobile app.
- "User Interviews: Order Customization Preferences," Coffee Chain UX Team, April 2024.
  - Qualitative data from user interviews provide an in-depth understanding of user needs and preferences for order customization.
- "Behavioral Analytics: Reordering Patterns," Coffee Chain Analytics Report, October 2023.
  - Analyzes patterns in user behavior related to reordering customizations and identifies key features that drive repeat usage.

[Expanded] **Insight**: Users value the ability to customize their orders extensively and save preferences for future orders.

Customization Preferences:

- **Depth of Options**: Users want a wide range of customization options, including specific ingredient adjustments, portion sizes, and add-ons.
- **Control**: Users seek granular control over their orders, such as adjusting sweetness levels, milk types, temperature, etc.

Saved Preferences:

- **Convenience**: Users find it convenient to save their favorite customizations for quick reordering.
- **Consistency**: The ability to save and retrieve previous customizations ensures consistency in users' orders, which is particularly important for regular users.

CHAPTER 15   KEEPING YOUR PERSONAS AND JOURNEY MAPS IN THE AIR

- **Time-Saving**: Saved preferences significantly reduce the time spent customizing orders during each app interaction.

References:

- "Customization Trends in Mobile Apps," ACME Research, November 2022.
- "User Preferences for Order Customization," Coffee Chain Customer Insights, March 2023.
- "User Interviews: Order Customization Preferences," Coffee Chain UX Team, April 2023.

[Collapsed] **Insight**: Users desire real-time feedback on the cost and nutritional information of their customizations.

[Collapsed] **Insight**: Users want visually appealing and clear representations of their customizations.

[Collapsed] **Insight**: Users want personalized suggestions based on their past customizations.

You should treat each collection as a stand-alone set of insights on a focused topic. Depending on the tools you use to create your collection and available resources, you can format it as a simple set of bulleted insights or graphically styled in a newsletter format.

Identifying new collections to create should be a collaborative process between those providing knowledge and those consuming it.

Evolving Personas and Their Journeys over Time

The evolution of personas and their journeys over time is a complex process shaped by various factors, including natural evolution, demographic changes, technological advancements, and societal shifts. Natural evolution, such as the aging population and increased focus on health and wellness, significantly impacts user needs and behaviors.

CHAPTER 15 KEEPING YOUR PERSONAS AND JOURNEY MAPS IN THE AIR

Older adults, for example, require products with simpler interfaces and larger text sizes, while the health-conscious demand sophisticated fitness apps and health monitoring devices. This necessitates focusing on accessibility and personalization, ensuring products cater to different life stages and abilities.

Demographic changes, driven by globalization and migration, introduce a wider variety of cultural backgrounds and expectations. This diversity necessitates culturally sensitive and inclusive product designs and marketing strategies to appeal to a global audience. Additionally, shifts in lifestyle and values, such as a move towards minimalism or sustainability, influence consumer priorities, requiring organizations to align their values with those of their users, such as emphasizing eco-friendly practices or ethical sourcing.

Technological advancements have dramatically altered user expectations and interactions. With the increasing familiarity and proficiency with technology, users now demand more sophisticated and seamless experiences across various devices and platforms. The rise of new interaction modes, such as voice assistants, augmented reality, and virtual reality, has changed how users engage with products and services. Businesses must ensure an omnichannel experience, providing consistent and integrated interactions across different platforms and leveraging new technologies to create immersive and interactive experiences that enhance user engagement and satisfaction.

Societal shifts, including the pervasive influence of social media and economic changes, also play a crucial role in shaping personas and their journeys. Social media not only influences public opinion and trends but also shapes consumer behavior and expectations. Economic conditions, such as recessions or economic booms, affect purchasing power and consumer confidence, requiring businesses to offer flexible pricing models and value propositions that cater to varying economic conditions. Building strong online communities and fostering brand loyalty through social media and other platforms becomes essential for retaining users in this dynamic landscape.

CHAPTER 15   KEEPING YOUR PERSONAS AND JOURNEY MAPS IN THE AIR

The evolution of personas and their journeys is a multifaceted process influenced by natural, demographic, technological, and societal changes. Organizations must continuously adapt to these evolving factors to meet their users' changing needs and expectations, ensuring relevance and engagement in a rapidly transforming world.

Case Study: Evolution of a Fitness App Persona and Journey

Let's look at how the users of a fitness app changed over time.

Initial Persona in 2008:

- **Demographics**: Young adults, primarily male, tech enthusiasts
- **Goals**: Track workouts, monitor progress, and compete with friends
- **Challenges**: Limited smartphone capabilities and basic app functionalities

Journey in 2008:

- **Discovery** Through tech blogs and word of mouth
- **Engagement**: Basic workout tracking and manual data entry
- **Retention**: Gamification elements like leaderboards and badges

Evolved Persona in 2024:

- **Demographics**: Diverse age groups, gender-balanced, health-conscious individuals

299

- **Goals**: Comprehensive health management, integration with wearable devices, and personalized fitness plans
- **Challenges**: Privacy concerns, data accuracy, seamless integration across devices

Journey in 2024:

- **Discovery**: Social media, influencer endorsements, app stores
- **Engagement**: AI-driven personalized recommendations, real-time data syncing with wearables, and virtual classes
- **Retention**: Community features, regular updates with new content, responsive customer support

It's important to highlight these changes to help stakeholders understand how their users are changing over time and how to anticipate and plan for future needs.

The Impact of Major Disruptors on Personas

The impact of major disruptors on personas and their journeys can be profound, altering how people complete tasks, their perceptions, expectations, goals, and overall behaviors. Disruptors such as generative AI, the COVID-19 pandemic, and AR/VR technologies reshape the content of existing personas and journey maps. These disruptors change how tasks are completed, alter user perceptions and expectations, and shift goals and behaviors.

CHAPTER 15   KEEPING YOUR PERSONAS AND JOURNEY MAPS IN THE AIR

How COVID Changed Our Personas

The COVID-19 pandemic has significantly changed how people work, changing their personas and journeys.

Pre-COVID, the typical office professional operated within a centralized office setting. Daily commutes, in-person meetings, and a clear separation between work and personal life characterized this environment. Technology use was moderate, relying on office suite software and basic collaboration tools. Professional development primarily occurred through in-person training sessions and networking events.

The goals of the persona are essentially the same before and after the pandemic:

- Efficiently manage tasks and team projects
- Maintain a work-life balance
- Grow within the company through networking and professional development

301

However, this disruption has resulted in new challenges, opportunities, and ways of working to accomplish these goals.

Post-COVID, the work environment has shifted for many to a decentralized, home-based, or hybrid model. This new landscape demands a high proficiency with digital tools and cloud-based solutions to maintain productivity and collaboration. Virtual meetings and digital communication tools have become the norm, replacing face-to-face interactions. Consequently, the boundaries between work and personal life have blurred, necessitating new strategies for managing work-life balance. Professionals now rely on virtual training sessions and online networking to continue professional development.

Overall, the shift has driven an increased dependence on technology and digital platforms to support remote work, highlighting the need for flexible work environments and tools that cater to the evolving needs of a more distributed workforce.

CHAPTER 15   KEEPING YOUR PERSONAS AND JOURNEY MAPS IN THE AIR

As major disruptors occur, your personas must reflect the most up-to-date insights about these users and highlight the key changes that would most impact their experience.

Key Takeaways

- **Integration and Alignment:** Personas and journey maps should not be static; they must be tightly integrated into organizational decision-making processes. This alignment ensures they remain relevant and impactful in guiding who the organization designs for and setting goals.

- **Measuring Impact with KPIs:** Linking personas and journey maps to Key Performance Indicators (KPIs) helps measure their effectiveness. This connection ensures that organizational success metrics, such as revenue growth or customer satisfaction, are directly tied to user experience improvements.

- **Performance Metrics:** Utilizing user experience performance metrics (efficiency, utilization, satisfaction, learnability) provides a comprehensive view of how well personas and journey maps support organizational goals. These metrics help identify areas for improvement and validate successful strategies.

- **Hypothesis-Driven Approach:** Developing clear hypothesis statements based on personas helps focus efforts on achieving specific outcomes. By defining actions and measurable targets, organizations can validate their strategies and iterate based on results.

- **Centralized Knowledge Management:** Establishing a centralized repository for research insights and user data fosters organizational knowledge. By consolidating all research findings and insights into a searchable system, teams can easily access and utilize information to inform decision-making and innovation. This approach ensures that knowledge about personas and their journeys is effectively shared across departments, facilitating a cohesive understanding of user needs and behaviors throughout the organization.

- **Continuous Learning and Adaptation:** Evolving personas and journey maps over time are essential to reflect changes in user behavior, technology advancements, and societal shifts. This ongoing adaptation ensures that organizational strategies remain relevant and aligned with user needs.

In the next chapter, you will learn how to use personas and journey maps in conjunction with other artifacts and how to integrate them into organization processes.

CHAPTER 16

Using Personas and Journey Maps with Other Artifacts

This chapter explores the uses of personas and journey maps with other tools commonly used in product and service design. You will learn how personas and journey maps complement product and service-centric artifacts like user stories, story mapping, Jobs to Be Done (JTBD), ecosystem maps, and service blueprints. You will also learn strategies for using different personas and journey maps together as part of a larger ecosystem that examines an end-to-end user experience.

CHAPTER 16   USING PERSONAS AND JOURNEY MAPS WITH OTHER ARTIFACTS

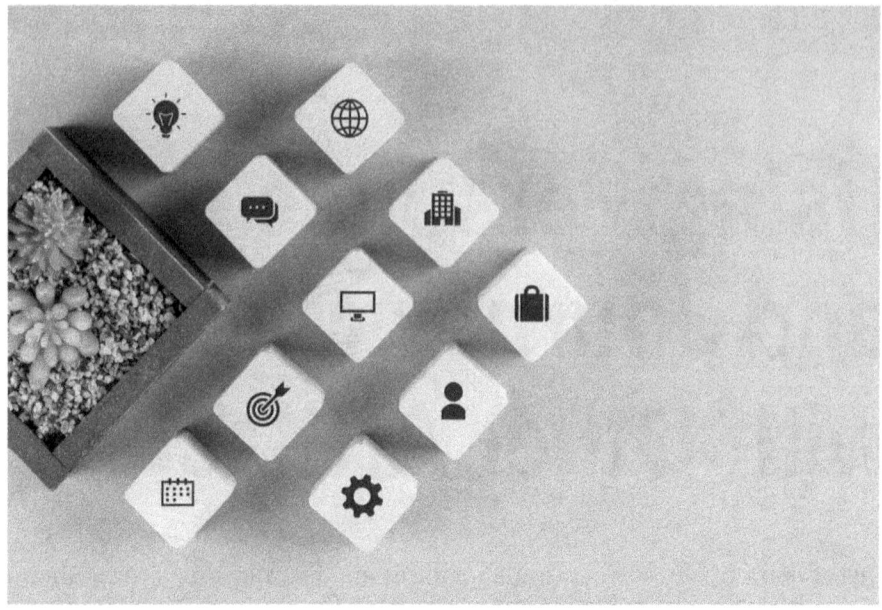

Using Personas with Other Personas

When multiple personas are used within an organization, their interplay, relationships, and interconnectivity can significantly enhance the design and strategy process.

Utilizing Research Insights Across the Persona Family Tree

Developing a comprehensive persona family tree that maps relationships and hierarchies between different personas created by various teams, such as product, customer experience (CX), marketing, human resources, and finance, provides a holistic view. This mapping helps to highlight the interconnections and overlaps between different personas, enhancing the overall effectiveness of the persona-based research.

Fostering collaboration between different teams to share insights and update the persona family tree is essential. Regular meetings and workshops can facilitate discussions on new findings and their implications for different personas. Cross-functional collaboration ensures that the persona family tree remains current and comprehensive.

It is important to continuously expand the persona family tree by adding new personas as new user segments are identified. Regularly updating existing personas with new research insights keeps them relevant and accurate. By maintaining an up-to-date persona family tree, organizations can ensure that their research remains relevant and actionable.

Connecting insights from different teams to create a comprehensive view of each persona provides valuable context for strategic decision-making. Using this connected knowledge can inform various aspects of the organization, from product development to marketing strategies. By leveraging collective insights, organizations can enhance their overall effectiveness and drive innovation.

Identifying Commonalities and Differences

Identifying commonalities and differences among personas is essential for creating effective and inclusive solutions. You can use personas at different altitudes to compare overarching attributes and needs that all of these personas share. For instance, in a project management tool, multiple user personas such as project managers, designers, and clients might share common goals like tracking project progress efficiently and pain points such as dealing with missed deadlines. Recognizing these commonalities allows for the development of universal solutions, like an intuitive dashboard, that benefits all user groups. However, it is equally important to understand the distinct needs of each persona. Project managers need advanced reporting features, while design team members require easy task updates. Avoiding a one-size-fits-all approach ensures these unique requirements are met.

Balancing the interests of different personas is crucial, especially when their needs conflict. For example, clients might want frequent updates, whereas team members might find constant reporting disruptive. Understanding these conflicts enables the design of solutions that strike a balance, such as implementing automated status updates that satisfy both groups. In situations where resources are limited, comprehending the needs of various personas aids in making informed trade-offs. For instance, if development resources are tight, prioritizing features like a robust task assignment system that provides the most value to project managers and design team members ensures efficient use of resources.

A balanced focus prevents any single user group from dominating the decision-making process. For example, focusing solely on client needs might lead to neglecting team members' productivity tools, resulting in project inefficiency. Ensuring equitable attention across different segments, such as enhancing both client communication and team collaboration features, leads to a well-rounded solution. Moreover, personas serve as effective tools for negotiation and compromise. For instance, when deciding whether to allocate resources to a mobile app or a desktop version, understanding the impact on different user segments—clients preferring mobile updates versus project managers needing detailed desktop views—helps make balanced, informed decisions.

Designing Holistic and Inclusive Experiences

Designing holistic and inclusive experiences involves considering multiple personas to ensure that diverse user needs are comprehensively met. By mapping the journeys of different personas, organizations can optimize all touchpoints and interactions for various users, creating a cohesive end-to-end experience. For example, understanding student and teacher personas' interactions in an educational platform helps design a seamless experience where both parties can communicate and collaborate effectively. This cross-persona interaction is essential for creating a cohesive ecosystem.

Aligning different teams, such as marketing, design, and development around user personas ensures everyone is on the same page regarding user needs and priorities. This alignment helps maintain consistency and coherence in the user experience across all aspects of the product. Personas are a shared reference point, fostering better communication and collaboration across departments. For example, when the marketing team understands the specific needs of a teacher persona, they can craft targeted campaigns that resonate with this user group. Simultaneously, the design and development teams can create features that enhance the teaching experience. Using personas for alignment and shared understanding leads to more inclusive and user-centric solutions.

Feedback and Iteration

Incorporating feedback and iteration when considering multiple personas is essential for developing a product that meets the needs of a diverse audience. For example, in a fitness app, collecting feedback from various personas such as beginners, professional athletes, and personal trainers provides a comprehensive understanding of how different user groups perceive and interact with the product. Beginners might struggle with complex features, while professional athletes might seek more advanced tracking options. This diverse input is crucial for making iterative improvements that cater to a broad audience, ensuring that updates and enhancements address the specific needs of all user segments.

Building robust scenarios involving multiple personas allows for testing the product's resilience and effectiveness in real-world situations. A scenario where a personal trainer uses the app to create a workout plan for a beginner can reveal how well the app supports user collaboration and customization. Inclusive testing, which includes a variety of personas, ensures that usability testing captures the experiences of different users. Ensuring the app is tested by users of different fitness levels, ages, and technical proficiencies leads to more inclusive and user-friendly designs.

CHAPTER 16   USING PERSONAS AND JOURNEY MAPS WITH OTHER ARTIFACTS

This approach improves the overall user experience and helps create a product that is accessible and valuable to everyone, whether they are just starting their fitness journey or are seasoned professionals looking for advanced features.

Using Journey Maps with Other Journey Maps

Journey maps can be connected to create a more comprehensive view of the user experience. This is useful when each journey map represents a different segment of a larger end-to-end experience.

End-to-End Continuum

Journey maps should be part of an end-to-end continuum, where each journey map is a piece of the larger experience. This helps in understanding how different phases of the user experience connect and contribute to the user's overall and longer-term goals.

Consistent Persona and Overarching Goal

All connected journey maps should be related to the same persona and the overarching goal they want to achieve. This consistency ensures that each part of the journey map aligns with the same user's needs and expectations contained within a shared higher altitude journey. Let's look at two interconnected journey maps for a cruise traveler:

- **Finding and Booking a Cruise:** One journey map might focus on the traveler's experience of finding and booking a cruise. This includes researching destinations, comparing prices, and making reservations.

- **Checking In and Boarding**: Another journey map covers the experience once the traveler is about to begin their vacation. This includes checking in, exploring the ship, and participating in a safety orientation.

Despite focusing on different parts of the travel journey, both maps relate to the same user and contribute to the overall vacation experience.

Connecting Journey Maps

To create a seamless experience, it's important to connect sequential journey maps. This can be done by adding phases before and after other parts of a journey. For example, the journey map for booking a cruise might end where the journey map for the check-in experience begins. Another journey segment could also be introduced between these two, which are related to communications and activities between booking and boarding. Here's how you can connect journey segments effectively:

- **Aligning Altitude Levels**: Ensure that connected journeys are created at the same altitude, meaning they should have a similar level of detail and scope. This alignment helps in maintaining consistency and coherence across different segments.

- **Sequential Phases**: Define clear transitions between phases. For example, the transition from booking the cruise to the boarding experience should be smooth, with clear indications of what the user expects next.

By connecting different journey maps in this way, you can create a comprehensive and cohesive view of the user's entire experience. This approach helps identify gaps, pain points, and opportunities for improvement across the entire journey. By mapping out each phase and connecting them logically, you ensure a fluid and satisfying experience for the user from start to finish.

Product-Centric Artifacts

Personas and journey maps can complement product and service development artifacts, including user stories, story mapping, Jobs to Be Done (JTBD), and ecosystem maps. This multifaceted strategy ensures that products and services are designed with the user in mind and aligns them with broader business objectives and environmental contexts.

User Stories

In product development, personas and user stories are integral to capturing product functionality from the user's perspective. Understanding these personas is the first step toward writing effective user stories narrating how users interact with the product. Without this understanding, user stories may become a disjointed wish list rather than a coherent set of functional requirements. Once personas are established, their goals are used to derive epics—broad, high-level functionalities that the product must have to address users' problems and create desired benefits. These epics are then broken down into detailed user stories,

CHAPTER 16   USING PERSONAS AND JOURNEY MAPS WITH OTHER ARTIFACTS

each capturing specific aspects of the functionality from the persona's perspective. User stories are often expressed in a simple sentence, structured as follows:

"As a [persona], I [want to], [so that]."

Let's look at several examples of user stories related to building a store location finder for a large coffee chain.

> **Example 1**
>
> **As a**: Late shift worker
>
> **I want to**: see the operating hours of nearby coffee chain locations
>
> **so that I can**: plan my visit when the store is open
>
> **Example 2**
>
> **As a**: Remote worker
>
> **I want to**: find coffee chain locations with available seating and Wi-Fi
>
> **so that I can**: work comfortably outside my home or office
>
> **Example 3**
>
> **As a**: Daily commuter
>
> **I want to**: locate coffee chain stores with drive-thru services
>
> **so that I can**: conveniently pick up coffee without leaving my car

User stories are designed to be used tactically to help product teams add prioritized features to their backlog. The major problem with user stories is that they encourage teams to think in small incremental steps without understanding the big picture. Personas should be used with user stories strategically to determine:

- **Scale and Scope**: The number of features that are important to the broadest set of personas with common goals; these should be examined with higher altitude personas.

- **Context**: The location in the journey map where the feature would help the user accomplish their goal. These should be examined at the phase, milestone, and action level.

Referencing personas in user stories effectively ensures that product teams consider requirements from a human-centered perspective.

User Story Mapping

Journey maps and user story mapping are complementary tools in product development, each focusing on different aspects of the user experience. Journey maps provide a visual representation of the user's experience with a product or service over time, capturing emotions, pain points, and interactions at each touchpoint from start to finish. This holistic view helps build empathy, identify pain points, and uncover opportunities for improvement. On the other hand, user story mapping organizes and prioritizes user stories to reflect the user's workflow, illustrating how different functionalities fit together to support user tasks and goals.

By starting with journey maps, teams gain valuable insights into the overall user experience, which inform the creation of user story maps. These insights ensure that the user stories reflect real needs and contexts.

Journey maps help identify critical moments and goals that translate into high-level epics, which are then broken down into detailed user stories in the user story map. This process ensures a structured, prioritized, and user-focused development approach. Integrating journey maps with user story mapping allows teams to align product functionality with the user's experience, addressing their needs at every stage and ensuring a coherent, user-centered design.

Jobs-to-Be-Done (JTBD)

JTBD is a framework that focuses on understanding the underlying tasks or "jobs" customers are trying to accomplish when using a product or service. It emphasizes the context in which customers use a product, the specific problem they are trying to solve, and the expected outcomes. This approach shifts the focus from the customer's characteristics to the needs and circumstances driving their behavior. Let's look at a JTBD example related to customers of a large coffee chain.

> *"I want to get a quick caffeine boost when I am on my way to work in the morning so that I can stay alert and focused during my early meetings by finding a convenient, quick, and effective caffeine source along my commute that helps me feel energized, prepared, and appear engaged and productive, despite any limitations such as time constraints, availability, and cost."*

JTBD provides a helpful frame to look at the user's needs in context without being overly prescriptive with a specific solution. Personas include details about user goals similar to those in JTBD descriptions but are also enriched with attitudinal and behavioral insights that can provide a well-rounded set of considerations to guide product teams in decision-making. Instead of creating separate personas and JTBD artifacts, consider incorporating the JTBD framework into your personas to represent user goals. When combined, organizations can use personas and JTBD to create a clearer picture of what the users are trying to accomplish, the motivations behind those needs, and the challenges they face in their pursuit of a solution.

Ecosystem Maps

An ecosystem map is a visual tool that outlines the various elements and their interactions within a system, providing a holistic view of the environment in which a product or service operates. It includes stakeholders, such as users, customers, partners, and competitors, as well as the processes, technologies, and resources involved. This map helps to identify relationships, communication flows, dependencies, and value exchanges among these elements. Let's look at the content for an ecosystem map for a large coffee chain store experience:

Core Elements:

- **Customers**: Various types of customers such as regulars, occasional visitors, and first-time visitors
- **Staff**: Baristas, cashiers, and managers
- **Products**: Different coffee beverages, food items, merchandise, and loyalty programs
- **Physical Store Environment**: Store layout, seating areas, ambiance, Wi-Fi availability, and cleanliness
- **Digital Touchpoints**: Mobile app, website, social media, and online ordering system
- **Suppliers**: Coffee bean suppliers, equipment providers, and other vendors
- **External Stakeholders**: Local community and regulatory bodies

CHAPTER 16 USING PERSONAS AND JOURNEY MAPS WITH OTHER ARTIFACTS

Interactions and Relationships:

- **Customers and Staff**: Interactions include ordering, payment, customer service, and feedback. Regulars might have personal relationships with staff.

- **Customers and Products**: Preferences for certain beverages, customization options, and loyalty program usage.

- **Customers and Physical Store Environment**: Experience influenced by store ambiance, seating availability, and Wi-Fi connectivity.

- **Customers and Digital Touchpoints**: Use of the mobile app for ordering, loyalty points tracking, receiving promotions, and engaging with the brand on social media.

- **Staff and Suppliers**: Coordination for inventory management, quality control, and equipment maintenance.

- **External Stakeholders and Store**: Community events, regulatory compliance, and competition influencing store operations and customer experience.

Personas help identify and categorize the various users and stakeholders within the ecosystem, ensuring that their specific needs and interactions are represented. Journey maps contribute by detailing the user interactions and touchpoints within the ecosystem, allowing for a comprehensive understanding of the flow of experiences and identifying areas for improvement or innovation. Together, personas and journey maps ensure that an ecosystem map reflects the complexities and interdependencies of the broader system, facilitating more effective and strategic design and decision-making.

Service Blueprints

A service blueprint provides a detailed, visual representation of the entire product and service process, highlighting customer interactions, employee actions, support processes, physical artifacts, and performance metrics. It focuses on:

- **People**: Understanding who (i.e., a persona) is involved, their wants/needs, and mental models
- **Process**: Understanding how things currently get done (i.e., a journey map) and uncovering bottlenecks, disruptions, miscommunications, inefficiencies, etc.
- **Technology**: Understanding what technologies are currently being used and how new digital solutions could be introduced

The experiences visualized in a service blueprint follow a journey and represent how people, processes, and technology help a specific persona achieve its goal. A journey map focuses on the user's actions, while a service blueprint highlights how the organization supports them while completing these activities. This would include representing the same phases, milestones, and actions from the journey map into the service blueprint. Journey maps and personas should be created first, as they serve as the foundation and backbone of a service blueprint.

Frontstage and Backstage Personas

A service blueprint relates to the experience of a single primary persona. It often includes multiple personas to demonstrate how they support the goals of the primary persona and how they interact to accomplish this. Some secondary personas interact directly with the primary persona, while others support operations from behind the scenes, also known as the backstage. Each persona has its own swim lane that runs horizontally across the service blueprint.

CHAPTER 16   USING PERSONAS AND JOURNEY MAPS WITH OTHER ARTIFACTS

In a service blueprint for a large coffee chain that focuses on the customer's experience, the primary frontstage persona would be a specific type of customer, such as regulars familiar with the menu and staff. In this scenario, the barista acts as a secondary frontstage persona, handling orders and engaging with customers.

Backstage personas include support staff such as inventory managers who maintain stock levels and ensure ingredient freshness and maintenance staff who handle equipment repairs. Logistics personas, like delivery coordinators, manage supply deliveries to various locations. Corporate management personas include regional managers overseeing multiple cafes to ensure they meet company standards and training coordinators developing employee training programs. These personas collectively capture the coffee chain's comprehensive operations and customer interactions.

Establishing the Who, What, and How

Personas, journey maps, and service blueprints should not be used as stand-alone artifacts but as an integrated part of understanding the user and how the organization supports them in achieving their goals.

CHAPTER 16   USING PERSONAS AND JOURNEY MAPS WITH OTHER ARTIFACTS

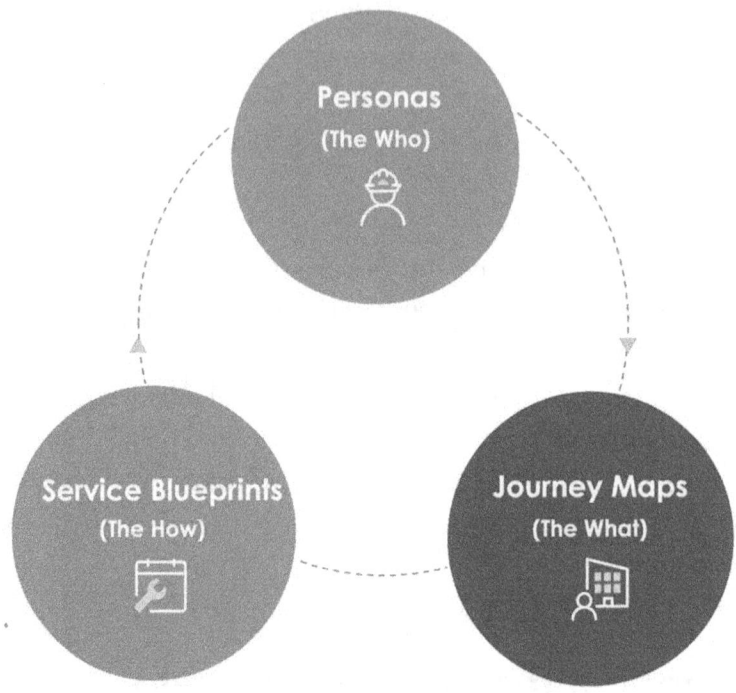

It is essential to first establish **who** your users are by creating a persona. Next, you should determine **what** the persona wishes to achieve and **what** they do to achieve their goal in a journey map. The persona along with its journey will be reflected in a service blueprint to demonstrate **how** the organization supports the persona in achieving its goal.

Key Takeaways

- **Using Personas with Other Personas**: Recognize common attributes and needs shared among personas to develop universal solutions while addressing unique requirements through tailored features and functionalities. Foster collaboration between teams to regularly update the persona family tree, ensuring it remains current and comprehensive through shared insights and workshops.

- **Using Journey Maps with Other Journey Maps**: Connect multiple journey maps to provide a seamless view of the user experience across different phases, ensuring consistency and identifying opportunities for improvement. Ensure each journey map contributes to the larger overarching goal, maintaining focus on meeting user needs consistently throughout their journey.

- **Leveraging Product-Centric Artifacts**: Strategically use personas with user stories and user story mapping to effectively align product development with real user needs and workflows. Integrate journey maps with user story mapping and Jobs-to-be-Done frameworks to prioritize and develop product features that address critical user moments and enhance usability. Utilize ecosystem maps and service blueprints to visualize persona interactions throughout the organization along a particular journey aligned with the user's goals.

In the next chapter, you will learn how to look toward the future to develop future state personas and journey maps.

CHAPTER 17

Charting Future Courses for Your Journey Maps

In this chapter, you will delve into envisioning an ideal user experience by creating a future state journey map. You will learn how to ground your future state journey maps in current realities, ensuring that solutions are practical, actionable, and directly address identified pain points. By exploring methods to prioritize pain points, brainstorm and evaluate solutions, and measure improvements, you will understand how to transform user experiences and achieve long-term success.

CHAPTER 17   CHARTING FUTURE COURSES FOR YOUR JOURNEY MAPS

Why You Should Envision the Ideal User Experience

Creating a future state journey map provides a shared vision of the ideal user experience, aligning all departments toward common goals. This proactive planning allows the organization to anticipate user needs and design experiences that exceed expectations. By envisioning the optimal journey, organizations can work toward delivering seamless, delightful interactions at every touchpoint. Additionally, the future state journey map helps the organization see the optimal user experience once they have addressed the pain points associated with the current state journey map. This comprehensive approach ensures that all aspects of the user journey are refined and improved, leading to a superior overall experience.

CHAPTER 17   CHARTING FUTURE COURSES FOR YOUR JOURNEY MAPS

Strategic Focus

A future state journey map helps identify and prioritize initiatives that will have the most significant impact on achieving the desired future state. This prioritization ensures that resources are allocated effectively, focusing investments on areas with the highest potential for improvement. By having a strategic focus, the organization can systematically work toward long-term goals, driving overall success. Addressing current state pain points through the future state journey map allows the organization to eliminate inefficiencies and enhance satisfaction in a targeted manner.

Innovation and Competitive Advantage

Envisioning a future state encourages creative thinking and innovation by removing the constraints of the current state. This process helps organizations identify opportunities for differentiation and stay ahead of competitors by continuously improving the user journey. By fostering innovation, organizations can develop unique value propositions that attract and retain customers. The future state journey map serves as a blueprint for innovation, ensuring that the solutions implemented effectively address the pain points of the current state, leading to a more competitive and compelling experience.

User-Centric Culture

Developing a future state journey map fosters a deeper understanding of user needs, behaviors, and pain points, promoting a user-centric culture within the organization. It engages team members in envisioning and creating the future state, boosting morale and ownership. This approach ensures that every decision and action is aligned with delivering value to those the organization serves. By focusing on the pain points of the current state, the future state journey map drives the organization to prioritize user satisfaction and empathy, embedding these values into the organizational culture.

Stakeholder Alignment

A future state journey map aligns stakeholders with a unified vision and strategy for improving the user's experience across the organization, ensuring everyone works toward the same goals. This alignment fosters a cohesive effort, maximizing the impact of initiatives and driving collective success. By integrating solutions to current pain points into the future state journey map, the organization ensures that all stakeholders are committed to addressing these issues and achieving a shared vision of the optimal experience.

Creating a future state journey map helps organizations to strategically plan for an enhanced user experience, drive innovation, improve operational efficiency, foster a user-centric culture, mitigate risks, measure impact effectively, and align stakeholders toward common objectives. By addressing the pain points identified in the current state journey map, organizations can work toward an optimal user experience, ensuring sustainable growth and long-term success.

Defining the Future Based on Insights and Practical Solutions

Allowing organizational fortunetellers to create a future state vision of a journey map is risky because their projections are often based on speculation, intuition, and vague aspirations rather than concrete data and a deep understanding of the current state.

CHAPTER 17 CHARTING FUTURE COURSES FOR YOUR JOURNEY MAPS

This approach can lead to unrealistic and impractical plans that fail to address your users' actual pain points and root causes. Without a solid foundation in the current state, these speculative visions risk creating a disconnect between the proposed future and the organization's real capabilities and constraints, leading to wasted resources, unmet goals, and diminished stakeholder confidence. Future state journey maps must be grounded in detailed analysis and evidence-based solutions to ensure actionable and effective improvements.

Rooted in Current Reality

Future state journey maps are effective planning tools because they are deeply rooted in an organization's current reality rather than speculative aspirations. This grounding is achieved through a meticulous analysis of the current state journey map, which involves a comprehensive understanding of existing processes, user experiences, and pain points.

CHAPTER 17   CHARTING FUTURE COURSES FOR YOUR JOURNEY MAPS

By thoroughly examining the present circumstances, organizations can identify specific areas that need improvement. This foundational knowledge ensures that the future state journey map is based not on guesses or hopes but on concrete data and insights from the current operational environment. This approach allows organizations to build on their strengths and address weaknesses with targeted interventions.

Directly Address Pain Points

Every solution in the future state journey map is a targeted response to specific issues identified in the current state, ensuring a pragmatic progression. By directly addressing these pain points, organizations can eliminate inefficiencies and enhance user satisfaction. This method ensures that the proposed changes are not arbitrary but are instead focused on resolving actual problems. By mapping solutions one-to-one with identified pain points, the future state journey map provides a clear and logical progression from the current state to the desired future state. This direct approach helps prioritize actions with the most significant impact, making the improvement process more efficient and effective.

Clear Articulation of Solutions

Each solution in the future state journey map is clearly articulated, explaining how it resolves particular pain points. This clarity helps stakeholders understand the rationale behind proposed changes and how they will improve overall processes or experiences. Detailed descriptions of solutions ensure that everyone involved has a shared understanding of the goals and methods. This transparency fosters buy-in from stakeholders, as they can see the direct benefits of the proposed changes. Furthermore, clear articulation aids communication and collaboration, providing a common language and framework for discussing improvements and measuring success.

CHAPTER 17   CHARTING FUTURE COURSES FOR YOUR JOURNEY MAPS

Feasibility and Practicality

Future state journey maps are also designed with feasibility and practicality in mind. They consider the organization's resources, capabilities, and constraints to ensure that proposed solutions can be realistically implemented. This realistic approach prevents the creation of overly ambitious plans that are unlikely to succeed. By considering factors such as budget, personnel, technology, and time, organizations can develop actionable plans achievable within their existing framework. This consideration of feasibility helps set realistic expectations and timelines, thereby increasing the likelihood of successful implementation and adoption of new processes or solutions.

Measurable Improvements

The future state journey map outlines measurable improvements, including specific metrics and KPIs to assess the solutions' success. This quantifiable approach provides a clear pathway for evaluation and continuous improvement. Organizations can track progress and make data-driven decisions by setting concrete goals and performance indicators. These metrics help identify areas performing well and those needing further attention. Measurable improvements also facilitate accountability, providing a basis for assessing the effectiveness of implemented changes and making necessary adjustments. This ongoing evaluation ensures that the organization continues evolving and improving over time.

By grounding future state journey maps in a comprehensive understanding of the current state and directly addressing identified pain points with well-articulated, feasible solutions, organizations can create realistic, actionable plans that drive meaningful improvements. Through careful analysis, clear articulation, feasibility consideration, and measurable improvements, organizations can confidently and precisely navigate the path to their desired future state.

CHAPTER 17   CHARTING FUTURE COURSES FOR YOUR JOURNEY MAPS

Let's look at an example of a scenario that highlights the pain points of an existing journey and how the organization optimized the experience in an envisioned future state.

The Journey of a Nightmare Flight Experience

John is a seasoned business traveler, accustomed to the rigors of frequent flights. This trip, however, was proving to be a nightmare from the start. His troubles began with the airline's mobile app.

As John tried to select his preferred seat online, the app's interface was confusing and cluttered. Options were buried under several layers of menus, making it difficult to navigate. After struggling to find the seat selection option, he encountered a poorly designed form that led to multiple error messages. Frustrated, he switched to his laptop to access the airline's website, but it was equally difficult to navigate and had numerous distracting pop-ups and advertisements. Eventually, John had to call customer service. After being on hold for nearly 45 minutes, he finally spoke to a representative who confirmed his seat. However, his preferred seat was unavailable due to a "system error."

Arriving at the airport, John needed to check his bag. He decided to use the self-service kiosks, which had a small, nearly unreadable screen and an unintuitive interface, making the baggage drop-off process difficult.

The mobile boarding pass provided by the app had a poorly designed barcode that wouldn't scan. The TSA agent directed John to the airline's customer service desk, where he had to wait in line to obtain a printed boarding pass and then wait again in line at security.

John hoped to catch up on emails at the gate using the airport's complimentary Wi-Fi. However, the connection process was overly complicated, requiring multiple steps and personal information inputs. The app's gate notifications were inconsistent, providing outdated information.

CHAPTER 17   CHARTING FUTURE COURSES FOR YOUR JOURNEY MAPS

Onboard, the in-flight entertainment system was another disaster. The touch screen was unresponsive, and the available content was hard to browse due to poor categorization. When he tried to purchase Wi-Fi to work, the payment gateway required several unnecessary steps and information, leading to multiple failed attempts.

After arriving at his destination, John reached his hotel and decided to leave feedback using the airline's app. However, the feedback form was buried deep within the app and had unclear instructions. After finally filling it out, it wouldn't submit, repeatedly showing an error message without explanation. Switching to the desktop version didn't help either; it was plagued with the same issue.

John's experience highlighted a series of usability failures at every touchpoint with the airline, both digital and analog. From the initial check-in process to the in-flight services and baggage handling, the combination of poorly designed interfaces and inadequate customer support made this a trip to remember for all the wrong reasons. Let's deconstruct John's experience into a current state journey map:

Current State Journey Map

1. **Booking and Check-in**

    - **Mobile App**: -4

        - They struggled with a confusing and cluttered interface, making it difficult to navigate the check-in process.

    - **Website**: -3

        - The website was slow and filled with ads and pop-ups, obstructing important information and frustrating John.

- **Customer Service Call**: -2
    - They experienced long hold times, and the customer service representative informed him that his preferred seat was unavailable due to a system error.

2. **Arrival at Airport**
    - **Self-service Kiosks**: -3
        - The self-service kiosks had tiny, unreadable screens and an unintuitive interface, making the baggage drop-off process difficult.
    - **Security**: -4
        - The mobile boarding pass had a poorly designed barcode that wouldn't scan, causing delays and a workaround to obtain a printed boarding pass.

3. **At the Gate**
    - **Airline App Notifications**: -3
        - The app's gate notifications were inconsistent, providing outdated information and leading to missed updates on flight delays.
    - **Airport Wi-Fi**: -1
        - The Wi-Fi connection process was overly complicated, requiring multiple steps and personal information inputs.

4. **Onboard**

    - **In-flight Entertainment System**: -3

        - The in-flight entertainment system was unresponsive, and the content was hard to browse due to poor categorization.

    - **In-flight Wi-Fi Purchase**: -4

        - The payment gateway required several unnecessary steps and information, leading to multiple failed attempts and a slow connection.

5. **Post-flight Feedback**

    - **Airline App**: -3

        - The feedback form was buried deep within the app and had unclear instructions, resulting in repeated error messages.

    - **Website**: -1

        - The desktop version of the feedback form was plagued with the same issues as the app, preventing submission.

Once the organization fully understands this persona's situation and identifies potential ways to address these issues, it can envision an optimized scenario in the future. Let's look at John's story, which shows how the organization addressed his previously experienced pain points.

CHAPTER 17   CHARTING FUTURE COURSES FOR YOUR JOURNEY MAPS

The Improved Future Experience

John, a seasoned business traveler, had grown accustomed to the rigors of frequent flights. However, his upcoming trip turned out to be a pleasant surprise, thanks to significant improvements made by the airline through AI and personalization.

John started his journey by checking in through the airline's mobile app. The interface was easy to understand and intuitive, with a clear menu that guided him effortlessly to the check-in option. The app used AI to pre-fill most of his information based on previous flights, making the process quick and seamless. The remaining form fields were straightforward, with mandatory fields clearly marked. He completed the process in minutes, chose his preferred seat from a selection curated based on his past choices, and received a confirmation instantly.

Arriving at the airport, John noticed the self-service kiosks had been upgraded with large, user-friendly screens. The kiosks instantly recognized him through a quick facial scan and pulled up his booking information. He quickly printed his baggage tag and dropped his bag off without any hassle. The streamlined design and clear instructions made the process efficient and stress-free.

At security, John no longer had to present his boarding pass or ID as the TSA system entirely relied on facial recognition. He breezed through security and headed to the gate.

John used the airport's complimentary Wi-Fi to catch up on emails. The connection process was simplified, requiring only a single step to log in. The app's gate notifications were timely and accurate, providing real-time updates on his flight status. Even though the flight was slightly delayed, John received an alert well in advance, allowing him to adjust his schedule accordingly.

Onboard, John was impressed with the in-flight entertainment system. The touch screen was highly responsive, and the content was well-organized, making it easy to find something enjoyable to watch. AI-driven recommendations suggested movies and shows based on his previous viewing history, enhancing his experience. When he decided to purchase Wi-Fi, the payment process was quick and efficient, and the connection was strong and reliable throughout the flight.

Once at his hotel, John decided to leave feedback using the airline's app. The feedback form was easily accessible, and the instructions were clear. AI analyzed his comments and provided instant responses to any issues he mentioned. He quickly submitted his positive comments and received a confirmation email thanking him for his feedback.

John's experience highlighted a series of well-designed touchpoints with the airline, both digital and analog. From the initial check-in process to the in-flight services and baggage handling, the combination of AI-driven personalization and excellent customer support made this a trip to remember for all the right reasons.

Let's deconstruct John's experience into a future state journey map to see how his experience has changed:

Future State Journey Map

1. **Booking and Check-in**

    - **Mobile App**: 5

        - The intuitive mobile app used AI to pre-fill most of their information, making the check-in process quick and seamless.

2. **Arrival at Airport**

    - **Self-service Kiosks**: 5

        - The user-friendly self-service kiosks recognized them through a facial scan and quickly printed their baggage tag.

CHAPTER 17   CHARTING FUTURE COURSES FOR YOUR JOURNEY MAPS

- **Security**: 4
  - There is no longer a need to present a boarding pass or ID as the TSA system entirely relies on facial recognition.

3. **At the Gate**
   - **Airline App Notifications**: 4
     - The app's gate notifications were timely and accurate, providing real-time updates on John's flight status.
   - **Airport Wi-Fi**: 4
     - The Wi-Fi connection process was simple, requiring only a single login step.

4. **Onboard**
   - **In-flight Entertainment System**: 4
     - The responsive in-flight entertainment system had well-organized content with AI-driven recommendations.
   - **In-flight Wi-Fi Purchase**: 4
     - The quick and efficient payment process for Wi-Fi provided a strong and reliable Internet connection throughout the flight.

5. **Post-Flight Feedback**
   - **Airline App**: 4
     - The easily accessible feedback form had clear instructions, allowing them to submit their comments effortlessly.

- **Website**: 4
  - The website version of the feedback form was user-friendly, with AI analyzing comments for instant responses.

In addition to highlighting solutions for every pain point in the future state, the journey map shows the anticipated improvement in the experience score. This score should be a realistic determination based on user research, including existing data from surveys, usability tests, and available behavioral and attitudinal sources. Not every solution will generate a top score, and improvements should be considered incremental toward reaching the optimal future state.

Creating a Future State Journey Map Based on a Current State Journey Map

Align to a Specific Altitude

Creating a future state journey map begins with considering the different altitude levels. Higher altitude journey maps help inform the bigger picture, longer-term solutions, and North Star visions. In comparison, lower altitude maps focus on more tactical problems that can be solved in the short term on product roadmaps. Deciding on the appropriate altitude level is crucial as it determines the scope and focus of the future state journey mapping process.

Extract Insights from the Current State Journey Map

The process starts with extracting insights from the current state journey map. A cross-functional team is assembled to analyze all of the pain points and their root causes. Each insight and pain point is documented on sticky notes and placed on a physical or digital collaboration board, such as Miro or Mural, to visualize the findings and facilitate discussion.

CHAPTER 17   CHARTING FUTURE COURSES FOR YOUR JOURNEY MAPS

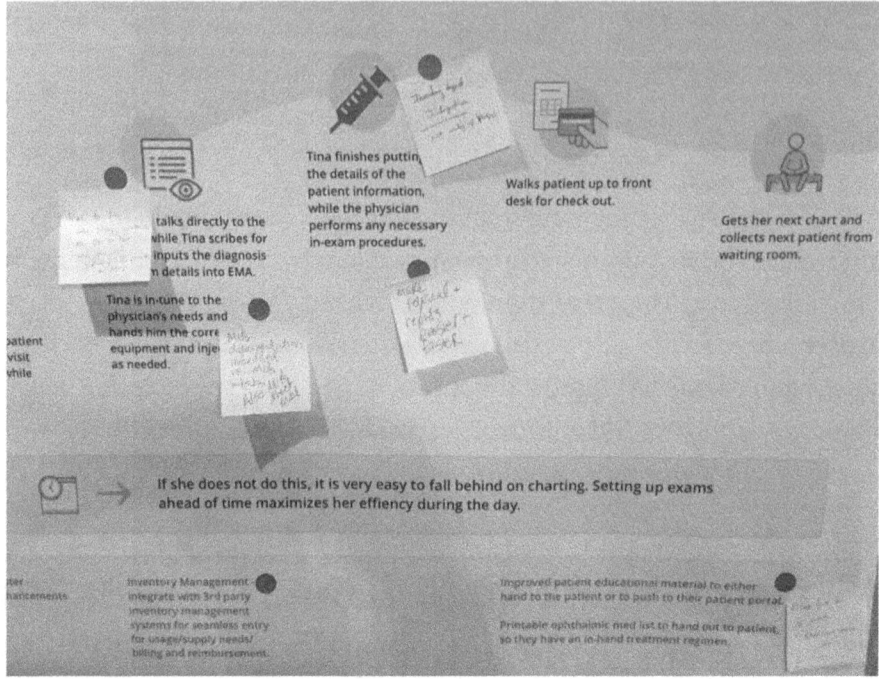

Conduct a Workshop to Align on Pain Points and Solutions

It's important to involve the team members who will ultimately be responsible for championing, designing, building, and measuring the future state experience that the organization will create. Your workshop should utilize the double diamond method to ideate and align your team. This method involves two main stages: aligning on the problems and developing and delivering solutions.

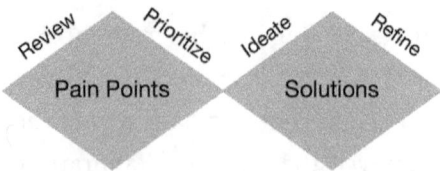

During the first diamond stage, your team will diverge and converge on the current state problems to align on a set of prioritized issues to be addressed in the future state journey map. Begin the activity by delving deeply into the persona's key characteristics, goals, and motivations so that all pain points are considered in the context of a specific type of user. Next, discuss each pain point the persona encounters. Ensure the group completely understands each pain point and how it impacts the user's experience.

Prioritize Pain Points

The team should focus on solving issues that would most help the user to achieve their goals. One effective prioritization method is a variation of the MoSCoW method. The acronym MoSCoW represents four categories of priorities: must address, should address, could address, and will not address.

- **Must Address**: Aspects that must be addressed. They represent non-negotiable needs for the user to successfully achieve their goals.

- **Should Address**: Aspects that should be addressed. They would greatly enhance the user's experience and directly contribute to their success in achieving their goals.

- **Could Address**: Aspects that could improve the user's experience but do not directly contribute to their success in achieving their goals.

- **Will Not Address**: Aspects that would have a minimal impact on improving the user's experience and do not directly relate to the user's ability to achieve their goals. They should not be a priority for the organization to address.

A facilitator should ensure that the group continually focuses on pain points directly associated with the persona and problems identified in the journey map tied to a specific user goal. The persona and journey map should be highly visible and referenced throughout the workshop. By the end of the workshop, your group should have prioritized all of the pain points reflected in the current state journey map. Prioritization methods such as MoSCoW help the team focus on the most critical issues that need to be addressed to improve the experience for a specific persona and journey.

Brainstorm and Evaluate Potential Solutions

Once the issues are prioritized, the team moves to the second stage, where they brainstorm potential solutions to address the pain points. Not every solution will be a good fit, so the team must evaluate and select those that provide the most value. This is evaluated during the cause and effect activity to determine which solutions best address the root causes of the issues.

Encourage the team to brainstorm solutions that directly address the root causes identified. For each proposed solution, articulate how it will solve the specific pain point, using clear, actionable language to describe the solution and its direct impact on the user experience.

CHAPTER 17 CHARTING FUTURE COURSES FOR YOUR JOURNEY MAPS

Create a visual map showing the relationship between each pain point (cause) and the proposed solution (effect). Highlight how the solution will change the user's experience and alleviate the pain point. Clearly articulate the expected direct result for the user if the solution is implemented, describing the improved experience and how it aligns with the persona's goals and needs.

For each solution, complete the sentence: "We will know the user is successful when ___." This statement should clearly define what success looks like for the user after the solution is implemented. Additionally, complete the sentence: "This will result in ___," specifying the positive outcomes and benefits for the user. These statements should be specific and measurable, indicating the direct impact of the solution.

Evaluate the practicality of implementing each solution within the current constraints. Consider the resources, time, and potential challenges associated with each solution. Ensure that the proposed solutions are clearly articulated and understandable to all stakeholders, using specific examples and scenarios to demonstrate the impact of the solutions.

Before finalizing the solutions to be represented in the future state journey map, review the proposed solutions with the team, refining the solutions based on feedback to ensure clarity and feasibility.

Develop the Future State Journey Map

The next step involves introducing the chosen solutions into the future state journey map. This map should illustrate the ideal experience after addressing all pain points. It is important to include target experience scores the team wants to achieve incrementally and benchmark against. These scores help measure the success of the implemented changes and ensure that the desired improvements are realized.

Final Review and Alignment

To finalize the future state journey map, the team presents it to all stakeholders for feedback and alignment. Based on stakeholder input, any necessary adjustments are made to ensure the map accurately reflects the envisioned future state. Once finalized, it contributes to an actionable roadmap and clear North Star vision to bridge the gap between the current and desired states. For future state journey maps to have the highest long-term impact, your organization's solutions must be achievable and should consider incremental progress toward the optimal future state.

Creating a Bridge from the Current to the Optimal Future State

The journey from the current state to the optimal future state can be envisioned as constructing a long metaphorical bridge. This bridge is supported by various foundational pillars, each representing a critical aspect of the progression. These pillars provide the necessary support for incremental solutions to realize the optimal future state.

CHAPTER 17   CHARTING FUTURE COURSES FOR YOUR JOURNEY MAPS

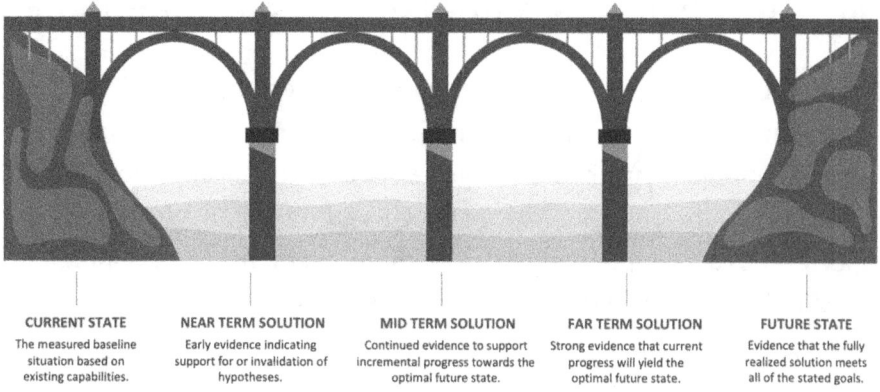

CURRENT STATE	NEAR TERM SOLUTION	MID TERM SOLUTION	FAR TERM SOLUTION	FUTURE STATE
The measured baseline situation based on existing capabilities.	Early evidence indicating support for or invalidation of hypotheses.	Continued evidence to support incremental progress towards the optimal future state.	Strong evidence that current progress will yield the optimal future state.	Evidence that the fully realized solution meets all of the stated goals.

Here's how each stage of the bridge-building process is structured:

Current State: Establishing the Foundation

In the current state, objective measurement involves developing detailed personas, blueprints, and journey maps that accurately reflect the present conditions. This thorough analysis provides a clear baseline from which to measure future progress. Proactively identifying trends and mapping opportunities for improvement helps create a roadmap for the journey ahead, ensuring clarity and direction.

Near-Term Solution: Constructing Initial Pillars

As incremental improvements are identified and implemented, data-driven decisions ensure that each change is validated and effective. Hypotheses about potential improvements are tested and validated through pilot projects, with performance measured against business and experience quality metrics. This iterative process ensures that the bridge's initial sections are strong and aligned with organizational goals, with data providing clarity at each step.

Mid-Term Solution: Refining and Strengthening

With significant progress made, continuous monitoring of trends and performance helps refine and enhance the bridge. Proactive stress testing and benchmarking ensure the bridge can handle increasing demands and future expansions. Data-driven insights guide identifying new opportunities and implementing further improvements, maintaining clarity and alignment with evolving business goals.

Far-Term Solution: Ensuring Long-Term Stability

A forward-looking approach, supported by data, helps identify emerging trends and opportunities, ensuring the bridge is future-proofed. Regular performance benchmarking against internal and external standards maintains progress, while proactive solutions to potential risks ensure the bridge's long-term stability. Data provides the clarity needed to adapt and evolve organizational priorities, aligning them with long-term business goals.

Optimal Future State: Continuous Monitoring and Improvement

The optimal future state is when all previously identified pain points have been addressed. Reaching these goals is a major achievement, but it is not the end of the journey.

Ongoing research and data collection about your users foster a dynamic and responsive organizational structure and ensure the bridge remains a reliable conduit to future opportunities. Data provides the clarity needed to navigate each step forward.

By following this structured, evidence-based methodology, organizations can successfully navigate the journey from the current state to the future state, building a robust bridge to support ongoing progress and adaptation.

CHAPTER 17   CHARTING FUTURE COURSES FOR YOUR JOURNEY MAPS

Key Takeaways

- **Envisioning the Ideal User Experience**: Create a future state journey map to align teams toward common goals and exceed user expectations by designing seamless interactions. Prioritize impactful initiatives and allocate resources effectively to drive significant improvements and long-term success.

- **Defining the Future Based on Insights and Practical Solutions**: Address pain points with practical, measurable solutions to ensure the future state journey map is grounded in current reality. Avoid relying solely on speculative visions; instead, emphasize data-driven insights and a clear understanding of current conditions to ensure feasibility and achieve measurable improvements.

- **Creating a Future State Journey Map Based on a Current State Journey Map**: Begin by selecting the appropriate altitude level to define scope and focus. With a cross-functional team, analyze pain points and root causes to extract insights from the current state journey map. Conduct workshops using the double diamond method to align on prioritized problems and develop targeted solutions, ensuring alignment with team members responsible for future state implementation.

- **Creating a Bridge from the Current to the Optimal Future State**: Build the journey from the current to the optimal future state by constructing a metaphorical bridge supported by incremental improvements, data-driven decisions, and continuous adaptation to ensure alignment with evolving business goals and user needs.

In the final chapter, you will learn how to launch a successful user artifact program at your organization.

CHAPTER 18

Launching a User Artifact Program

In this final chapter, you will learn how to launch a successful user artifact program at your organization by following a structured approach through various phases. You will discover how to align your teams and stakeholders, meticulously plan and manage the program, and effectively engage with key individuals to gather valuable insights. This guide will help you understand how to tie the initiative to organizational goals, drive team outcomes, and maintain a user-driven focus, ultimately leading to the successful implementation and continuous improvement of your user artifact program across the Align, Assess, Enable, Educate, Design, and Refine phases.

CHAPTER 18   LAUNCHING A USER ARTIFACT PROGRAM

Welcome aboard the journey to launching a successful user artifact initiative. Your aim is to align, educate, and provide the necessary resources to your organization, ensuring a smooth and effective launch plan that drives organizational goals and team outcomes. Fasten your seatbelts as you dive into each phase of this process.

Align Phase: Planning and Stakeholder Engagement

The align phase, which focuses on planning and stakeholder engagement, is a crucial starting point for your user artifact program. It sets the foundation for the entire process, much like the thorough preparation passengers undergo before a long trip.

CHAPTER 18   LAUNCHING A USER ARTIFACT PROGRAM

Program Management

The first crucial step involves comprehensive program management, where you will meticulously plan all activities to initiate a user artifact program. This planning encompasses setting timelines, allocating resources, and defining project milestones to ensure a smooth and organized launch.

Teams must understand that they collectively own the creation and management of their user artifacts. An essential part of this planning is creating a RACI matrix, which clarifies roles and responsibilities within the project. The RACI matrix stands for Responsible, Accountable, Consulted, and Informed, ensuring everyone knows their part in the program. Here is an example of a part of a RACI table indicating how different organizational roles will be involved in the program.

Responsible	Accountable	Consulted	Informed
UX Researchers	UX Leads	Product Strategists	Business Stakeholders
Data Analysts	UX Directors	Product Managers	Executives
UX Designers		Business Analysts	Customer Service Leads
		Customer Experience (CX) Leads	Technical Leads
			UX Content Strategists

Once you have established who will be involved in the program, you must plan how the work will get done. Use a Gantt chart to build a schedule representing all phases and activities. This visual tool helps set quarterly goals, providing a realistic time frame to accomplish each phase's activities while including buffer time to account for any changes and identifying dependencies, such as research activities needed to inform the design of personas and stakeholder sign-offs.

Depending on the program's scale and scope, multiple teams might work on developing user artifacts simultaneously, each at different process phases. For example, the sales and finance departments may each have their persona and journey map initiatives, requiring coordinated efforts to ensure consistency and alignment across the organization.

Stakeholder and Leadership Interviews

Engaging stakeholders and leadership is akin to the pre-boarding call, ensuring decision-makers are ready for the program to launch. Conducting interviews with executives, department heads, and team leaders helps us understand their expectations, values, priorities, and concerns. Key questions to ask include

- How have you used user artifacts such as personas, journey maps, and service blueprints in the past?
- What types of users are most important to focus on?
- What are the primary goals that your users are looking to achieve?
- What are the primary business goals for the year?
- What KPIs are used to measure success?

These interviews provide insights into stakeholders' understanding of personas and journey maps and their expectations for these artifacts. Be prepared that many stakeholders may need to be made aware of these artifacts or have misconceptions about their use and value. Your program should ensure that all stakeholders have a shared understanding of how these artifacts can help them understand, strategize, and measure user experience outcomes. Stakeholder buy-in is essential for securing the necessary resources, time, and focus commitments to make the program successful.

SME "Deep Dive" Interviews

In-depth discussions with subject matter experts (SMEs) are crucial, as these individuals often have extensive knowledge of the organization's users and may hold valuable data to jumpstart user research. SMEs may have direct interactions with users as part of their roles and may already possess existing user artifacts or insights that can inform our process. These experts should be continually consulted as partners, adding their expertise to the development of the program. Once all your team members are aligned, it is time to move on to the next phase to identify and evaluate existing organizational artifacts.

Assess Phase: Inventory and Gap Analysis

This phase involves determining what the organization already knows about its users, including past reports, presentations, and other documents stored on shared networks or research repositories.

Inventory Existing Artifacts and Knowledge

Contact individuals who have been with the organization for a long time and may know of past activities that generated personas, journey maps, and other user artifacts. Also, reach out to individuals in different departments about what their teams have created. For example, the marketing team may have already created personas to focus on specific market segments and mapped out customer journeys during the awareness and acquisition phases. Taking inventory of existing artifacts helps to prevent rework by leveraging existing knowledge and identifying areas needing further research.

Review Current Data

This assessment involves meeting with teams that hold data about your users, such as data analytics, Voice of the Customer, customer support, and user research teams. The team should assess the quality and applicability of currently available data to identify any missing information needed to create personas and their journeys. Key considerations include

- The type of data (i.e., qualitative or quantitative)
- The level of rigor associated with the data (e.g., sample size, data triangulation)
- How closely the data relate to the target audience
- How recent the information is

This assessment concludes with a clear understanding of what the organization knows about its users and gaps that need to be addressed through further research. This understanding informs the amount of research necessary to inform the activities in the design phase.

Enable Phase: Documenting Processes and Resources

Empowering your team with everything they need will enable them to create user artifacts that contain relevant information, use a consistent format, and follow your organization's established human-centered design practices. This phase establishes the resources for the organization's processes, templates, and best practices.

Provide Templates

To support teams in creating user artifacts, provide easily accessible templates in various formats such as collaboration tools like Miro, Figjam, and Mural or more sophisticated design tools like Figma to take advantage of established design system patterns. These templates help standardize the process and ensure consistency across the organization.

Develop Documentation

Create a how-to guide that explains your organization's process for creating user artifacts. Use annotations to explain the different parts of each artifact, and use examples and case studies so that team members can understand the end result.

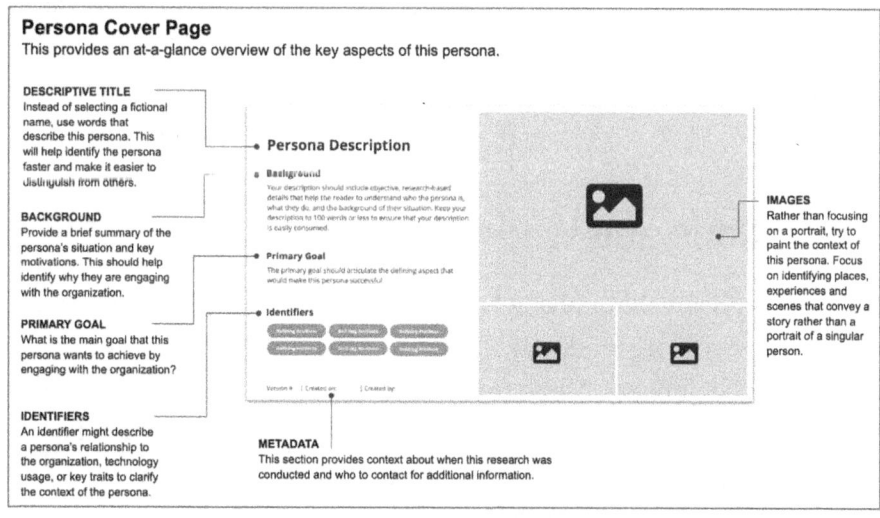

Align with other parts of the organization that oversee operations in product and service management to ensure that the proper use of user artifacts is also reflected in their documentation.

CHAPTER 18   LAUNCHING A USER ARTIFACT PROGRAM

If your organization has a platform for sharing resources, such as Sharepoint or Confluence, establish a dedicated page for creating, using, and managing user artifacts. This page serves as a central hub where team members can access the artifact library, download templates, and access best practices.

Education Phase: Workshops and Ongoing Support

Training sessions ensure that everyone understands best practices and is equipped to contribute to the initiative. Training your team on best practices should not be a one-size-fits-all approach. Product directors may need a high-level understanding, while UX designers require detailed instructions for creating journey maps. Educating your organization can take many forms that are focused on being informative and interactive and can be synchronous, such as a workshop or asynchronous using video recordings.

Orientations and Workshops

Orientation sessions should align teams on a shared understanding of user artifacts, how they are made, and how they can be used in the human-centered design process. These sessions should include a wide range of individuals across the organization who may be involved in creating or utilizing user artifacts in their role. Orientations should be provided to everyone at the start of your program, and then periodically for new team members, and as a refresher for others.

CHAPTER 18   LAUNCHING A USER ARTIFACT PROGRAM

Workshops provide an excellent opportunity for hands-on learning, allowing teams to practice creating user artifacts in a collaborative setting. Sessions should be conducted with team members from the same department to focus on the problems that the team is trying to solve, the types of users, and the goals that they are focusing on. Attendees should gain experience brainstorming attributes to generate personas as part of the persona family tree. They should examine existing workflows and user goals and practice incorporating them into preliminary journey map flight paths.

Ongoing Support and Guidance

Establish office hours where anyone can drop in for assistance with creating user artifacts or using them as part of their team's human-centered design process. Provide a dedicated contact person on your team if someone has questions or needs help. This ongoing support ensures that teams have the knowledge and resources they need to succeed.

Design Phase: Creating User Artifacts

The design phase involves all the steps needed to create user artifacts, pulling together all the necessary knowledge to develop research-based artifacts. This should be an iterative and collaborative process where teams synthesize insights, create persona trees, outline personas, and establish initial journey flight paths.

Iterative Development

Teams may start with proto-personas and proto-journey maps based on SME interviews to identify knowledge gaps and hypotheses that need to be tested. Research insights will help the user artifacts take shape as knowledge gaps are addressed. Early drafts can be low fidelity and require multiple iterations, team feedback, and representative user validation.

The teams will then begin connecting personas with journey maps to understand how certain types of users go about activities to achieve their goals. The personas and journey maps will then be integrated into service blueprints to know how the various people, processes, and technology support the user in achieving their goals.

The final stage of the design phase concludes with artifacts that the team feels confident in using to understand and create experiences for their target users.

Refine Phase: Continuous Feedback and Expansion

The refine phase includes ongoing feedback, measurement, and evolution of your user artifacts. This phase helps establish an infrastructure to continually update and expand artifacts. It also provides continual guidance and ensures adherence to best practices. This requires ongoing coaching and mentoring for teams to create their own personas and journey maps and ensure they follow established best practices.

Feedback and Refinement

The refinement process is based on feedback from those using the templates and processes. The organization should conduct quarterly reviews to learn how teams utilize the resources and how well user artifacts inform design decisions. This input should inform further iterations of the artifacts as part of continual improvement to ensure they remain relevant and valuable.

Updating and Expanding Artifacts

The phase includes continually updating and adding to the user artifacts as the team learns more about its users. Your program should have a process for ingesting new user insights from teams that conduct user research and manage data sources about users. The latest information about personas should be tagged and integrated into the knowledge repository. The organization's persona tree should grow to support other user types and add lower altitude personas as needed to support more specific use cases.

Measuring Effectiveness

Your organization should measure the impact of its user artifacts on decisions that improve user experiences. This can include the number of team members accessing artifacts, how often they appear in user stories and product roadmaps, and how many are associated with KPIs.

Data streams about your users should be visually represented to stakeholders to indicate the current "health" of your personas and how well the organization supports their goals along their journey. This process starts with creating an operating model where data is regularly infused into personas, journey maps, and service blueprints.

Create a template to standardize reporting on the status of each persona and what each team is doing to make progress on specific milestones within a user's journey. As your program evolves, your organization can invest in creating interactive dashboards that represent the latest data about our users. These dashboards can be queried to gain new insights and used as a model to predict future user needs.

Engagement Strategies: Tying the Program to Organizational Goals

Developing and maintaining a user artifact program requires a lot of work and dedication, but it is essential to helping your organization create a successful human-centered strategy. An overarching engagement strategy is vital to the long-term success of your program.

Align with Organizational Goals

Tying the initiative to strategic objectives and KPIs is crucial to keep team members and stakeholders engaged throughout the process. Highlight how user artifacts can help achieve these goals and demonstrate their value to the organization.

Focus on Team Outcomes

Emphasize the impact on team outcomes rather than the artifacts themselves. Explain how understanding users through personas and journey maps can lead to better decision-making and improved performance.

User-Driven Experience

Maintain a user-driven approach, ensuring that the focus remains on understanding and meeting user needs rather than getting bogged down in product requirements and technical issues. This user-centric approach helps teams stay aligned with the ultimate goal of creating valuable and meaningful user experiences.

Following these phases and engagement strategies will ensure the successful launch of our persona and journey map initiative, drive organizational success and achieve team outcomes.

CHAPTER 18   LAUNCHING A USER ARTIFACT PROGRAM

Key Takeaways

- **Align Phase: Plan and Engage Stakeholders**
  Start with comprehensive program management by meticulously planning activities, setting timelines, and allocating resources. Create a RACI matrix to clarify roles and responsibilities and use a Gantt chart to visualize schedules and dependencies. Engage stakeholders and leadership through interviews to understand their expectations KPIs, and ensure their buy-in.

- **Assess Phase: Inventory and Analyze Existing Data**
  Take inventory of existing user artifacts and knowledge within the organization. Meet with various teams to assess the quality and applicability of current data. Identify gaps in information about user personas and their journeys to inform the necessary research in the design phase.

- **Enable Phase: Establish Processes and Provide Resources**
  Develop comprehensive documentation and provide easily accessible templates to support the creation of user artifacts. Use collaboration and design tools to standardize the process across the organization. Conduct training sessions and workshops to ensure teams understand best practices and can effectively contribute.

- **Design Phase: Create and Iterate User Artifacts**
  Collaboratively create user artifacts by synthesizing insights, outlining personas, and establishing journey maps. Use an iterative process, starting with low-fidelity drafts and refining them based on feedback and validation from representative users. Ensure the artifacts are research-based and helpful in understanding and creating user experiences.

- **Refine Phase: Continuous Improvement and Expansion**
  Provide ongoing guidance and support to teams, ensuring adherence to best practices. Continuously update user artifacts based on new insights and feedback. Align the initiative with organizational goals and KPIs to maintain engagement and demonstrate the value of user-centric approaches in achieving better decision-making and performance.

Index

A

Altitudes
  alignment/decision-making, 53
  artifacts
    attributes, 42
    business traveler goals, 45
    high altitude artifacts, 44
    mid/high/low, 43
    small business, 45, 46
    traveler goals, 44
  characteristics, 42
  detail/context levels, 39
  framework, 52
  high/low altitude, 52
  human-centered approach, 40
  landscape, 41, 42
  organizational alignment, 39, 40
  organizational
      alignment/fog, 52
  relationship
    high persona, 47, 48
    low altitude persona, 48–50
    personas/journey map, 46
    primary goal, 49
  tree structure, 51
  visualization, 51, 52

Artifacts
  balanced focus, 308
  commonalities/differences,
      307, 308
  connecting insights, 307
  family tree, 306, 307
  feedback/iteration, 309, 310
  fostering collaboration, 307
  holistic/inclusive experiences,
      308, 309
  personas, 306
  product/service
      development, 312
    backstage, 318
    derive epics, 312
    ecosystem map, 316, 317
    interactions, 317
    JTBD framework, 315
    mapping, 314
    service blueprints, 318
    user stories, 312, 314
  strategies, 305
Atomic design patterns, 152, 153

B

Backstage personas, 318–319

INDEX

C

Construction
- articulating considerations, 145
  - customized solutions, 146
  - feedback loops, 147
  - hesitancy, 145
  - human-centered experience, 146, 147
  - human touchpoints, 147
  - hybrid approach, 146
  - virtual consultations, 147
- benefits, 126
- business implication, 143, 144
- components, 125–148
- considerations, 142
- consistent structure/framework, 128
- constraints, 137
- contextual factors, 127, 138
  - demographics, 141
  - formal/informal roles, 138
  - knowledge/experience, 139
  - people/relationships section, 140
  - psychographics, 141
  - responsibilities, 138
  - tools/resources, 140
- cover page, 128
- dependencies, 137
- descriptive title
  - altitudes, 129
  - background information, 130
  - florist crafts, 130
  - identifiers, 132
  - metadata, 133, 134
  - primary goal, 131, 132
  - tech-savvy wedding florist, 131
  - wedding florist coordinates, 130
- design implications, 142
- empathy, 127
- evidence-based insights, 127
- goals definition, 134
- implications/considerations
  - accessibility, 143
  - design process, 142
  - flows/navigation paths, 142
  - prioritization, 142
  - user interface/interaction design, 143
- industry trends, 135
- pain points, 137
- referrals, 136
- scannable, 128
- strategies, 126
- tasks definition, 135

Cooper, Alan, 5

D

Data synthesis
- themes (*see* Themes)

E

Experience quality score
- fundamental challenge, 228

INDEX

mental models, 227
root cause analysis (*see* Root cause analysis)
scoring metrics
    actions, 231
    baseline score, 231
    benefits, 229, 232
    cart review process, 235
    checkout process, 235
    considerations, 232
    delivery process, 237
    determination, 229–231
    email confirmation, 236
    frustration, 231
    login process, 233
    online shopping experience, 233
    order history, 234
    reorder items, 233
    tracking process, 236
structural design, 262

F

Family tree
    cross-functional collaboration, 73
    organizational wide, 72
    relationship structure, 71
    transparency/alignment, 72, 73
    tree visualization
        components, 73
        foundation, 74
        governance structure, 75, 76
        hierarchical/relationship structure, 76
        hierarchy diagram, 77
        primary branches, 75
        relationships, 78
        secondary branches, 75
        Venn diagram, 76, 77
    visualization methods, 80
Flight paths
    actions
        addressing nonsequential actions, 224
        progress markers, 223
        transition points, 224
    charting approach
        attributes/implications, 220
        concepts, 214
        high altitude, 215–217
        low altitude, 217, 218
        phases, 219
        review/evaluate/order, 219–223
        right altitude, 215
    creation, 213
    identification, 221, 222
    landing point, 225
    milestones, 223, 226
    takeoff point, 220, 221, 225

G

Growing organizational knowledge
    COVID-19 pandemics, 301–303
    disruptors, 300

INDEX

Growing organizational
knowledge (*cont.*)
    evolution, 297–299
    fitness app, 299, 300
    knowledge systems, 289, 290
        aggregating insights, 293
        collections, 293–295
        customization, 294
        customization options, 296
        Dovetail dashboard, 290
        integration, 290
        mobile app, 294–297
        tagging information, 291
    societal shifts, 298
    strategies, 288
    technological
        advancements, 298

H

HCD, *see* Human-centered
design (HCD)
Human-Centered Design (HCD)
    collaboration, 3
    ethical considerations/
        inclusive, 4
    feedback, 3
    foundational principles, 1
    holistic view, 4
    key principles/elements, 2–4
    ongoing evaluation, 4
    personas (*see* Personas)
    problem-solution, 3
    problem-solving/innovation, 2

I

Ideal user experience
    address pain points, 328
    altitude levels, 337
    clear articulation, 328
    competitive, 325
    comprehensive approach, 324
    current reality, 327, 328
    current state, 331–333
    development, 342
    entertainment system, 331
    exploring methods, 323
    extract insights, 337
    feasibility/practicality, 329
    feedback and alignment, 342
    feedback form, 335
    frequent flights, 334
    future state, 335, 336
    future state vision, 326
    innovation, 325
    measurable improvements,
        329, 330
    nightmare flight experience,
        330, 331
    optimal future state
        bridge-building process, 342
        current state, 343
        forward-looking
            approach, 344
        mid-term, 344
        near-term solution, 343
        ongoing research/data
            collection, 344
        optimal future state, 344

self-service kiosks, 334
stakeholder alignment, 326
strategic focus, 325
unrealistic/impractical plans, 327
user-centric culture, 325
workshops
   brainstorm potential solutions, 340–342
   diamond stage, 339
   prioritization method, 339, 340
   stages, 338
   visual map, 341

J

Jobs-to-Be-Done (JTBD), 315
Journey maps, 24
   alignment, 311
   altitudes, 46
   artifacts, 305–321
   collaborative research, 212
   construction
      actionable, 254
      contextual framing, 254
      core principles, 254
      empathetic, 255
      scannable, 254
   end-to-end continuum, 310
   experience quality score, 233–237
   flight paths, 213–226
   fundamental building blocks, 253
   ideal user experience, 323–346
   identification, 211
   individual experience, 211
   KPI, 286–288
   measurement process, 276
   overarching goal, 310, 311
   product/service development, 312–319
   research (*see* Research methods)
   sequential Phases, 312
   structure (*see* Structural design)
   synthesis, 189–212
   Who, What, and How, 319, 320

K, L

Key Performance Indicators (KPIs), 24, 127, 254, 272
   benefits, 286–288
   coordination/resources, 287, 288
   measurement process, 277
KPIs, *see* Key Performance Indicators (KPIs)

M, N, O

Measurement process, 276
   articulating goals
      actions, 283

INDEX

Measurement process (*cont.*)
    e-commerce company, 285
    healthcare, 284
    hypothesis statements, 283, 284
    solutions, 283
    structured approach, 282
    targets, 283
  centralized repository, 304
  continuous learning/adaptation, 304
  goals, 277, 278
  growing organizational knowledge (*see* Growing organizational knowledge)
  hypothesis statements, 303
  indicators, 281
    financial indicators, 281
    improvements, 282
    longitudinal analysis, 281, 282
    multiple metrics, 281
  integration/alignment, 303
  Key Performance Indicators (KPIs), 277
  performance (*see* Performance metrics)
  performance metrics satisfaction, 280
  representation (KPIs), 286–288
  return on investment, 278
Modular persona design, *see Systematic, modular approach*

P, Q

Performance metrics, 278, 303
  capabilities/limitations, 280
  efficiency metrics, 279
  learnability, 279
  satisfaction, 279
  utilization metrics, 279
Personas, 19
  altitude levels
    business-to-business (B2B), 62
    buyer types, 63
    considerations, 68
    distinct types, 63
    lower altitude, 64–66
    strategic/bigger-picture view, 62
    workshops, 66, 67
  altitudes (*see* Altitudes)
  attribute framework, 56
    altitude level, 58
    characteristics, 58
    granular details, 59
    traffic control coordinates, 56, 57
  attributes, 7
  bad personas, 33
    disengagement, 34
    distractions, 33
    distrust, 34
    misinformation, 34
  characteristics, 55
  Chuck/Cynthia/Rob, 5–7

INDEX

common personas
    disengagement, 35
    generalization, 36
    quality/quantity, 35
    reasons, 36
    trust, 36
components, 7–10
confusion, 31
construction, 125–148
design process, 10, 11
difficulties, 32
failures, 21–37
    design/research teams, 22
family tree, 71–80
foundational discovery research, 10
geographic location, 7
goal-directed design, 5
health information, 26–30
    extraneous, 27
    harboring junk, 27
    hyperspecification, 29, 30
    irrelevant, 27
    stereotyping/oversimplification, 28, 29
    unsupported information, 30
    vague, 27, 28
ideation sessions, 10
isolation, 24
iterative design, 10
journey maps
    biases/assumptions, 17
    booking process, 14
    broader fields, 12
    building blocks, 12–14
    components, 13
    confirmation/payment, 15
    designing products, 17
    fake characters, 17
    inspiration/research, 14
    iterative processes, 16
    qualitative/quantitative insights, 15
    solution-driven entities, 18
    strategies, 17
    visual representations, 11, 12, 19
local small business, 61, 62
neglect, 24
numerous, 32
organization, 23
postmortem, 23
prevent persona failure, 37
redundancies, 31
representation, 5
Sally, 21, 22
symptoms, 26, 27
synthesis, 109–123
systematic, modular approach, 149–170
unique roles/activities, 6
unique types, 61
user-centered approach, 5

R

RACI, *see* Responsible, Accountable, Consulted, and Informed (RACI)

INDEX

Research methods, 171
  attitudinal insights, 185
  behavioral data, 90, 91
    analytics, 174–176
    qualitative insights, 176
    sources of, 174
    workflow patterns, 175
  behavior patterns, 103
  contextual inquiries
    delivery person, 184, 185
    documentation, 180
    formal/informal
      structures, 182
    key principles, 179
    observation, 180
    observations, 182
    people, 182
    place/environment, 183
    planning/preparation,
      179, 180
    real-life settings, 178
    recommendations, 181, 182
    things, 183
  current/aspirational
    personas, 83
  data analyzation
    affinity diagramming map,
      105, 106
    affinity map, 106
    findings, 104, 105
    hoc tagging, 105
    labeling groups, 107
    relationships, 106
    tagging strategy, 105
    trends/themes, 105
  data triangulation, 87, 88
  diverse backgrounds/roles, 85
  existing knowledge, 173
  external sources, 88
  frequent vs. infrequent users, 91
  goals, 82
  healthcare startup company, 85
  interviews
    conversations, 95
    funnel approach, 97–99
    leading questions/
      language, 99, 100
    pilot testing, 100
    saturation, 100
    "3 P's" questioning
      technique, 96
  iterative approach, 86
  mixed-methods approach,
    81, 87, 88
  mixed methods/triangulate, 173
  new/returning users, 91
  novice vs. advanced users, 91
  objective data, 82
  objectives, 172, 173
  proto personas, 83
  qualitative research
    methods, 94
  recruiting representation, 101
    screener, 101–104
    wide representation, 101
  SMEs possess, 85, 86

INDEX

strategies, 82
surveys
   behavioral/attitudinal
      data, 92
   branching logic details, 93
   limitations, 94
   statistical analysis, 92
user data, 94
user data types, 88
user session
   screen capture page, 176
   session replays, 178
   task information, 177
utilizes existing knowledge, 84
Research methods planning
      process, 172
Research synthesis
   affinity diagramming, 207
   assumptions/
      interpretations, 206
   collaborative approach, 205
   data familiarization, 207
   debrief session, 209
   details, 208
   feedback, 211
   group activity, 206
   identification, 208
   introduction, 207
   plan validation sessions, 210
   preliminary themes/
      concepts, 210
   preparation, 206
   structured approach, 210
   visualization, 209

Responsible, Accountable,
      Consulted, and Informed
      (RACI), 349
Root cause analysis, 237
   bottlenecks, 247
   constraints, 246
   dependencies, 248
   disruptions, 247
   distractions, 248
   effectiveness, 244
   efficiency, 245
   emotion classification, 249, 250
   error handling, 245
   expectations, 240–243
   "5 Whys" technique, 238, 239
   inconsistencies, 246
   learnability, 244
   mental models, 238
   ontology/taxonomy, 251
   qualitative methods, 245
   relevant knowledge, 239
   tech startup project, 246
   troubleshoot issues, 239
   TurboTax software, 240
   turbulence, 251
   usability, 244
   workarounds, 249

S

SMEs, *see* Subject matter
      experts (SMEs)
Structural design
   business objective snapshot

INDEX

Structural design (*cont.*)
    components, 257, 258
    large-scale coffee shop
      chain, 258, 259
    metadata, 260
    organization's goals, 259
    persona snapshot, 260, 261
  components, 255
  high-fidelity templates, 256
  insights track/effects, 263
    categorization, 265
    contextual factors, 266–268
    effective descriptions,
      269, 270
    evidence, 268, 269
    research, 269
    user experience, 266
    user experiences, 264, 265
    visual elements, 272
  low-fidelity templates, 255
  mobile ordering customer
    journey, 270
  stage setting, 256, 257
  templates, 255
  visualization
    actions, 262
    experience quality
      scores, 262
    flight path, 260, 261
    milestones, 261
    phases, 261
subject matter experts (SMEs), 173
Subject matter experts (SMEs),
  85, 86

Synthesis
  booking phase, 203
  collaborative approach, 205–210
  context information, 190
  data organization, 191
    annotations/
      descriptions, 191
    categorization, 192, 193
    recording, 191, 192
    tagging segments, 192, 193
    transcription tools, 191
  evaluation phase, 202
  qualitative/quantitative
    data, 189
  quantitative/qualitative data,
    201, 202
  research phase, 202
  sketching process
    contextual
      inquiries, 196–198
    identification, 198–200
    participant's
      journey, 193–195
    pre-purchase phase, 195
    touchpoints, 196, 197
  themes, 200
  unanswered questions
    booking process, 205
    evaluation, 204
    research phase, 203
Systematic, modular approach
  atomic design patterns, 152, 153
  atomic design principles, 170
  block-style format, 154

design fidelity templates, 150
high-fidelity designs, 170
high-fidelity templates, 151
list format, 155
low-fidelity designs, 150, 151, 170
narratives, 153, 154
photos, 163
    artifacts, 166, 167
    diversity, 168, 169
    situational photos, 164
reusable templates, 149
tabular format, 154
templates, 150, 170
visual hierarchy, 157, 170
    bar charts, 162
    bright/saturated colors, 158
    elements, 158
    iconography, 159
    information visualizations, 160
    pie charts, 163
    radar/spider maps, 161
    Venn diagrams, 160
    weight, 157
    white space, 159

T

Tech Neophyte Cruise Veteran, 145, 146
Themes
    attributes, 118, 123
    B2B customers/wholesale business, 111, 112
    combination, 122
    considering findings, 111
    consistent supply/reliable delivery, 114
    cost effectiveness, 114
    cruise booking experience, 118
    customer service, 114
    domain knowledge/experience, 117
    flexibility, 114
    four quadrant diagram, 119, 120
    plot representation, 121
    qualitative insights, 122
    quantitative data, 121
    similarities, 113–115
    similarities/differences, 111, 115
    sustainability, 115
    synthesis, 200, 201
    tech savviness, 118
    Venn diagrams, 115–117
    visualization, 116
"3 P's" questioning technique, 96

U

User artifact program
    align phase
        planning/stakeholder engagement, 348
        program management, 349, 350

INDEX

User artifact program (*cont.*)
    RACI matrix, 349
    stakeholders/leadership, 350
    subject matter experts
      (SMEs), 351
  assess phase, 351
    analyze data, 352
    inventory, 351
    key considerations, 352
  design phase, 356
  education phase
    ongoing support, 356
    orientation
      sessions, 354–356
    training sessions, 354
    workshops, 354, 355
  enable phase
    documentation, 353, 354
    resources, 352
    templates, 353
  engagement strategies, 359
    organizational goals, 359
    team outcomes, 359
    user-driven approach, 359
  iterations, 357
  refine phase, 357
    data streams, 358
    feedback/refinement
      process, 357
    measuring effectiveness, 358
    updating program, 358
  structured approach, 347, 348

V, W, X, Y, Z

Visual design, 151–170

GPSR Compliance
The European Union's (EU) General Product Safety Regulation (GPSR) is a set of rules that requires consumer products to be safe and our obligations to ensure this.

If you have any concerns about our products, you can contact us on

ProductSafety@springernature.com

In case Publisher is established outside the EU, the EU authorized representative is:

Springer Nature Customer Service Center GmbH
Europaplatz 3
69115 Heidelberg, Germany

www.ingramcontent.com/pod-product-compliance
Lightning Source LLC
LaVergne TN
LVHW010334260326
834688LV00036B/704